Workbenches

From Design & Theory to Construction & Use

Revised Edition
Christopher Schwarz

ABOUT THE AUTHOR

Christopher Schwarz is the former editor of *Popular Woodworking Magazine* and is a long-time amateur furniture maker and hand-tool enthusiast.

He began working with wood as a boy when his family members built their first home on their farm outside Hackett, Ark., using hand tools because there was no electricity. After studying journalism at Northwestern University and The Ohio State University, Chris became a newspaper reporter but studied furniture making at night at the University of Kentucky and joined the staff of *Popular Woodworking* in 1996.

Today Chris is the editor of Lost Art Press where he has published books on handwork since 2007. He builds custom furniture for clients and teaches woodworking classes all over the world.

He lives in Fort Mitchell, Ky., with his wife, Lucy; two daughters, Maddy and Katy; and five cats.

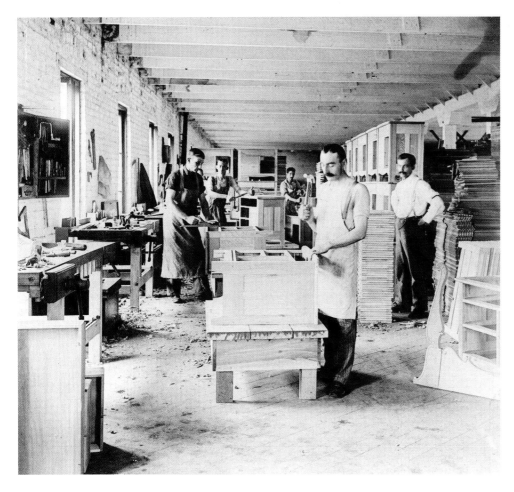

ACKNOWLEDGMENTS

I began writing this book in 2005 as a manual for my students after explaining for the 100th time why their workbenches weren't working. It was written on the couch at night with the kids by my side, on weekends and in hotels from California to Germany.

Luckily for me, lots of people around me gave their time, effort and goodwill in generous measures. At the top of the list are my wife and daughters: Lucy, Maddy and Katy. They tolerated me being chained to my laptop without a single complaint.

John Hoffman, a fellow woodworker in arms, read every word of this book in both its rough and polished form, helped me shape the narrative and listened to untold hours of me droning on about workbench obscura. Also without complaint.

Louis Bois, a professional draughtsman and amateur woodworker, made the construction drawings in this book and also edited every chapter for style and substance.

Gary Roberts, who runs the excellent Toolemera Press web site (toolemera.com) provided many of the old photos and engravings from his personal collection. His web site is an excellent resource for anyone investigating the written record of early woodworking.

Other illustrations, photos and research materials came from a fair number of readers and woodworking friends, including: Michael Gladwin, Stephen Fee and Wiktor Kuc.

After the book was written and (basically) designed, Linda Watts, my art director at *Popular Woodworking*, spent a few days cleaning up behind me. And Megan Fitzpatrick spent several of her lunch hours copy editing my book and rooting out numerous typographical errors.

And finally, I'd like to thank one person who probably doesn't know this is coming. David Raeside, one of my most enthusiastic students, suggested one day during a class on handwork that I should write a book. While I'd been asked several times by publishers to write books on a topic of their choosing (and then declined their offers) it was his suggestion that set me in motion. Without his casual remark, this book simply would not exist.

Contents

86 NEVERS. — École Professionnelle Supérieure. — Atelier de Menuiserie. —

Workbenches

From Design & Theory to Construction & Use

Cabinetmaker's bench from the book
*Holtzapffel's Construction, Action
and Application of Cutting Tools.*

"Portable cabinet bench" from *Spons'
Mechanics' Own Book.*

NICE WORKBENCH (AND HAT): Note how the legs, stretchers and almost certainly the front edge of the benchtop are all in the same plane. This is one of the oft-missed fundamentals of workbench design.

Introduction to the 2nd Edition

Every piece of lumber has three kinds of surfaces: edges, faces and ends. A good workbench should be able to hold your lumber so you can easily work on these three kinds of surfaces. Any bench that falls short of this basic requirement will hold you back as your woodworking skills advance.

It took me years to come to this conclusion – years of frustrating fits and starts, observation and – eventually – success. Though the maxim above looks so obvious when written down, it sometimes eludes both the woodworkers who set out to build their own benches and the manufacturers of commercial workbenches.

Even today, 10 years after I started writing the first edition of this book, I see many beginning woodworkers struggle with designing or buying their first workbench.

Part of the problem is that to a beginning woodworker, almost every tool, vise, workholding appliance and bench looks useful and viable. It takes experience and hard knocks to realize that many commercial products are designed by non-woodworkers, or are poor copies of trusted designs that lack some important component.

The second problem is that the beginning woodworker (and the advanced one) can actually find too much information out there on workbench design. Thanks to the Internet, you can find thousands of differing opinions on the ideal workbench, vise setup and even workbench height.

If you pay close attention to this endless noise, you will find some patterns. Here's the most common one: Sam builds a workbench. It works. Sam is estatic and tells everyone about it. Someone asks Sam: "What bench should I build." Sam answers: "Why this one, of course. It's the best I've ever used."

My experiece with workbenches began when I was about eight years old when my grandfather and I built my first bench from construction lumber and plywood. That bench was a challenge to use as a boy. The workholding was terrible for hand tools (and hand tools were all my family would allow me to use for safety reasons).

I can still remember struggling to hold pieces for sawing and planing on that bench. It was a pattern that would be repeated again and again throughout my life. I inherited my grandfather's European workbench right after college and quickly reached its limits.

I became an editor at *Popular Woodworking Magazine* in 1996, and that's when the real journey began. Suddenly, I was exposed to workbenches of all types used by woodworkers all over the world.

Our shop at the magazine was outfitted with benches that were little more than glorified kitchen cabinets with a vise at one corner. During the next 15 years, however, I was sent to work with craftsmen in their shops and was amazed at the wide varieties of benches out there – vintage, commercial and sometimes silly.

I got to work on these benches and started to find that some benches worked better for certain operations than others. Mostly, however, I found a lot of commercial workbenches that seemed like a cruel joke. They were lightweight, they wobbled and getting them to hold anything was as frustrating as working on my first bench as a kid in an Arkansas garage.

The turning point for me was discovering old woodworking books and 19th-century magazines. The benches in those books were fundamentally different. They were more massive. They had vises and features I had never seen before.

My first instinct was to seek out an old workbench for myself. At the time I was fixing up vintage woodworking hand tools, so an antique bench seemed the right answer.

If you've ever gone down this path, then you probably know what happened. Old workbenches are a special challenge. Unlike vintage handplanes and chisels, they don't suffer abuse as well. Or maybe the problem is that they are administered a special kind of abuse.

> *"At its most basic we are only discussing a learned skill, but do we not agree that sometimes the most basic skills can create things far beyond our expectations? We are talking about tools and carpentry, about words and style ... but as we move along, you'd do well to remember that we are also talking about magic."*
>
> — Stephen King, *On Writing*

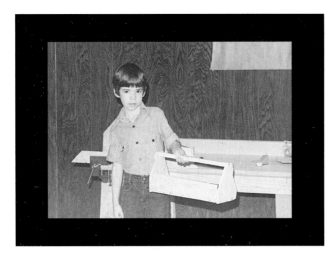

IT WAS THE 1970S: Even our garage was fully clad in ugly dark paneling (you should have seen my room). Here is my first workbench and the first project I ever built on it, a tool tote that probably fell apart within a few years – I can't remember its specific fate. Note the nice hammer marks on the bench's legs from my expert pounding.

They end up outside, in barns or are stripped of their useful bits to become a kitchen island or wet bar. Their wooden threads are destroyed by children who play with the benches in the garage or barn. Chickens take up residence in the shelf below. The top is used for butchering livestock.

And these examples could cost $800 to $1,000.

Like any normal woodworker, I looked at the price tag, scoffed and said, "Heck, I can build that."

My First Real Bench

After a few years of – I wouldn't call it "begging" exactly – I was permitted to build my first workbench for the magazine. But there was a catch. Like anything in woodworking journalism, you need a "hook" for the story. It's not enough to build a router table, you need to build "The Ultimate Router Table."

The hook for my workbench was that it had to be built for $175 – that included the wood, hardware and vises. I actually enjoy limitations such as this because they force me to become creative.

In this case, my $175 budget drove me back to my childhood in Arkansas. While growing up there, we spent many weekends on our farm building two houses – the first one was built entirely with hand tools because there was no electric service.

All of our framing lumber was yellow pine. And I remember it being incredibly heavy, dense and difficult (for a kid) to work with hand or power tools. My dad said it was the sap, and once the sap set up in the yellow pine it became almost rock-like. You would be hard-pressed to drive a nail into it without a pilot hole.

Because I couldn't afford maple or beech for my bench, I went to the home center and bought enough yellow pine 2x12s to make the bench. I'll be honest, I knew that yellow pine was great joist material, but I wasn't sure how it would be in a bench. I'd never seen a yellow pine bench before – though they were out there, I'm sure.

As it turns out, yellow pine is a spectacular workbench material. It is almost as stiff as maple, and once it dries it barely moves seasonally. And it is so inexpensive that you really can build a workbench for less than $200. This experience opened my eyes as to what I could use to

HOLDS TOOLS BETTER THAN IT HOLDS WORK: I see a lot of workbenches in professional cabinetshops that look like these benches in our shop. They store a lot of tools below and are useful for piling stuff on. But if you ever want to plane or saw anything, you have to start improvising.

build workbenches. It didn't have to be a seasoned hardwood. In fact, I soon discovered it could be almost any wood.

In the early 2000s I was sent on a woodworking show circuit for a few years and our shtick was that we would build a bench in every city and give it away to a lucky attendee.

They don't have untreated yellow pine in Los Angeles. But they do have Douglas fir. Other cities had "hem-fir" or hemlock. So we'd shrug our shoulders and build the bench out of whatever was available in the framing lumber section of the home center.

The benches turned out just fine, and I realized that just about any species can be used to build a workbench – if you use the correct design that properly exploits the material. And somehow researching workbench designs became my life's work. This chapter of my career began, oddly enough, in a Manhattan apartment.

Meet Monsieur Roubo

During a trip to New York City, I stopped by the Tools for Working Wood store and the owner, Joel Moskowitz, invited me to his apartment to see his collection of tools and woodworking books. The tools were nice, but the books were fantastic – many volumes I had

10 Rules for Building Workbenches

RULE NO. 1: Always overbuild your workbench. There is a saying in boatbuilding: If it looks fair, it is fair. For workbenches, here's my maxim: If it looks stout, then make it doubly so. Everything about a workbench takes punishment that is akin to a kitchen chair in a house of 8-year-old boys.

RULE NO. 2: Always overbuild your workbench. Use the best joinery that you can. These are times to whip out the through-tenon, the dovetail, whatever you've got.

RULE NO. 3: You must remain married as you overbuild your workbench. Every project is a strain on everyday life. And when I build a workbench, I feel soreness in my joints and sorry for my family. If something isn't right on a project, I'll tear it out and start again. A bench has to be perfect – like a highboy, but in a different way.

RULE NO. 4: After you sketch out your workbench design but before you cut the wood, do yourself a favor. Compare your design with other historical designs of benches. If your bench appears to be a new design or looks unlike anything built before, chances are your design is flawed. I hate to be the one to stomp on innovation, but we're not talking about the latest fashions from Milan. We're talking about a table designed to grip bits of wood.

RULE NO. 5: Your bench design cannot be too heavy or too long. But its top can easily be too wide or too tall.

RULE NO. 6: All benches should be able to grip the wood so you can easily work on the faces, the ends and the edges. Submit your bench to what I call the *Kitchen Door Test*. Imagine a typical kitchen door that is ¾" thick, 15" wide and 23" long. How would you affix that door flat on your bench to level its joints and then sand (or plane) it flat? How would you clamp the door so you could work on the ends to trim the top rail and tops of the stiles so the door will fit its opening? And how will you secure that door on edge so you can rout its hinge gains and plane off the sawblade marks without the door flopping around? Does your bench pass this test? OK, now ask the same questions with a door that is ¾" x 15" x 38".

RULE NO. 7: Showcase benches made from exotic materials with a fancy finish are nice. No argument there. But focus on the functions before you work on the flash. I'd rather have a construction-lumber bench that followed these rules than a beautiful European beech Ulmia bench that skipped even one of these basic concepts.

RULE NO. 8: When finishing a workbench, less is more. A shiny film finish lets your work scoot over the bench. And a film finish will crack when struck by a hammer or dead-blow mallet. Choose a finish that is easy to apply, offers some protection from stains and doesn't build up a thick film. I like an oil/varnish blend (sold as Danish Oil), a straight boiled linseed oil or a completely bare bench.

RULE NO. 9: Avoid bolting your bench to the floor or the wall. You should be able to move your bench, but not too easily. Some operations require you to pull your bench away from the wall. However, a bench on a mobile base can be a problem. If the bench rests on casters (even if the casters lock) it will move easily.

RULE NO. 10: Your bench is a three-dimensional clamping surface. Anything that interferes with clamping work to your benchtop (aprons, a drawer bank, doors, supports, etc.) will frustrate you in short order.

Fig. 2940

STILL SPINDLY: Modern manufacturers don't have the market cornered on workbenches that are small and puny. Check out this vintage example from a William P. Walters tool catalog. This bench would frustrate anyone who wanted to make anything other than small boxes.

No. 100

THE GNOME BRAND: This "bench" was one of Hammacher Schlemmer & Co.'s Gnome Brand benches. Why Gnome Brand? My guess is that the benches were too small for the average-sized woodworker.

only heard of but had never seen. Chief among them was the 1976 Leonce Laget editions of *l'Art du menuisier* by A.J. Roubo. Until that day I had only seen a few plates of this 18th-century masterpiece. And so for a long time, Joel and I pored over the full-size plates in the three volumes and discussed what we saw.

Because Roubo is such a massive work, you can get lost in one particular thread. If you are obsessed with planes, you will find enough material there to consume a lifetime of further research. Same with marquetry, jigs, finishing or millwork. At that point in my life, I was diving deep into handwork and chairmaking, and I was trying to get my $175 workbench to hold odd-shaped parts. I'd modified my bench quite a bit since building it – I'd shifted the benchtop so its front edge was coplanar to the front legs for planing edges of boards. I'd added a sliding deadman, plus holes in the benchtop for hold-downs.

When I saw the French workbench in *l'Art du menuisier*, it was like I was struck by lightning. Not because of the famous Plate 11, which explains the bench and its accessories. But because the bench was in use throughout all the volumes. It was being used for everything from carriage-making to building garden trellises, marquetry, casework, finishing and so on.

I knew right then I had to build one to find out if it was the answer to my questions about workbench design. I did just that. I then put the bench to hard use and it became the first French workbench featured in this book. It's made from construction lumber and inexpensive vise components, and yet it could easily be the only bench you need for the rest of your life. I honestly have yet to find anything that this bench form cannot do. And it does it with ease.

For the next 10 years I taught woodworkers all over the world how to build this bench from a wide variety of materials, from fir construction beams to French oak that had been cured to repair belltowers in Germany. I learned a lot more about building the many

THE $175 WORKBENCH: This bench is an excellent first bench because you can modify the heck out of it without worrying too much about how much the raw materials cost. It's like customizing an old Volkswagen Beetle, I suppose. Chop it. Drop it. Paint flames on it if you like.

STARTING SPINDLY: When you look at old catalogs of workbenches, they would list a line for pros and a line for *Manual Training*. The manual training benches, such as the one above, were almost always lacking. A bench like this isn't a tool for your shop. It's a challenge to overcome.

variants of this form. And eventually I built a version of this bench that was true to the 18th-century Plate 11 bench shown in Roubo. I used the same sliding-dovetail and tenons, massive components and traditional wooden vise screws and blacksmith hardware. That bench is the second French bench featured in this book, and it is the bench I currently work on in my small basement shop.

Using those two chapters, I feel certain you can design your own French bench using almost any budget.

And though the French probably won't admit it, this bench does pose some difficulties, mostly in construction. You need a lot of wood to make the massive top, legs and stretchers. Obtaining big slabs can be a challenge, as you'll see. And laminating up a lot of small pieces to make the large components can be time-, glue- and clamp-consuming.

So to balance this bench out, I looked across the English Channel.

Engineered Effectiveness

Peter Nicholson's *Mechanic's Companion* (1831) was the next important woodworking book after Roubo's masterwork. Like Roubo, Nicholson was a trained practitioner, not just a writer. So this book is a deep dive into all aspects of joinery (and other topics).

The workbench in Nicholson's book looks absolutely nothing like the French bench. It's huge, yes, but it's made of flat panels that are assembled into what is effectively a torsion box. Nicholson's bench (though I'm sure he didn't invent the form) achieves the same goals as the French bench. But with much less material – about half the material by my estimates.

Because Great Britain is an island that has had to import wood for more than 500 years, this bench makes a lot of sense. If you can build

DON'T FORGET THE EDGES: Your workbench is a three-dimensional clamping surface, so don't give up the ability to clamp items vertically against your legs, aprons (shown above) or a sliding deadman.

an effective and professional bench with half the wood, an English joiner would likely jump at it.

The other advantage to this form, from a modern perspective, is you can build it with few machines or clamps. All the material can be purchased from a home center already surfaced and ready to go. So if you are short on time or money, this design deserves a good look.

I've included two versions of the English bench in this book. The first is a fairly tricked-out design with a wagon vise, a jack-leg face vise and angled legs. The second is designed to be built quickly and knocks down flat in less than 10 minutes. Both English benches can perform the full variety of tasks required by a furniture maker, joiner or carpenter.

Beware the New — Fight Progress

I hope this book also will prevent you from venturing down unnecessary paths. If you can see in your mind's eye a workbench device that no one has ever invented before and that you think you need, then I caution you. Chances are that someone has come up with a way to do what you want to do, and they used simple technology to do it. Or your particular need is so specialized and narrow that few people would ever need to do that to a piece of wood. So take a moment to look around at what already exists before you build a triple-screw vise with pneumatic suction panels. Or a bench that is attached to a barber's chair (yes, that one exists). Or a bench that is 42" high with vises on all four corners.

Whenever I build a bench, it's inevitable that someone will ask me if this is the last bench I'll ever build. They ask if I have found perfection. I don't think there's an answer. Since I started woodworking at age eight, my needs as a woodworker have changed. And they will continue to change.

But the benches in this book fulfill all the basic needs of a furniture maker. I have yet to stumble into any serious limitations of either design. Would I change things if I built them again? Sure. Would that change they way they functioned? No, not really.

So these benches are a good place to begin. And that's what this book is for: To give you a head start in the craft by building a bench that is capable of doing things you might not be ready to do yet. And when you are ready, your bench will be willing and waiting.

The Most Common Workbench Questions (and the Answers)

When woodworkers approach the question of building a bench, they usually have a series of questions that generate quite a bit of debate among veteran craftsmen. Here are some of the most common questions, and the answers (from my experience).

1. SHOULD I BUILD OR BUY MY WORKBENCH? This gets to the heart of many questions in woodworking (buying used tools v. new tools, buying rough lumber v. surfaced stock). Whenever I face a question such as this, I answer: "What do you like to do? Work wood or fix up old tools? Spend a week at the planer or cut joints? Let your answer be your guide." But with workbenches, my semi-Socratic method falls apart. I think you should build your workbench, even if you aren't looking for a career in workbench building. Building a workbench teaches you a lot about woodworking, including: traditional joinery, integrating hardware into a design, balancing form and function and making assemblies that are demonstrably flat and square. And you get to learn all this on a piece of furniture that doesn't have to go in the living room and embarrass you if you stumble.

2. WHAT STYLE OF WORKBENCH SHOULD I USE? Workbench purists will push you toward building a copy of a tested or classic design. I know craftsmen who have built benches that are doppelgangers of benches built in the 19th century. I say that you should use your good judgment instead. While you shouldn't re-invent the wheel when you build a workbench, you shouldn't be afraid to combine elements of different benches, as long as the result meets the minimum requirements for size, mass and workholding. Then I think you'll have a fine workbench. Most workbenches (even the holy relic ones) are hybrid designs with features from other cultures. (The earliest workbench that I know of is an Egyptian rock. That one has mass in spades, but the workholding is lacking.)

3. CAN I MAKE MY BENCH MOBILE OR HEIGHT-ADJUSTABLE? Unless your bench is bolted down, it is already mobile. Every mobile base I've seen for benches has wheels that are too small, a mechanism that is too complex, a design that makes the bench unstable or a price tag that has too many zeros. I move my bench all the time and it weighs 350 pounds. Push. Shove. Done. Height-adjustable benches are for hospitals. If you need to get closer to your work to see details, buy a stool and sit down. Build your bench so it's comfortable for common operations then adjust yourself up or down for the uncommon ones. Few people need a height-adjustable bench unless they also do dentistry or barbering there, too.

4. HOW HIGH SHOULD MY BENCH BE AND WHAT WOOD SHOULD I USE TO MAKE IT? OK, now you're getting ahead of the class. Turn the page and we'll dissect those two questions like frogs in a high school biology class.

Holdfast holes

Planing stop

Note front of leg is flush with front edge of benchtop

Holdfast holes

Crochet (hook)

Sliding deadman

Parallel guide for leg vise

Stretcher

Face vise position (a leg vise is shown in this position)

End vise position (wagon vise shown in this position)

Square dog holes

Holdfast holes

Jack-leg leg vise (in face vise position)

BENCH ANATOMY: The nomenclature to describe the parts of a bench can confuse (though it's not as tricky as understanding your own preteen children or the geometry of sawteeth). Here's the most important thing to remember: the terms *face vise* and *end vise* refer to the position of the vise on the bench. A quick-release iron vise is a face vise when it's mounted on front, and it's an end vise when it's on the end.

The Basics of Workbench Design

Few people dispute that the workbench is the single most important tool in the workshop, yet there is surprisingly little written about the details that are critical to its design, construction and — most of all — its use.

There are plenty of books that offer a guided tour of workbenches built by contemporary woodworkers around the globe. They offer plans for a handful of handsome workbenches. They show you photographs of the woodworkers using the benches and discuss how some have added a sailing ship's galley of storage to the bench. Or a lift mechanism that raises the benchtop like a dentist's chair.

I own those books and like them. But this isn't that kind of book.

This book is everything that I thought was missing from the other workbench books. This book focuses on how you solve everyday problems with a workbench that resides in your garage or basement. Professional woodworkers I know use either rudimentary workbenches designed for production work or specific purpose-built workbenches that solve a thorny problem that crops up every day in their work. In other words, the professionals I know use benches that are designed for that person's business, which might be kitchen cabinets, millwork, veneering panels or laying up butcher-block tops. Such benches as those are not for the generalist.

Workbench Design

It's my belief that the enthusiastic modern-day home woodworker needs a workbench that has much in common with the workbenches used by 18th- and 19th-century craftsmen. Home woodworkers tend to build a wide variety of projects (shelves one month, chairs the next, followed by picture frames). So they need a workbench that excels at the garden-variety woodworking tasks and yet is flexible enough to be adapted to the oddball stuff.

Old-school workbenches are well-suited for a jack-of-all-trades woodworker.

So the chapter on workbench design isn't about how a Shaker-style workbench is different from a Tage Frid-style workbench. Instead, it's about how the construction details of a workbench — any workbench — affect the way you work. Workbenches are far more than a strong table. When designed, built and used properly, a workbench is a four- (sometimes five-) legged dance partner that will add fluidity and speed to your work. A poorly designed bench is one of the most frustrating obstacles in the craft.

Here are some of the critical points to consider as you design your own workbench or buy a commercial one:
- The species of wood.
- The size of the top and the amount of its overhang.
- The size, location and existence of a tool tray.
- The placement of the completed bench in your workshop.
- The placement of the legs — flush or recessed from the top's front edge.
- The selection and placement of vises.
- The addition of dog holes and stops in the benchtop and legs — including their size, shape and composition.
- The height of the benchtop from the floor.
- The use (or misuse) of the space beneath the top.
- The design of the support structure beneath the benchtop.
- And most of all, designing a workbench around the tasks you need to perform instead of designing a workbench around ideas, names or nationalities. Here, we'll list all the typical things you can do with a workbench and match them to the devices and features above. That is the heart of this book. Many woodworkers end up building several benches as their skills grow and they realize their first bench-building efforts were inadequate. By understanding all the common tasks performed on a bench, you can draft a work bench you will never outgrow — even if you've never taken hammer in hand.

"He (the wheelwright) had no band saw to drive, with ruthless un-intelligence, through every resistance. The timber was far from being prey, a helpless victim, to a machine. Rather it would lend its own special virtues to the man who knew how to humour it."

— George Sturt, *The Wheelwright's Shop*
(Home Farm Books)

Building a workbench is simple. The joinery is straightforward. The materials are inexpensive and plentiful. There is a now a wide variety of hardware available. I've built more than 50 workbenches and worked on many commercial benches as well, everything from Ulmia to Sjoberg to Lie-Nielsen to no-wonder-it's-got-no-name.

Choose a Good Material

The first question that bench builders ask is what sort of material they should use for making a workbench. It's the first barrier: "Where will I get the wood? And what kind of wood?" There's a lot of confusion on this topic. Most European benches were built using beech, and sometimes fine-grained steamed European beech. And so a significant number of woodworkers go to lengths to purchase precious beech for their workbenches. After all, who wants to argue with several hundreds of years of tradition?

I do. European apprentices, cabinetmakers and joiners didn't choose beech because of some magic quality of *Fagus sylvatica*. They chose it because it was dense, stiff, plentiful and inexpensive. In the United States, beech is dense, stiff, hard to find and (sometimes) a bit spendy. You can, of course, use it to build a bench (it's your bench, not mine), but you will pay for the privilege. And it will have no demonstrable advantage over a bench built from a cheaper species.

Other woodworkers, tacking toward the sensible I suppose, use hard or soft maple for their benches, rationalizing that it's like the beech of the New World. And indeed, the maples have all the desirable qualities of a species for a workbench (save its expense — boy howdy, it's expensive in the United States).

Maple is stiff, resists denting and can span long distances without much of a support structure below it. But so can other species. In fact, if you went by the numbers from the wood technologists alone, you'd build your bench from shagbark hickory, despite its difficult nature. Once you look at the characteristics that make a species good for a workbench, you see that white oak, Southern yellow pine, fir, poplar or just about any species will perform brilliantly. The real challenge is in how you scale and assemble the parts (which we'll discuss) to increase the top's stiffness or its resistance to loading.

So don't get hung up on the species of your material. There are many other workbench properties that are more important than the particular species.

Here's one important property: How stiff is the wood? You want the wood to remain stiff over long spans so you don't have to build a complex undercarriage that could impede clamping things to the top. And a monolithic top is the way to accomplish this. Among the wood scientists there are several ways to describe the stiffness of a board, including, most critically, the modulus of elasticity. Tip: *modulus* is just a fancy word for *measure*.

I don't intend to get technical here, but I do want to say that I think one of the most striking failures of woodworkers is that they don't understand the material. Wood's structure is complex, though no more complex than a plunge router. Years ago I read R. Bruce Hoadley's masterwork *Understanding Wood* (The Taunton Press) and it changed the way I looked at wood. Instead of seeing boards, I saw my shop filled with snippets of a cone-shaped organism. That is a bigger shift in viewpoint than it might sound. I highly recommend the book for the mindful woodworker.

Find a Source for Southern Yellow Pine

When people see my workbenches they always ask: Where did you get that beautiful clear pine? It must have been expensive.

Hardly. It's construction-grade stuff found in floor joists in the Midwest and South. Of course, some people can't find yellow pine where they live, so they don't think it really exists. Here is the true story:

I grew up in Arkansas, and every lumberyard had Southern yellow pine in the construction section. When we lived in South Carolina, it was the same story. Lexington, yup. Now we live in Northern Kentucky, and there is still lots and lots of Southern yellow pine.

It is stacked up in huge piles, clear and kiln-dried at every Lowe's and Home Depot in town. When I build a bench, I generally push one of the orange wheeled carts up to the bunk that holds the 2x12 x 12's. These are generally the clearest boards in the store, and you really don't get charged a premium for them. I never, repeat never, buy 2x4s. These are knotty, twisted, poorly dried and generally nasty.

I start sifting through the stack and reject usually about half the boards. I look for clear stock (some pin knots are OK). I look for twist, severe cupping and damage (forklifts are murder on the edges). Then I feel the weight. If a few feel too heavy, they probably are waterlogged. I reject them if I can.

I've always been able to find enough Southern yellow pine for a workbench by making one visit to a store. The only time I had to visit more than one store was when I was teaching a class on building a sawbench and had to buy enough 2x12s for a dozen students. I bought $600 worth of pine that day.

If you don't have Southern yellow pine in your local home center, I'd check with the Southern Pine Council; yes, the wood even has its own cheerleading organization. The organization's web site (southernpine.com) has a product locator that has helped many people find yellow pine in unlikely locations, such as New Jersey.

One more detail: Many people have asked me if they could use pressure-treated lumber for their workbenches. After all, the treated stuff is Southern yellow pine and is available everywhere. The Environmental Protection Agency warns against allowing the sawdust from CCA-treated material to accumulate indoors and recommends protection when sanding it. With those precautions, I don't feel comfortable allowing that product into my home as something I work on every day. Perhaps I'm overly cautious. Perhaps that trait is why I have all 10 fingers intact.

If you're still having trouble finding the wood, drive your truck here to Cincinnati and load up. It's a nice town with a fair supply of Southern pine and German beer.

A HEAVY FRENCH MEAL: I move my bench at least once a week – and not for exercise. A tricky setup or clamping job can be easier with access to the rear. But sawing and planing are easier with the bench braced against the wall.

The Stiffness of Common Workbench Woods

SPECIES	E VALUE
Hemlock, eastern	1.20
Chestnut	1.23
White pine	1.24
Sycamore	1.42
Basswood	1.46
American cherry	1.49
Hemlock, western	1.49
Red oak (Northern)	1.49
Poplar	1.58
European beech	1.63
Red (soft) maple	1.64
Black walnut	1.68
American beech	1.72
Ash	1.77
White oak	1.78
Hard maple	1.83
Southern yellow pine	1.93
Douglas fir	1.95
Yellow birch	2.01
Hickory, shagbark	2.16

Source: *Understanding Wood* (Taunton Press)

OK, back to numbers. The most important technical factor when choosing a species for a bench is its E value. The E value is the measure of stiffness, or how much strain a species exhibits under a certain amount of stress. The higher the E value, the stiffer the board. A board with an E value of 2 is twice as stiff as one with an E value of 1. When you dissect this chart, I think you'll understand why I choose Southern yellow pine or Douglas fir for workbenches (and joists). Use the chart at right to figure out how your local species fare on the stiffness scale.

E value aside, once a benchtop reaches 4" thick, it is plenty stiff enough for a standard woodworking bench. So be aware of the E value, but don't let it paralyze you.

Another characteristic of the wood that's important for building a bench is its weight. Unless you are building a bench that must be portable, a heavy bench is desirable. Heavy benches resist the pushing and shoving that comes with the craft. One of my first workbenches was an old walnut cafeteria door resting on a poplar sawhorse-style frame. It weighed no more than 70 pounds. During planing or sawing, the bench would inch down the wall until it kissed the drill press's table. Every few days I'd drag my bench back to the starting line.

There are definitely ways to make a lightweight bench function well. You can bolt it to (or through) your floor. You can capture its base using cleats that you attach to your floor with concrete anchors or screws. But these fixes prevent you from easily moving your workbench. And you will occasionally want to pull it from the wall or move it a few inches or a few feet. So the ideal bench is one that is difficult to move unless you are trying to move it.

My current French-style bench weighs about 500 pounds, all told. It does not move under any woodworking task. However, I can lift one end and pivot the bench to move it by myself within the shop. Two strong backs can move the bench onto a truck (we've done this several times). It is the heaviest bench I've ever used, and I'm well pleased with its weight.

The relative weight of wood is expressed by what is called *specific gravity*, which compares the weight of the wood to the weight of an equivalent volume of water. The larger the number the heavier the

THE DAILY BEATINGS WILL CONTINUE: Even if you don't like nails (and I do) you'll find yourself whacking your benchtop on occasion. If you don't like dents, choose a species that is high on the Janka scale.

The Weight of Common Workbench Woods

SPECIES	SPECIFIC GRAVITY
White pine	.35
Basswood	.37
Hemlock, eastern	.40
Poplar	.42
Hemlock, western	.47
Chestnut	.48
Douglas fir	.48
Sycamore	.49
American cherry	.50
Red (soft) maple	.54
Black walnut	.55
Red oak (Northern)	.59
Ash	.60
Yellow birch	.62
Hard maple	.63
American beech	.64
Southern yellow pine	.67
European beech	.68
White oak	.68
Hickory, shagbark	.72
Purpleheart	.77

Source: *Woods of the World*, a list of species at 12 percent moisture content, plus various industry publications.

wood is. A wood that approaches (or exceeds) 1 will be heavier than water and will sink in water. That's heavy.

Most texts tend to separate hardwoods and softwoods when they deal with specific gravity, but I think that's a taxonomic transgression. The difference between a so-called *hardwood* or *softwood* has nothing to do at all with the wood's woodworking properties. Instead, it has to do with how the trees reproduce. Yes, tree sex. Look it up if you don't believe me. Hardwoods are angiosperms, which means their seeds have a covering, such as an acorn. Softwoods are gymnosperms, which means their seeds don't. That's the major difference. Now, it's true that hardwoods are generally harder and denser than softwoods, but it's also an over-simplification. So don't discount the so-called softwoods when building a bench. Southern yellow pine is about the same density as European beech, and both species make a fine workbench.

Another important characteristic of wood is its resistance to blows and denting in general. Anyone who has purchased a white pine 2x4 bench from a home center can attest to this fact: These benches are easy to beat. They dent when you look at them wrong. A maple bench, on the other hand, won't dent even after you park a Ford F150 on it. Is this an important trait for a workbench? It depends. Do you hit your bench? I think that handwork is more likely to introduce a

lot of pounding and beating on the benchtop. Chop a few mortises by hand and you might agree. The power-tool workshop is much less reliable on percussion tools (such as mallets); the joinery is handled almost exclusively by cutting tools.

If you are worried about dents, get to know the Janka scale. It is a test that reveals the amount of force (in pounds per square inch) required to insert a .444"-diameter steel ball into a species of wood so that half of the pellet is buried in the wood.

If you study the chart, you'll note that some of the woods I've used for workbenches, such as Southern yellow pine, are pretty pitiful on the Janka scale. Truth is, I think that yellow pine is tough enough for a bench. I flatten my benchtops about once a year, and it's an opportunity to see how each top fared in use. I find very few serious dents in my yellow pine tops. Never do I see a dent from a clamp head. We use parallel-jaw clamps that can apply up to 1,000 pounds of pressure across the clamp's contact area. Occasionally I find a stray hammer mark, but all in all, yellow pine is tough enough to resist most percussion. In fact, it seems to get tougher with age.

So the bottom line is that you have a wide latitude when choosing a species with which to build your bench. In fact, almost any species will do. So select a species that is stiff, heavy, tough, plentiful in your

SHRINKAGE IS OK: When the top of my French bench shrank, it distorted the base into a slight A-frame shape. It's no problem to work on a bench with this shape.

The Janka Scale for Some Common Workbench Woods

SPECIES	PSI
White pine	380
Basswood	410
Hemlock	500
Chestnut	540
Poplar	540
Douglas fir	660
Southern yellow pine	690
Sycamore	770
American cherry	950
Red (soft) maple	950
Big leaf maple	1,000
Black walnut	1,010
Yellow birch	1,260
Red oak (Northern)	1,290
American beech	1,300
European beech	1,300
Ash	1,320
White oak	1,360
Hard maple	1,450
Hickory/Pecan	1,820
Purpleheart	1,860
Ipe	3,680

area and affordable. And if you are strapped for cash, you can always invest the most money on the wood for the top and use construction-grade white pine lumber for the base, which doesn't have to be as stout. There's nothing wrong with a mongrel, mixed species bench. Most benches end up that way after user modifications anyway.

Wood for Workbenches: Somewhat Seasoned is OK

When building cabinets and other casework, you generally want your wood to be at equilibrium with your shop environment. In other words, you want it to achieve a state where it is not actively giving off (or taking in) large gulps of moisture from the air. Any change in moisture content of wood at equilibrium is related to the changes in humidity with the seasons.

The usual advice is to bring the wood into your shop and allow it to acclimate to the shop environment, checking its progress with a moisture meter. That's good advice for cabinets, however you can use wood that is still in flux for a workbench if you are smart about it.

Here's how: Once you bring your stock into your shop, check each piece with the moisture meter, writing its moisture content on the surface of the board (I use a grease pen). Then separate the stock into

two piles: those boards that are close to the equilibrium moisture content in your shop and those that are way over (4 percentage points or more counts as way over). I've used stuff that is 9 points over, and I've tried using stuff that was even wetter. That was a bit of a disaster. The wood was Douglas fir and was probably 22 percent moisture. When I ripped it on the table saw, the blade sprayed a thin fan of water back at me, which was a weird way to work. When I'd leave the wood on a cast-iron surface for a couple hours, the iron would rust. So I try to avoid stuff that is too wet.

Once you have the two piles of wood, that's when you can start marking out your parts. First choose the driest parts for anything that will be a rail or a stretcher – anything that will have a tenon on the end of it. Now pick the wettest stuff for the legs or anything that will have a mortise bored into it.

Then set the other stuff aside as you build the base of the bench. As the legs dry out, the wet legs will shrink on the dry tenons (which won't change in size much). This will tighten your most critical joints. This is a basic chairbuilding technique used by some green woodworkers to make their projects last for centuries.

Once you've selected the parts for your base and built it, go back to your pile of wood for the benchtop and check the stock again with

17

LONG ENOUGH: This 1910 photo shows a bench at the Bristol Aeroplane Co. in Filton, Bristol. It is likely 14' long. Note the drawer and the frame clamped on edge in the face vise. Photo courtesy of Michael Gladwin.

your moisture meter. During the time it took you to make the base, the boards for the top all should have moved closer (sometimes much closer) to the equilibrium moisture content in your shop.

This strategy has worked well for several of my benches. It allows you to get to work on your workbench, it makes your joints stronger and it doesn't cause any splitting that I've found.

The Size of the Top

With your wood species selected, you should start sketching the skeleton of your design on your computer, graph paper or a napkin. The first issue is the top. Its thickness, width and length are key. And their dimensions are not arbitrary.

My first revelation about the size of the top came from my own early experiences as an adult in working wood. I started on our back porch in Lexington, Kentucky, which was sagging and reeked of the sweet but nauseating smell of rotting possum. I had my grandfather's bench out in the shed, but I didn't move it to the porch for some reason, which is now lost to me. Instead, I assembled all the furniture I built on the floor of the porch. I even had the table saw out on the porch, which would have made a half-decent assembly surface. But instead, I would move all the parts to the floor for fitting. Ridiculous? Yes.

Fast-forward seven or eight years and I'm trying to teach some fellow employees at *Popular Woodworking* magazine how to do some basic woodworking operations. I walked them through all the critical power-tool operations that could sever a digit. But then I left them alone for a few minutes to adjust their joints and assemble some parts while I returned some phone calls.

I'm out of the shop for 10 minutes, tops.

When I walk back in they are all working on the floor. It looked like I'd barged in on circle time at the local kindergarten. In the shop

BENCH EXTENSION: This is an odd bench with an unusual position for the end vise. But what's interesting is the fold-down extension. Long benches were the norm, especially for house carpenters and joiners. From *Carpentry and Building* magazine, October 1882.

we had six or seven workbenches and assembly benches the students could have used. We also had three table saws, two with massive outfeed tables that would have been great assembly tables. Instead the students chose the cold, hard concrete floor. Why?

I suppose we gravitate toward the support and space offered by the earth. It is the infinite assembly table, after all. And it offers unerring support. You rarely run out of floor space when moving cabinet parts around down there. So when I make a workbench top, I make it imitate the best qualities of the floor. I think your benchtop should be as long as possible. Find the wall where your workbench will go. (Hint: Pick the wall that has a window.) Measure that space. Subtract four feet from that and that's a good length for the top. Note: The benchtop should be at least 5' long unless you build only small-scale items. Furniture-sized parts typically range up to 48" long and you want to be able to support these fully and have a little room to spare.

I've made tops that are 10' long. I dream of a 12' top. It is difficult to make or imagine a workbench that's too long. The same goes for thickness. It is the thickness that allows the top to be that long. If you make the top really thick, 4 or more inches, then it will offer the

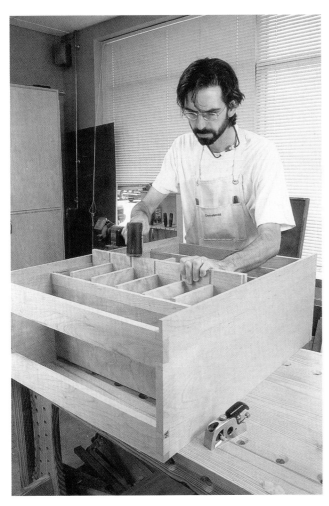

JUST WIDE ENOUGH: You can reach across a benchtop that is narrower than 30" to work on a typical cabinet. Benchtops that are wider than 36" force you to trot around them all day.

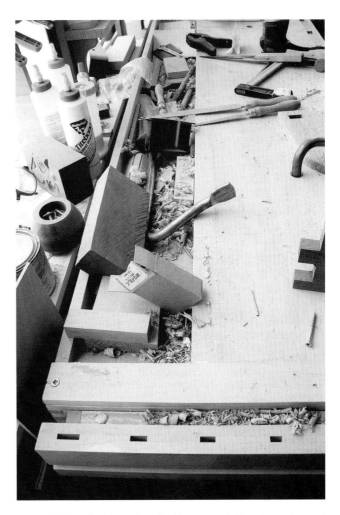

HAMSTER TOWN: The tool tray in this commercial bench gets cluttered during a project. Some people love tool trays, however.

erring support offered by the earth and allow you to build your bench without any unwieldy support system beneath. My current benchtop is 6" thick. The top can perch on your legs and will not sag under any normal weight.

But the width is a different matter. You can have benches that are too wide for a one-person shop. I've worked on benches that are 36" wide and they have downsides. For starters, if you park them against the wall you'll have to stretch to reach the tools that are hanging on the wall or have scooted across the top and are cowering against the wall.

But there's more. Cabinetwork is sized in standard chunks. These sizes come from the human body; they aren't arbitrary. A kitchen's base cabinet is generally 24" deep and 34½" high. This is important for a couple reasons. First: It means you don't really need a bench that's much more than 24" deep to build cabinetry. With that 24" depth, you actually gain advantages, including the fact that you can clamp the cabinet to your bench from as many as three sides of your bench. That is handy. A deep bench will allow you to clamp your cabinets to the bench on only two sides (with a couple exceptions).

Here's the other thing to keep in mind: Kitchen cabinets are themselves a highly studied work surface. There's a good reason that kitchen cabinets are 24" deep. And, if you think about it, it's the same reason you don't want your workbench much deeper either.

The height of the kitchen cabinets (and your workbench) are another important dimension. Keep that 34½" in mind for now.

Now I'm not going to argue with you if you build really big stuff or have a bench that you share with another woodworker facing you; you might need more depth. But if you are like the rest of us, a 24"-deep bench is a powerful and right-sized tool. In fact, I have been building benches that are even narrower – 18" is surprisingly stable, takes up less floor space in a small shop and allows me to sleeve drawers and carcases over it to plane their flat surfaces.

These guidelines for bench sizes aren't random. Check out illustrations of early benches for cabinetmakers or joiners, who outfitted homes with sashwork and doors. These benches usually follow these rules, especially the ones on length and depth. The top's thickness is another matter, and it depends on whether the cabinetmaker was French or English. More on that later as we'll get into the different styles of benches.

The Tool Tray: Do You Need One?

In general I don't like discussing religion or politics, so I was tempted to ignore the topic of tool trays. This recessed area at the back edge of your bench – or down the middle in some designs – is the subject of much debate. It can be a good place to keep bench tools handy, accord-

A BENCH IN THE BREACH: This bench has always interested me. It has so many qualities of 19th- and 18th-century benches, yet it has metal vise screws, the face-vise is built using finger joints (a machine-made joint) and the tools suggest it's an early 20th-century photograph. This bench was (and still is) a blend of old and new. Note especially how the top is flush with the legs and sliding deadman.

ing to some, and a great place to make a nest for the family hamster, according to others.

I've worked on all sorts of benches, with and without tool trays, and both perspectives are exactly right.

If you're going to have a tool tray in your workbench, make it deep. I'd say that 4" is right. The deeper the tool tray, the better it is at holding tools. Shoulder planes and right-angle drills will nest in a deep tray without poking up above the benchtop surface. Another excellent feature with a tool tray is to make the floor of it removable in sections. This cunning idea, which I first encountered in David Charlesworth's books, eliminates some of the features I dislike about tool trays. By removing the floor of the tool tray you can get a clamp in there to secure some work to the top. Plus, the tool tray is easier to clean of shavings and dust. The tool tray on my grandfather's bench has ends that are ramp shaped so you can sweep debris out of the tool tray — this also works, but the removable floor works better.

The most significant downside to tool trays of any design is that they reduce the amount of working and clamping surface you have available. There are times where you need the support of the benchtop right where the tool tray is located. I've encountered this obstacle a number of times when planing wide panels for case sides. I'll want to get a shim or wedge under the panel to make it sit firmly on the benchtop, but I cannot because of the tool tray. Also, a bench with a tool tray in the center can be tricky to flatten.

Also, no matter how fastidious you are, your tool tray is going to be a junk magnet. Dust and shavings collect there among your tools, and you can end up having to root around like a pig hunting truffles for your marking knife or carpenter's pencil.

The Placement of the Bench in the Workshop

Where you place your bench in your shop might not seem like something you should be concerned about at the design phase, but it is.

Workbenches for handwork thrive when they're placed near a wall with a window. The wall can brace the workbench as you are planing cross-grain and sawing. The light from the window points out the flaws in the work that your hand tools are trying to remove. (In fact, when I work with hand tools, I usually turn off the overhead lights in my shop. I can see much better with fewer light sources.)

There are some interesting theories about which direction your bench should face. One 19th-century maxim was that benches should

"I think that if I did not work with wood, my life would be a hollow emptiness. If I did not form and shape and build, what would I have done to leave my mark in this world? My eyes have been filled with the endlessly changing patterns of the grains. I have felt the warmth of a thousand suns in my hands every day. I have smelled the rich, tangy odors of the freshly hewn chips. These are the things that have made my life so fine. These are the most precious things I can leave for you, my son."

— Jonas Wainwright, Master Carpenter, from a letter to his son, 1832

Benches from the Old Countries

People tend to personalize benches – a Tage Frid bench, a Frank Klausz bench, a Michael Dunbar bench. I tend to nationalize them instead.

We could start with the Roman workbench, a low table with four to eight legs that's built like a Windsor chair. It's just about the earliest form of workbench in the literature, but it's disappeared from the workshop. The French workbench shown in Andre Roubo's 18th century masterwork *Description Des Arts Et Metiers* has a thick slab top, massive legs and narrow stretchers.

Work-holding is simple and ingenious. There's a planing stop on the benchtop, plus holes for holdfasts in the top. Early French benches sport a crochet, a planing stop for working edges of boards. The wood is supported below by holdfasts in holes in the legs.

German- and Scandinavian-style benches share similarities with French benches, with some engineering added. These benches – sometimes called continental or European benches – generally have a slab top, though the top is more complex. It can be thinner in the middle and ringed by a thick frame. For workholding, you get a tail vise on the right side of the bench with a system of dogs for pinching the work. Some benches also have holes for holdfasts. And there is a shoulder vise on the left. The shoulder vise allows you to clamp pieces for dovetailing or tenoning without interference from screws from the vise. The undercarriage of the bench can have sled feet, and the legs are rarely flush with the front edge of the benchtop. Instead of relying on the legs to support long work, these benches would use a bench slave – a separate stand with an adjustable shelf.

And then there is what I call the English bench, which appears in Peter Nicholson's *The Mechanic's Companion* (1831). Nicholson calls out this bench as intended for joiners – workmen who made sashes, doors and fittings for houses. There is no discussion of furniture being made on this bench. (An earlier book by Joseph Moxon also insists its bench is for joiners. And so does Roubo, though the bench is shown being used for fine furniture work).

The English bench has a thin top supported by interior ribs, and at least one wide apron. The English bench has a face vise, a planing stop and pegs on the front apron to support long boards on edge.

There are rarely dog holes in the top surface or a tail vise, which would make working the faces of wide panels quite a challenge. But that is a task for furniture makers more than joiners.

It is a material-efficient design and the English form survived into mid 20th-century America. My 1947 edition of *Audels Carpenters and Builders Guide* (Vol. 1) shows some typical English benches for house carpenters, but one form has a sliding deadman; another has dog holes in the benchtop. But neither has a tail vise! How did they secure the work between dogs? My guess: Wedging.

These three basic bench forms – French, continental and English – are the basis for most Western-style workbenches, with latter-day bench designers mixing and matching their features to suit their work or whim. Sometimes the mongrel designs work; sometimes they don't. Examining why a bench design succeeds or fails is why this book exists.

THREE TRADITIONS: The French bench (top) is massive, the Continental workbench (middle) is the most complex (and it's the dominant form today), and the English bench is cleverly engineered.

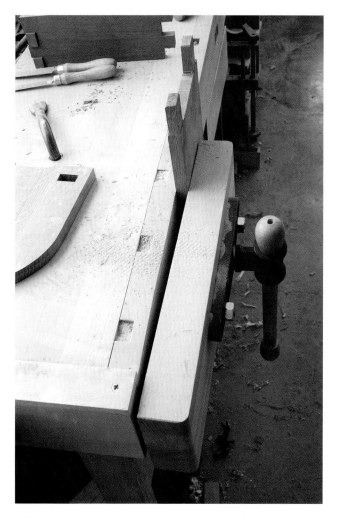

ABOUT FACE: Though its jaws are wooden, this is a face vise because it is located on the face of the bench. Quick quiz: If this were a twin-screw vise, what would you call it? Yup, a twin-screw face vise.

FACING FACTS: The quick-release metal vise is perhaps the most common form of face vise on benches today. That doesn't mean it's the best thing for woodworking. Its parallel guide bars interfere with clamping boards to work on edges and ends.

stand so the length runs north and south. There should be windows at the north and south, with no windows east or west.

My bench at home is under a window that faces north, and the light is constant and even throughout the day. My bench at work was under a west window. There, the light was harsh at the end of the day. This produced glare on lighter workpieces and the color of the light was warmer than at mid-day. The work looked different at the end of the day.

Your particular shop space may determine the ultimate length of your workbench. If you have an 8'-long wall for your bench an 8'-long bench isn't going to work. You need access to the ends and room for your tools (particularly your long planes) to complete their strokes without striking a wall.

Your shop space can also affect what sort of vises you choose. If you have to wedge your bench into a tight space, then a twin-screw vise on the end of the bench is a bad idea. It will be unusable if you cannot get your body in front of it for sawing dovetails or tenons.

When working with power tools, I tend to pull my workbench away from the wall so I can work on all sides of it. When working with routers, you sometimes have to work with odd clamping setups to avoid climb-cutting. So access to all four sides of the bench is handy.

Power tool setups thrive on overhead light — and lots of it. So being by the window is nice, but not as necessary as with hand work.

Because most shops use some sort of combination of hand and power tools, I bet you'll move your bench around a bit. Mine gets shifted a couple times during most projects. Keep this in mind when you settle on the ultimate length of the bench. Make it as long as possible while allowing the vises to work without hitting a wall.

Overhang: How the Top and Legs Interact

When you build a dining room table, the amount that the top overhangs the table's apron is a critical measurement. A well-sized overhang can add grace to the design. It's something I fuss over whenever I build a table. But when it comes to designing workbenches, I have concluded that the old ways are best. Here's exactly how much the old-timers let their workbench tops overhang the legs in front: zero.

Why? OK, erase from your mind that a workbench is a table. It's not a table. It shouldn't be built like a dining room table, and it shouldn't look like one either. Your bench is a three-dimensional clamping surface. If you're clamping work to the top only, you're missing out. The front of your bench (when made properly) is an amazing clamping surface. You can clamp an entryway door against the legs and top (if they're flush) to mortise in the hinges or lockset. You can clamp a carcase side for dovetailing. You can easily support long and wide boards to work their edges. Cabinet doors, face frames, tabletops — anything big and flat can be clamped there.

In fact, early French benches would even make the stretchers between the workbench's legs flush to the front of the bench. I have to agree here with the French — this feature has come in handy in my shop. English woodworkers also knew this trick. English workbenches have legs that are flush to the front of the bench and also have an enormous front apron that is flush to the legs and top. The apron offers unparalleled vertical clamping (it also gets in the way of clamping things to the workbench top).

RACKED WITH A WEAK GRIP: Many face vises, wooden or iron, will rack when pressure is applied on one end only. This racking saps your clamping power. You need a vise block (actually, you need several), that will even out the pressure on both sides of the vise's screw.

The Placement and Selection of Vises

Vises confuse many workbench builders. Vises are especially bewildering if you've never spent much time working at a bench developing a taste for the peccadilloes of all the idiosyncratic forms out there. There are a lot of weird configurations in the world, from a bench with no vises at all to the bench with a vise on every corner.

So let's start with first principles when you consider a vise. I think the first question you need to ask yourself is not how many vises you need, but if you need a vise at all.

Early benches didn't have the quick-release, iron-and-steel behemoths we use today. Early woodworkers used gravity, force and simple machines to solve workholding challenges, and they solved those problems well. Working on a bench without a vise is an interesting experience. A crochet on the left corner constrains work on edge; a series of pegs or a sliding deadman supports the work from below. For working on the faces of boards, a planing stop does the dirty work with the benchtop supporting the length of your board. A doe's foot or other battens can help restrain your work for travering.

So why do vises exist if you don't need them? They're handy, though not as useful as you might suspect. They can pinch small work to hold it for sanding, planing, rasping or chiseling, but when it comes

to other common tasks, metal bench vises are a challenge you have to work around. So with that in mind, let's take a look at the most common metal vise around. Most people call it the face vise.

Face Vise

The face vise is so named because it goes on the front face of a workbench. Almost any vise can be a face vise, though most people associate the term with a cast iron vise or a similar wooden-jawed vise. Right-handers generally place the face vise on the left side of the bench; lefties put it on the right. It is typically the workhorse of a modern bench. It will hold small pieces of work, generally up to about 24" in length, for a variety of handwork and power-tool tasks.

Many woodworkers will take the extra time to fit the rear jaws of a cast iron face vise into the front edge of the workbench top. This arrangement allows you to use the front edge of your workbench's top to support long boards. Many English woodworkers prefer the rear jaw to be proud of the benchtop. You will have to ask them why.

The garden variety cast iron face vise has charms and challenges. First the good stuff: A face vise will generally open and close rapidly and smoothly, sometimes by pulling a trigger on the screw, or sometimes by rotating the main vise screw counterclockwise for half a turn or so. These vises, called quick-release vises, can adapt to parts of wildly varying size in a jiffy.

More good stuff: The jaws are cast iron or malleable iron, which makes them fairly stiff and robust. Cast iron face vises generally require little upkeep and are quick to install.

All these nice features make the cast iron face vise popular. In fact, in all the commercial shops I've been in, virtually every workbench had one. And when I started work at *Popular Woodworking* in 1996, every bench had an iron quick-release face vise. And so did my grandfather's bench. And my father's. In fact, I was unaware that any other vises existed.

But here's the truth: The typical iron face vise has limitations that are rarely discussed. It's not a conspiracy cooked up by vise manufacturers. I just think that woodworkers have adapted to the form and developed clever ways to work around its warts.

So what's wrong with them? The biggest problem is they don't excel at clamping long boards vertically – like when you want to cut dovetails or tenons on an end. The vise's screw and parallel bars interfere with the clamping capacity of the vise. You're lucky if you can reliably clamp anything wider than 5". And if you try to use one corner of the vise to clamp something wide and long, you're in for a rude shock. The jaws can rack under pressure, so you can't clamp the work securely without putting a vise block (a block of wood that has the same thickness as your workpiece) on the opposite corner of the vise. And even with a vise block, you still can only grab one edge of the work and the other edge is free to shake about. So you clamp that side to the front edge of your workbench – assuming the jaws of the vise and the front edge of your bench are in the same plane.

And that's just for starters. You really should line the vise's jaws with something softer so you don't mar your work. Some people glue leather to the jaws. Other people secure plywood *skins* to the cast iron jaws. The jaws themselves can be a liability. I've scratched a number of plane soles on the iron jaw, chipped a few chisel edges and extracted a few saw teeth.

The best solution I found to these myriad issues was to add a long, thick wooden jaw to the movable jaw of the vise. This gave me more

THE OLD FRONTIER: Wooden vise screws are nice, if they are well made. They move quickly and won't damage your tools.

clamping capacity thanks to the added length of the jaw, and it kept my work surrounded by some extra wood, which protected the tools.

So why not buy one of those face vises that requires you to make the wooden jaw? These imported vises are rarely quick-release vises, but they are a bit less expensive. I've installed and used three or four of these and have found them OK, but not perfect. You need to install a long, thick and stiff jaw for them to be effective. That's not a big deal, but I have found them to be more prone to racking: I was reaching for the vise blocks more with a wooden face vise than I was with an iron face vise with an accessory wooden jaw.

If you're a traditionalist, you might like a wooden-screw face vise. The screws were once difficult to find, but now they are available commercially again. They move quickly because of their coarse tpi. Vintage examples use a rectangular section of wood that's parallel to the screw to keep the vise jaws parallel to the benchtop. It's basically like the parallel guide on a leg vise.

Some vintage versions of these vises lack a garter – this is a locking ring that keeps the screw married to the jaw. If you don't have a garter, then you have to manually slide the jaw back toward you after you back off the screw. It's not a big deal, but a garter is nice.

All in all, I think the cast iron face vise is a fair choice for a workbench. You can always remove it. But before you automatically choose one, it's good to look at what the other vises have to offer.

Shoulder Vises

The shoulder vise shows up on many European benches at the left end of the bench in the face-vise position. It is like a giant letter L that is stuck to the front of the bench. There is a clamping screw through the L that presses your work against the front edge of the benchtop.

It's a remarkable vise, particularly for dovetailing drawers. Because of the arrangement of the screw, there is nothing to interfere or obstruct clamping below the benchtop. That means you can clamp long work that goes all the way to the floor and work an end of the board with ease. With most of these shoulder vises, you have the ability to clamp right at the center of a 12"-wide board without racking the jaws – that's quite a feat for any vise. Once your boards get wider (and especially as they approach the width of a typical case piece) you are going to have to add a clamp to your setup to hold the piece against

Patternmaker's Vises: Friend or Foe?

Among some woodworkers, the Emmert Improved Universal Vise is the end-all, do-all vise. But after working with an Emmert copy off and on for a couple years, I think that it's probably overkill for woodworkers who deal mostly with flat, square stuff.

The Emmert was invented by Joseph F. Emmert in the late 19th century and was the vise that graced the workbenches of many patternmakers during its nearly 100 years of production. It was the vise that held the wood that made the patterns that made the molds that made the castings that made the machines that made many wooden objects obsolete.

The Emmert vise's allure is its adjustability. You can clamp odd-shaped objects in its versatile jaws and then move the jaws all around – even above the benchtop – to work the piece. I know chairmakers, carvers and luthiers (instrument builders) who love this vise. When I used the Emmert copy – made by the now-defunct AMT corporation – it was attached to a workbench in the classic face-vise position at the left end of the bench.

It worked entirely as advertised, though I almost never had much use for its unusual functions. It was a very nice and quite expensive face vise for me.

This is perhaps a condemnation of my work more than the vise. I build cabinets, tables and chairs for the most part. And I don't do a lot of carving. So perhaps my world view is just a little small. Emmerts can sell for $800 these days. A Taiwanese copy is also available through many suppliers.

the front of the benchtop. This arrangement is typical for most vises with a couple exceptions.

The vise also works as a typical face vise for holding one end of a long board for planing (a portable bench slave typically supports the far end of the board). And it handles small tapered pieces beautifully.

The only disadvantage I've ever pinned down on the shoulder vise is that it is more complex to construct and install than a quick-release vise or a wooden leg vise. Nor is the vise a simple retrofit to an existing bench. The vise generally requires its own (fifth) leg that is tied into the trestle base of the workbench. The cantilevered section of the vise is typically bolted to the benchtop with a very long threaded rod.

When I first used one, I was concerned that it would force me to lean forward when dovetailing. The vise assembly does, after all, stick out a foot from the front end of the main benchtop. But my concerns were for naught. I approached the work from the same position as I did with any typical vise. There is some close work that isn't as elegant as I'd liked. When chamfering or shaping the ends of boards, I would

WORTH THE EXTRA LEG: Woodworkers who like hand-cutting dovetails like shoulder vises, such as this version made by Louis Bois. These vises are much better as original equipment than they are as an add-on.

SUPER – TO A POINT: My twin-screw vise at the end of the bench is great for dovetailing – as long as I don't have stock that is wider than the space between the screws. Then I'm stuck.

sometimes strike the bench screw or the cantilevered section of the vise. There are probably ways to work around this problem, but I simply moved my work to a traditional face vise to finish the job.

Twin-screw Vises

Yet another style of face vise is the twin screw. I have hundreds of hours of experience with a twin-screw vise, and here is my short assessment. Twin-screw vises are a lot like my collegiate experiments with Southern Comfort: Both work sweetly on the mind and make you think that anything is possible (tapers, dovetails, tenons, a Pulitzer). But when you reach their limit, everything goes south in a hurry.

Twin-screws excel at clamping wide material for dovetailing right up until you reach the maximum space between the vise's two screws. If you cross that limit, you're kinda sunk. Regular face vises, leg vises and shoulder vises can be rigged with the help of a clamp or sliding deadman to clamp boards of any width, as long as you are willing to live with some extra steps and inconvenience. You can set a face vise on one edge of your work and then a clamp across the benchtop to hold the other edge of a wide board.

With a twin screw, you generally have little leeway once you reach the vise's limit. Clamping on the vise's corners outside the protective confines of the screws is a bit of a pain on many of these vises. And if you have the twin screw mounted on the end of the bench instead of the face, you're truly out of luck.

There are some other personality quirks to the twin screw. Releasing the screws can become a two-handed operation with some vises and some setups, and you end up using one of your knees to keep the work from dashing to the floor while you release the pressure.

The twin screws (even the modern ones with the screws linked by bicycle chain) can be a bit fussy to keep the jaws parallel and everything moving smoothly. And old-school wooden ones require a bit of skill to manipulate – some of them don't have garters and the screws operate independently.

It might not sound it, but I quite like twin-screw vises. When set up and used properly, they are a pure joy for dovetailing, tenoning and working the edges of boards. Lots of other woodworkers over the years have also agreed because this style of vise is a common sight on the left front corner of early benches in particular.

Personally, my favorite for of twin-screw vise is one you can remove when you don't need it. Sometimes called a "Moxon vise" or "double bench screw," this portable bench has many charms. (See the Appendix on page 178 for plans for one.)

Leg Vises

You don't see a lot of leg vises on commercial benches. Perhaps one reason is that they can require two separate adjustments for one clamping operation. As you advance the screw of a leg vise (one adjustment), there is a separate guide at the floor that helps keep the jaws parallel (the second adjustment). When you reach your desired clamping range, you insert a pin through one of the holes in the parallel guide and advance the screw some more. The jaw then pivots on your pin and is levered onto your work with remarkable force.

This type of leg vise requires some stooping and some extra movements, so it's little wonder that woodworkers and manufacturers came up with devices that eliminated the extra steps required by the parallel guide. Among the fancier leg vises, these enhancements took the form of a scissor device near the floor that kept the jaws in parallel. There were also some other devices that would do the job, including a second screw with a flat plate that spun on it like a jam nut on a drill press's depth stop.

Leg vises – which are almost always in the face vise position – have their rewards. They can clamp a flat piece against the bench's leg all the way to the floor. If you mount them on an angled leg, you can increase the width they can clamp all the way to the floor without hitting the screw – a 7"-wide leg vise at a 20° angle will clamp an 8"-wide workpiece vertically all the way to the floor. That's great for dovetailing drawer sides.

AN IDEAL ANGLE: A leg vise that's angled at 20° can grip wide boards all the way to the floor. This one handles boards up to 8" wide – perfect for most drawers.

PERCHED FOR PLANING: You don't need a vise to work across the grain or at an angle to the grain. Thin wooden strips cinched by hold-fasts stop the work from sliding side-to-side. A planing stop at the end prevents the board from shooting into space.

NO WONDER THEY'RE POPULAR: The Veritas Wonder Dog is a good substitute for an end vise. There are limitations – they're tricky to use with thin work. But for the price and the simplicity, they're good workers.

They are the best vise I've ever used for clamping doors, windows, face frames and long boards so you can work on their edges. They are inexpensive and easy to make. And you can simply unscrew them to remove them from the bench if you ever want to try a different vise arrangement. They also play nicely with a crochet for working on the edges of boards.

And as to the stooping, I don't have back problems so it's an irritation more than a pain. Usually, I'm working on ³/₄"- or ⁷/₈"-thick materials, which use the same hole in the parallel guide. So I'm not futzing with the thing as much as I thought when I first built it.

Tail Vises – Sometimes Called an End Vise

An end vise can actually be a number of different kinds of vises. What they all have in common is that they are mounted on the end of the bench and are in line with a number of dog holes in the benchtop. There are a number of forms. I'll deal with them in an evolutionary manner, starting with the simplest form: No vise.

I ran into this arrangement when perusing my old books on house carpentry and even older books on French woodworking. The early French books showed no familiar rows of bench-dog holes. Just a few holes for holdfasts and a planing stop or two. You work long boards using the forward and downward force of the tool (plus the some-times-helpful gravity) to immobilize the work against the planing stop. This arrangement, which I have tried to master for some time, requires skill with the tool. It requires you to skew the plane as you work to keep the stock against the stop and not careening across the benchtop. Wider boards are harder than narrow ones to control.

How do you work across the grain? Simple battens work fine. A notched batten – called a doe's foot – is an even better solution as it will resist all sorts of forces, both across and along the grain. If you want to work without a tail vise, the doe's foot is the first appliance you should make.

There are lots of solutions. A house carpenter's bench in *Audels Carpenters and Builders Guide* offers only a long row of bench-dog holes. No vise mechanism at the end to pinch the work. And no text to indicate how the dog holes should be used. My first thought was that you could use a couple wedges and two dogs to secure your work. And you probably could.

More likely, however, is that the house carpenter would use a vise-like portable metal device that would attach to the benchtop and grip the work from behind when a lever was engaged. This hook-from-behind device – sometimes called a bench knife stop – is not made anymore. But it is the missing link to the next step in the chain: The Veritas Wonder Dog.

The Wonder Dog, invented in 1992 and patented in 1996 by Lee Valley Tools, is a movable tail vise. It drops into any ³/₄"-diameter round dog hole in your benchtop. Once in place, you turn a small brass handle and it advances a screw that is attached to a rectangular

UNUSUAL BUT EFFECTIVE: A so-called wagon vise does a lot of things that more complex end vises do. It clamps assemblies and can work as a spreader to take things apart.

DOE'S FOOT: You can do a lot of work without a tail vise if you have a doe's foot, a simple notched batten secured to the benchtop with a clamp or holdfast.

dog. With a Wonder Dog, a round bench dog and a row of $^3/_4$" holes you can have an instant tail-vise setup that works for nearly all of your benchtop clamping needs.

Yes, the Wonder Dog has a couple inherent quirks in its design. First, the screw that advances and retracts the dog has a fine thread, about 14 teeth per inch. I wish the thing would advance and retract faster. The second detail is that the movable rectangular dog sits $^5/_8$" above the benchtop. That's fine when planing $^3/_4$"-thick material, but a bit tricky when doing thin work. I've mounted accessory wooden jaws to the Wonder Dog, but you still have to steer carefully around the dog because a handplane sole is going to be 9" long or more with smoothing planes – even longer with jacks and jointers. These are minor flaws in the Wonder Dog system, all in all, especially if you stack them up against not having a tail vise at all.

Wonder Dogs also do a lot of other benchtop tasks: I've used them as spreader clamps to dismantle a door assembly. You can also (with a couple Wonder Dogs and regular dogs) clamp up many oddball shapes. I typically use them to secure benchtop tools, such as my router table, temporarily to the benchtop.

The next simplest kind of tail vise is called a wagon vise in some French accounts. It essentially is a movable dog that rides in a slot in the benchtop. This dog also is in line with a row of bench dog holes in the benchtop. The wagon vise's strength is its simplicity and the fact that it has but a few moving parts. You can move the dogs up and down to clamp really thin work – which gives it one advantage over the Wonder Dog. But the wagon vise serves only one line of bench dog holes and cannot be moved around the bench for unusual situations. To make one (which is shown later in this book), you need only purchase a metal bench screw, which is a little more expensive than a Wonder Dog. The remainder of the components are wooden. There also are commercial versions available.

Your next simplest option is a quick-release face vise. It can be mounted on the end of the workbench and function as a tail vise, if it is equipped with a dog. Even if it doesn't come with a dog, you can add an accessory wooden jaw to the vise (you really have to do this anyway to keep your work supported) and equip that with a dog or two. The advantage to using a quick-release vise is that it's an easy way

to install a fully functional tail vise. And you get the additional bonus of being able to clamp your work between the jaws at the tail end of your bench. I've found that's a handy spot for some unusual sawing and planing chores.

The downside to this arrangement is mostly cost. Quick-release vises are going to set you back some coin. There's another disadvantage to this vise that you might run into if your dog holes are spaced far apart on your benchtop. When clamping some boards, you'll have to extend the vise's jaws out to the point that your work will be unsupported over part of its length. When planing thin material, this can be a problem. The solution is to keep your dog holes spaced closely together. I typically put them on 3" or 4" centers. One of my first benches had a quick-release vise as a tail vise and the jaws extended out about 10" or 12", once you took the accessory jaw into consideration. In an attempt to be a clever (but lazy and foolhardy) boy, I drilled my bench-dog holes on 10" centers. As a result, some boards would have very little support. It didn't take me long to realize the error of my ways.

Some modern workbenches mount a twin-screw vise on the end of the bench and use it as an end vise. I've done this as well. The twin-screw tail vise usually has two or three dogs in the movable jaw, which can be in line with two or three rows of dog holes in the benchtop. This arrangement allows you to clamp circular work, primarily, though some plain-old odd-shaped work can be accommodated as well. (I've had great luck clamping Windsor arm bows with this rig.) You should keep your bench dog holes spaced closely together to avoid the same lack-of-support problem when using a quick-release vise in this position.

"A simple bench is like Tuscan pasta soup. You think it will be better if you add more stuff. But getting the basics right is way more important, and the extras won't make up for poorly prepared stock."
— Adam Cherubini

PERFECT FOR PANELS: Tasking a twin screw to be an end vise is great if you work with wide panels or circular tabletops. If you use it only for clamping narrow boards you might be stressing the vise unnecessarily.

MIND THE GAP: When you clamp work with an end vise, the difference between correct clamping and over-clamping is a few degrees of spin on the vise handle. When clamping, tighten the vise until it doesn't move and isn't bowed. Then go to work.

I also was told by some fellow craftsmen that using a twin-screw as an end vise is inherently bad for the vise. You end up stressing one of the vise screws most of the time with the other one racking the vise and not being under pressure. I scoffed at this notion until one day – after about five years of daily use – I advanced the screw on some work and heard a large thunk from inside the mechanism. I took the vise apart and found that one of the beefy screw heads that mounts the vise to the moving jaw had been sheared off. A defective screw perhaps? Or was it the result of my stressing out the vise? The rest of the vise appeared to be in good shape. I replaced the broken screw with a beefier one and went back to work. Two years later, no problems. Yet. Veritas, the manufacturer of my twin-screw, shows the vise being used in this position on the end of the bench and says nothing about stressing one screw.

And then there is the classic tail vise: an L-shaped section of the bench that slides left and right at the end-vise position. It has a number of bench-dog holes (four to six holes is typical) that line up with the other bench-dog holes in the top. The vise opens and closes by turning a fast-moving screw. It keeps the work (almost) fully supported and you can even clamp some workpieces between the vise's big jaw and the benchtop – narrow drawers and drawer sides fit nicely. You also can use the tail vise as a spreader clamp, like the wagon vise or Wonder Dog vise setup.

On paper, a traditional tail vise looks like an obvious good choice. But once you work with one that droops, it doesn't seem so ideal. Drooping tail vises can shift the work around in undesirable ways. That is not to say that you should dismiss tail vises out of hand. Some premium tail vises seem to have eliminated drooping, though I don't have long-term torture tests to back that claim up. They are both useful and popular forms. So I encourage you to take a balanced view and investigate the merits and drawbacks of every style of end vise.

For all the forms of the tail vise or end vise, there is one thing you must be careful to avoid: overclamping. All the tail vise forms are capable of bowing your stock under pressure. Once you flatten the face of the board and release it from the vise mechanism, you'll find the board bows in the opposite direction. So snug the vise just enough to secure the work and no more. It takes practice, but it ensures your work will end up flat and true.

If you are having trouble getting things secured flat, try lining the faces of your bench dogs with some leather or suede. The leather adds grip and allows you to use less clamping pressure.

Sliding Deadmen and Slaves

Though a bench jack (sometimes called a sliding deadman) isn't usually a vise, it is for workholding. It slides along the front of a workbench and supports work that's too long to be held by the face vise alone. The jack can also be a stand that is separate from the bench entirely – sometimes called a bench slave – with some kind of height-adjustable mechanism so you can support boards of many widths.

Another typical setup is to have a board built into the workbench that slides back and forth on a rail between the front legs. The board has holes that receive a peg. You place the peg in a hole that will support the door or wide board that you want to work on and then slide the jack into position. Clamp one corner of your work in the face vise, and you can then work on the edge of the board or assembly.

English workbenches would approach this problem differently. Instead of a slave or jack, the bench would be built with a wide front apron. This apron would be bored with as many holes as needed for pegs. This front apron, of course, prevents you from applying a clamp to the top at the front of the bench.

YOU SHOULD KNOW JACK:
A sliding bench jack supports long and wide work from below. Sometimes called a deadman, it is infinitely adjustable.

SEPARATE SUPPORT: If your bench isn't capable of supporting long or wide work, you can make a bench slave to do the job. This one clamps in a tail vise; it also could be freestanding on a base.

PINCH IN A PINCH: Two handscrews can hold the tail end of your work. This isn't really the way you want to work, day-in and day-out. But it is a good trick to have when you are in a bind. Or need to get into a bind.

There are other tricks that work quite well. The front legs can be bored with holes and you can secure long boards of scrap to the legs with holdfasts. Then you rest the work on the ledge of scrap. You also can use two handscrew clamps to support the tail end of the board with the front corner held by the face vise. Or, if you have your benchtop perched on a bank of drawers, you can pull a drawer out to support your boards. This works well.

Bench Stops

On a traditional workbench, the front left corner of the benchtop is home to a bench stop (sometimes called a planing stop or a bench hook, a confusing term that also means a jig for crosscutting small parts). The bench stop can be wood or metal and can be moved up and down in the benchtop with a lever, a screw or a mallet. The stop immobilizes your work while planing. Raise the stop a little to plane thin work. Raise the stop a great deal (mine goes up to 8" above the benchtop) to work boards on edge. This is a nice feature: The work is fully supported by your benchtop and is easy to control as you work the edge.

Some of the stops are toothed, which will bite into the end grain of your work. There are dozens of commercial versions that you might stumble upon at flea markets or on vintage benches. But the bench stop does not have to be a piece of toothed metal to be effective. In fact, the oldest bench stops were made entirely of wood, as were many of the British-style workbench appliances and jigs from the 19th and 20th centuries.

Bench stops for thin work are (in my experience) ideal when they are metal. A couple screws driven into a workbench act as finely adjustable stops for thin work – down to about 1/8"-thick stock. Need to plane something thinner? Use escutcheon pins.

When you look at old drawings of bench stops, the illustrations typically feature one stop. This is ideal for narrow stock but is a trick to use when working on panels. Some benches will feature two stops: Raise one for narrow stock and two for panels. Working on wide panels is a task typically performed by the furniture maker. Joiners (who made doors, sash windows and mouldings for homes) could probably manage with one stop.

Another option is a planing board. These ingenious trays are essentially large flat surfaces with raised stops around the edges. They might have adjustable planing stops at one end. You'd mount the planing board to your benchtop, perhaps with clamps, holdfasts or dropping it into dog holes. Then you'd work against the planing stops when working with the grain, the far lip when working across the grain, or into a corner when working diagonally.

The other bonus to a planing board is that you don't have to worry much about your benchtop's flatness – just the flatness of the planing board. And if the planing board casts (another name for warp) you pitch it and make another.

Holdfasts and Hold-downs

Other bench accessories for the benchtop are devices that hold the work down using single-point pressure from above. The oldest form of this is probably some sort of rope that is cinched by the worker's foot. But the earliest furniture-making and joiner's books discuss the holdfast as the tool of choice.

Style E

COMMERCIAL PERFECTION: If I didn't have to work on the edges of wide boards, this bench is a near-perfect specimen. In this old catalog, Hammacher, Schlemmer & Co. advertised this bench as handmade using 4"-square timbers. Sign me up.

The Stanley No. 203 – Better than a Peg

Usually a sliding bench jack uses a peg to support the work. This is pretty much all the support you need because when you are working on the edge of a board most of the forces involved are directed at the floor. However, the peg solution can allow the board to flop forward and back quite a bit.

Of course, there is an accessory from Stanley Works that solves this problem.

In 1915, Stanley patented a bench bracket that combines the support of a wooden peg with the holding power of an F-style clamp. It was manufactured as the Stanley No. 203 (also the number used for a Stanley block plane, by the way). And this item turns up at flea markets and on eBay. I bought a couple of them to try with the Roubo bench jack to see if they were useful.

The Stanley No. 203 works best in a 1"-diameter hole in an apron or bench jack that is ⅞" thick. Use thicker stock and the No. 203 won't grab. Use thinner and the bracket will not create a square ledge for your work. That was my first problem with the No. 203; my material ended up being a little under ⅞", so the clamp head came in at an angle to my boards. As a result, sometimes the head would dent the work on one edge.

While staring at the bracket, I noticed a small hole at the bottom of the device. It looked like there could be some sleeve of metal inside it. Could this small hole be used in some way to square the bracket in its hole? With no answers coming to mind, I decided to ask the U.S. Government. Patented devices have nice drawings and sometimes instruction-like information on file at the U.S. Patent Office.

I typed in the patent date (03-16-1915) and immediately had beautiful drawings of the No. 203, plus drawings of a similar bracket that may not have been made commercially and two pages of details on how the bracket works. The small hole at the bottom of the bracket is for a nail, according to the application, "to steady the lower end of

IT SUPPORTS & SECURES: A Stanley No. 203 bench bracket is like a peg that supports long work. The clamping function presses the work against the sliding deadman. When used properly (watch that clamp pressure) it is effective.

the clamp...." Hmmm, that's not my problem. So I made a little shim and am going to epoxy that to the bracket tonight. That should fix it. And the material in the hole that I thought could be a sleeve? Just junk.

After a couple years of experience, I have found the No. 203 to be useful. When I'm dovetailing boards that are too wide for my face vise, I use the No. 203 in the topmost pegs to clamp the workpiece to the bench jack. But mostly, I like the No. 203 because it holds wide boards or doors motionless and in perfect position when I am working their edges or mortising hinges in place.

One little detail: Don't clamp the No. 203 directly to your work. The pad on the vise screw will ding your work. Use a small scrap of wood between the No. 203 and the workpiece – just like you would with a holdfast.

EDGE WORK ON THE TOP: Many times you can work the edges of individual boards by bracing them against the bench stop and planing the edge. This is faster than clamping the board up with a sliding deadman – plus you get more support.

WHACK A HOLDFAST: These traditional holdfasts work by striking the hooked area. You release them by striking the back of the device. They work well – usually. Some workbenches have trouble with them but most do not. Just remember to keep your hole tight on the holdfast's shaft.

OLD SCHOOL STOP: This metal stop, made by a blacksmith, drops into a wooden bench stop. The toothed end will bite into your work, which is no big deal if you build period furniture where you hide the end grain. More modern work is trickier with this stop.

Traditional holdfasts are a steel hook – many look like a shepherd's crook. The shaft drops into a round closely fitted hole in the benchtop. Pound the hook with a mallet. The hook wedges into the hole and secures the work. Pound the back of the crook and it releases its grip on your work instantly.

During the last decade, holdfasts have come back with a vengeance. When I first started woodworking the holdfasts barely worked. Now they are available at all price levels. The two common patterns are a holdfast with a pronounced curve and those that are basically an L shape. The curvy ones are great for holding work for mortising or sawing. Heck I use them to hold patterns to my benchtop for pattern-routing. The L-shaped ones are ideal for setups where a hand plane might be involved. The L-shaped ones keep a low profile to the bench, so you are less likely to plow into them with your plane. But mine don't seem to hold as tenaciously as the curvy ones.

In general, here are the rules for holdfasts that require a beating: Very thick workbenches can make it difficult for the holdfast to wedge in place. Once the bench is 4" thick, you might have some trouble. The easiest way to fix this problem is to pimple the shaft of the holdfast using a metal punch. This fixes most problems.

Some woodworkers will also counterbore the underside of the benchtop around the holdfast hole, effectively making the benchtop appear thinner to the holdfast. This works, but the solution that uses the punch is easier than crawling under your benchtop.

If you have trouble getting holdfasts to work, consider using a pair of Veritas Hold-Downs. These are bit slower to use than the holdfasts, and they aren't as showy as bashing a holdfast, but they always work. Turn the brass knob on top, and the ribbed shaft engages the hole. Turn the knob the other way, and the hold-down releases. Thin tops or thick tops, it matters not.

There are a bunch of other hold-downs on the market that are less expensive and also work using a screw principle, but they have major disadvantages. The main one is that you usually have to secure the hold-down to the benchtop with a threaded nut located beneath the benchtop. In truth, deep-throat F-style clamps are faster than these boys. But they are inexpensive. And now you know why.

You rarely use a holdfast by itself and directly on the work. When securing pieces for mortising, a small scrap of wood or leather under the pad of the holdfast or hold-down protects the work from denting. When using a holdfast with planes, I generally use them in conjunction with scraps that are thin, narrow and long, typically $1/4$" x 2" x 18". I was turned onto these so-called battens by other woodworkers who have gone the old-style woodworking route.

A couple other readers of our magazine have pointed out to me that these battens – useful as they are – are not shown or discussed in early woodworking texts (except in one old plate I've found that's in Chapter 3 of this book). I couldn't imagine working without battens, but early woodworkers might have had a better way that relied more on skill than scraps. Sometimes these old drawings can be misleading. There are early engravings that show woodworkers using holdfasts directly on marquetry work without a pad to protect it – even though the text discusses using a pad. Illustrators make mistakes, too.

NEVER FAIL: The Veritas Hold-Down never lets me down. The one thing I don't like about it is the barbs on the shaft sometimes hang up on the hole – making it hard to extract the Hold-Down. These are a bit slower to use than a hit-me harder holdfast, but speed isn't everything.

SECURED FROM THE SIDE: Battens are ideal for restraining your work from the side. This allows you to plane or saw across the grain without having to clamp down your work. Using the force of the tool to hold your work speeds you up.

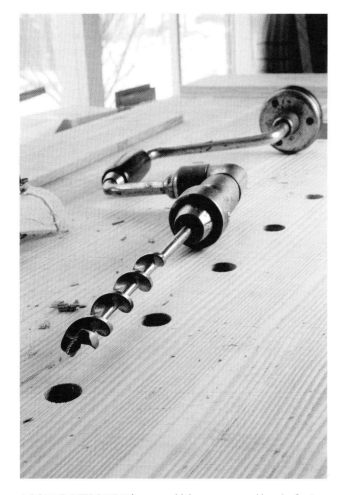

A ROUND RETROFIT: When you add dogs to your workbench after its completion, you are typically limited to using round dogs. Round dogs are best at gripping stuff that's low to the bench, and at odd angles.

Holes and the Dogs that Inhabit Them

Most workbenches have some sort of dog-hole system. Usually this can be anything from a wide array of holes across the top to a couple holes in line with the face vise. The most typical arrangement is to have a line of holes across the length of the benchtop that is in line with whatever end-vise system is in place. The line of holes is usually about 2" from the front edge to hold work for fenced planes.

The dog holes can be round (³/₄" diameter is the norm) or square with a rectangular section at the top where the dog emerges from the benchtop. The dogs can be metal or wood. So what's best?

The round holes are the best solution for a bench where the holes are a retrofit. It's easier to bore a round hole with an auger bit than it is to chop an angled mortise for a square dog. Square dogs will not rotate when put under pressure. And having four square dog faces to work against can be very handy. If you are building your bench from scratch, you can consider both.

I personally prefer wooden dogs, whether they are round or square. Wooden dogs won't damage your tools if you slip. Some people contend that metal dogs hold better. Well, that's true. But when you are applying the maximum grip with a metal dog, I bet you are bowing or marring your work. I find that wooden dogs hold great. Here's a tip to make any wooden dog hold even better: Glue a rectangle of leather to the face of the dog (yellow glue works great). You will be impressed.

The round dog is typically metal, which can be a hazard to your tools. And it is a bit slower to move up and down in the round holes. Of course, speed isn't everything.

Benchtop Height

Many bench builders worry about the height of the bench's working surface from the floor. There is a wide variety of rules, guidelines and advice on the matter. The bottom line is that you have to make the bench fit you and your work. And in the end, there are no ironclad rules. Really. I wish there were. Some people like low benches; some like them high.

COW MEETS DOG: A small scrap of leather adds gripping power to a wooden dog. I buy little scraps of leather or suede from the craft store or Tandy Leather stores. I never cut up my wife's shoes.

DOGS WITH BITE: The steel dogs with their pointy fangs do grip better, but sometimes at the expense of bruising your work. With practice, you learn their limits.

So consider this advice as a good place to start. After taking in my crackpot theories, your next stop should be a friend's house or a woodworking supply store to use their benches and get a feel for what feels like a right height (it could be as simple as having a bad back that prohibits you from a low bench, or a love for wooden handplanes that pushes you to a 31"-high bench).

Here's how I came to my best bench height: I started with a workbench that was 36" high, which seemed right for someone who is 6'-3⅝" tall. And for machine woodworking I was spot-on. The high bench brought the work close to my eyes, allowing me to see exactly what I was doing with the router as I wasted away hinge gains and mortised stock. I loved the high bench. Everything in the world was right by my eyes and I never stooped to work.

Then my love of handwork reared its ugly head.

Once you start getting into hand tools, a high bench becomes less attractive. I started out with a jack plane and a few smoothing planes. They worked OK with a high bench, but I became fatigued fast. My arms would get tired, weak and wobbly while planing, even after months of practice. I knew something was wrong because I'm not a weak fellow.

After reading the screed on bench heights, I thought about lowering the height of my 36" bench. It seemed radical surgery. But one day I got the nerve and sawed 2" off the four legs. Those two inches changed my attitude toward planing. Something serious in the equation had changed. I couldn't put my finger on it at the time, but here is how I see the world from 34".

The 34" bench height allowed me to do several things while planing. I could lock my left arm which grasped the front knob, and shift my weight to the tool, which held it down during the cut. And I could use my long leg muscles to propel the plane forward at that height. I found that I used my arms less to push the tool forward. The arm muscles kept the tool under control and on track. But it was the rest of my body that assisted in moving the tool forward.

Now, before you go to the shop and build your next bench at 34" high, stop for a minute. It might not be right for you. Do you use wooden stock planes? If so, you need to consider that the wooden body can hold your arms about 3"- 4" higher off the workbench than a metal plane can. As a result, a wooden plane user's workbench should be lower than one who favors metal-bodied planes. In my work with wooden planes, 31" is a good working height.

Also, if you use wooden-stock planes, a key part of using them correctly (according to my experience) has been to get on top of them to press them down against the work. This is as good a reason as ever to get to know someone who has a good shop you can visit and discuss your ideas with. You cannot make this decision on paper alone. You must make it with the help of a couple trips to a shop along with some thoughtful questions. The rewards are worth it.

But there are other factors you must consider when settling on the bench's height. How tall are you? If you are over 6' tall, as I am, you will be best served to try to scale your bench just a bit higher. Start a bit higher and cut it down if it feels too high after a while. And prop it up on some blocks of wood if it's too low. Experiment. It's not a highboy; it's a workbench.

Here are some other things to consider: Do you work with machinery? If so, a bench that is 34" from the floor – or a bit lower – is a good idea. The top of a table saw is typically 34" from the floor, so a workbench could be (at the most) a great outfeed table or (at the least) not in the way of your crosscutting and ripping.

Of course, everyone wants to know where to start. They want a ballpark idea. So here it is. Stand up straight and drop your arms against your sides in a relaxed manner. Measure from the floor to the place where your pinky finger joins your hand. That has been the sweet spot for me. It might not be right for you, but it is right for someone who uses metal-bodied planes, has really long arms and is 6' 3⅝". And likes cats and osso buco.

It's all very personal.

GET OVER IT: Wooden planes work better (for me) if I'm able to use my body weight to press the tool down into the work. I have more control and less fatigue. The mass of a metal plane does some of this for you, but at the expense of being more weight to push around.

VANITY OR WORKBENCH? These workbenches are ideal for storing tools, but aren't designed for holding your work steady. You can do nice work on these benches, but you'll be solving workholding problems as often as you are woodworking problems that crop up during a project.

The Misuse of the Space Under the Top

We had a phase at *Popular Woodworking* magazine where we tried to design a cup holder into every project. It started innocently with a sling chair for the deck. Who doesn't want a cool beverage next to them? Then there was the dartboard. What goes better with darts than a beer? (Besides an adhesive bandage for the resulting puncture wounds, that is.) I think we came to our senses when we designed cup holders into a Gustav Stickley Morris chair reproduction. Do you really need a Big Gulp-sized hole in your Morris chair?

The point is to illustrate a trend in workbench design that's troubling. It's a knee-jerk reaction to a common American complaint: We don't think we have enough space in our shops to store all our tools and accessories. And how do we solve this problem with our workbenches? By designing them like kitchen storage cabinets with a countertop work surface.

This design approach gives us lots of drawers below the benchtop, which is great for storing all the little tools and accessories you reach for everyday. What it also does is makes your bench a pain in the hinder to use for many common operations.

Filling the space below the benchtop can prohibit you from using decent holdfasts or hold-downs. There's just not enough space below the benchtop, typically, to make a holdfast or hold-down function (unless it has a short shank or you have designed space for a long shank). Believe me, I've made this error myself when designing a bench for my home shop. It's agony to admit the stupidity of the mistake.

If you build drawers below the top, how will you clamp objects to the benchtop to work with them? Typically, the banks of drawers below the benchtop prohibit a typical F-style clamp from sneaking in there and lending a hand with the set-up. So you can't use a typical clamp to affix a router template to the bench. And the drawer bank prohibits you from clamping things to the workbench from above. There are ways around these problems (a tail vise comes to mind). But the tail vise can be a challenge to install, set and use.

You can try to cheat (as I have) and install the drawer bank so there is a substantial space underneath the benchtop for holdfasts and clamps. This can work with holdfasts, but clamps come in such a variety of lengths that it's hard to anticipate everything you will need to clamp there. And that's why I like workbenches that are wide open in the undercarriage department.

That said, you can incorporate some storage in your bench that will not compromise basic functions. Early 18th-century woodworking texts by A.J. Roubo illustrate a bench that has two drawers below the stretchers of the bench – essentially they are tucked between the floor and the bottom stretchers. This bank of drawers is unlikely to interfere with any clamping and will hold a fair number of tools.

And for those of you who have one single drawer below the bench, I've been there as well. It always seemed that the drawer was right where a clamp needed to be. And one of the drawer sides happened to be under a dog hole, which wasn't my fault because it was a commercial bench. Plus the drawer filled up with sawdust that dropped through the dog holes. All in all, the one drawer in the dead center of the benchtop was a bad idea.

The Support Structure Below the Top

Because wood seems expensive, it's tempting to build a bench with a thin top – or perhaps make the center of the top thin. If you look at inexpensive modern commercial workbenches, this is exactly the trend you'll see. The center section of the top is thin, just 2" or so, and there's a wide apron that bands the top and gives the illusion of beefiness. And the apron banding the top does indeed lend support.

Another common strategy is to build a thin top and then support it from below using a system of aprons, much like a dining table.

When you are drafting a plan for a workbench, these strategies seem sound and material-efficient. The problem is that a short period of work with these kinds of benches will point out a few limitations you should consider when you have an eraser nearby.

FIG. 249. THE "COMPOSITE" BENCH.

AH (BATHROOM) VANITY: This bench from the Wm. P. Walter's Sons 1888 catalog shows a bench I hope never to work on. There's no way (none) to hold boards for cross-grain work. There's no way to work edges. And that backboard stops you from clamping across the bench (a trick that usually gets you around other problems).

DIG A DEEPER HOLE: The storage cabinet below this benchtop holds lots of tools, but the holddown can't hold anything. The drawer bank is too close to the benchtop. So now what? Remove the drawer bank or get one of the inexpensive (and inconvenient) plastic holddowns.

NO NEED FOR CLAMPS: Wanting storage space in a bench is nothing new. This ridiculous bench – called the Composite Bench – was published in 1904. The authors suggest you mount a table saw in the top. It's proof that old designs can be as bad as new designs.

With the commercial benches that feature a thin top banded by wide boards, the risk is that the top can flex a little bit under heavy pounding or other loads. This is more of a concern with hand work than it is when using the bench with power tools.

However, it's also quite difficult to clamp your work to this style of benchtop using common F-style clamps. The wide edging around the top interferes with any clamping you might want to do that approaches the center of the benchtop. In fact, this thin top/wide apron configuration makes some setups almost impossible.

The thin top also reduces a workbench's weight – so the bench might be more likely to skitter across the floor under planing pressure if you haven't bolted your bench to the floor.

The other sort of benchtop strategy, where you have a thin top supported by aprons (what I call the dining table workbench) has many of the same issues as the inexpensive commercial benches. The aprons below the benchtop prevent the top from flexing without using a lot of material. But the aprons impede clamping. Maneuvering clamps around the aprons can be a challenge if the aprons are narrow; and clamping can be impossible if your aprons are wider than the length of the screw on the clamp.

So as you plan the support below your top, think of the benchtop as a three-dimensional clamping surface. Your clamps are going to interact with both the top surface of your benchtop as well as the underside. After working on benches built in both of the styles mentioned above (aprons below the top or a thin top banded by wider boards), I can say that these are the most frustrating benches to use, both with hand tools and with power tools.

That's why I usually prefer a benchtop that is thick (4" or more) and unsupported by aprons. This feature lends flexibility with clamping. It also allows you to retrofit vises to the bench easily. Say that you

didn't add an end vise to your bench at first. If you wanted to add a quick-release vise to the end of the bench the aprons might get in the way of the screws and rods of the vise. If you don't have an apron, you only have to deal with interference from the legs.

There is, of course, an exception to every rule. The English-style workbench in this book breaks the above rules. It has extremely wide aprons and a thin top. You cannot clamp a thing with those aprons in the way. But because of the bench's system of dogs and its wagon vise you can clamp panels against the top. And with the help of holdfasts and the face vise, you can clamp boards on edge against the apron with ease. In short, it allows you to clamp boards to work faces, edges and ends. So it's a functional bench.

The English-style bench is what I prefer for woodworkers who need to make a bench that is material-efficient. The English bench uses less than half the wood of the similarly sized French bench in this book. Unlike your typical dining table workbench, the English bench doesn't have a top that overhangs the aprons, and that feature alone makes it a decent bench in my opinion.

Pl. 18

À la Forge Royale

"L'IDÉALE PRESSE"
Brevetée S. G. D. G. (N° 153.925)

à Serrage Instantané pour Établis de Menuisiers, Ébénistes, Modeleurs, Charpentiers, Carrossiers

N° 217

Longueur des Mâchoires 25 % — Ouverture maximum de la Presse 30 %

Les Mâchoires en acier sont montées sur des mordages en bois

PRESSE à CHARIOT

complète pour Établi

212

ÉTABLIS ORDINAIRES en HÉTRE
montés avec
L'IDÉALE PRESSE Brevetée

218-219

ÉTABLIS en HÉTRE
montés avec PRESSE PARISIENNE
et "IDÉALE PRESSE"

220-221

Fabrique d'Outils à travailler le bois

IT'S A GIFT TO BE SIMPLE: There is a long list of vises you can put on a workbench. Perhaps that list is too long. Workholding should be as simple as possible. When you begin to devise jigs that fit in your workholding jigs, it's time to take stock of the way you grip your stock.

Match Features to Functions

Here's the goal: Avoid unworkable workbenches. It sounds simple, but with all the different vises available, plus all the different designs for benches that are floating around, it's child's play to design a bench that is quite ridiculous.

Here's a quick example: I was talking to a guy who designs and builds custom workbenches, and he had a customer who wanted a workbench that had two twin-screw vises. One vise for the right end of the workbench that was matched to work with two long rows of dogs along the length of the benchtop. And the customer wanted the second twin-screw vise on the face of the bench that was matched to two more rows of dogs that were lined up across the width of the benchtop.

Now I'm certain that there are woodworkers who need this arrangement – perhaps someone who has to simultaneously work on a circular tabletop on one end of the bench and a Windsor chair seat at the other. And, in truth, I have seen a couple workbenches with two twin-screw vises (a quad-screw bench perhaps?) that made sense. But for most people who build cabinets and furniture, this setup is redundant in many ways and (as you'll see later in this chapter) neglects some functions of a bench that are critically necessary.

Making a misstep like this in designing a bench is common. When people begin working in the craft, the first thing they need to address is finding a place to work. Second on the list is obtaining a workbench to build things on (it's what all the books and magazines say you should do, and it beats building on the floor). If you haven't done much woodworking yet, your expectations and impressions of how a workbench should function and look will be colored by the fact that you haven't done much woodworking. So having two tail vises might seem logical. Or putting the face vise on the right corner of the benchtop might seem correct for an inexperienced right-hander.

To figure out the world of workbenches, you might take a class, go to a woodworking store to check out the commercial benches or even buy a book on workbenches. These are all good things to do, but these efforts might still lead you astray. Some woodworking schools and stores stock commercial workbenches that are designed to cost a certain number of dollars, even if they don't make sense. And many workbench books have designs in them that range from fantastic to fantastical, and it's up to you to figure out what is reasonable and

what is the sideshow. The difference isn't always obvious. A hydraulic height-adjustable bench base can look like a good idea to a person who has never worked with one.

Go take a look at the workbenches on the floors of woodworking specialty stores. Vise? Check. Dog holes? Check. Though this might look like a useful workbench, its shortcomings would fill an entire page. For starters: How would you work on the edge of a typical cabinet door? Benches like this give you an instant place to work, but you will also quickly outgrow them. I see a lot of these workbenches pushed into corners of shops, being used as a tool stand. For less than the cost of the top of that commercial bench, you can build a workbench that will stick with you the rest of your life.

Most woodworkers don't ask these questions. So the woodworker buys or builds a bench and starts working on it. And that's when the real education begins, and the shortcomings of the workbench (no workbench is perfect) become apparent. And so the woodworker buys or builds another bench, or he attempts a retrofit of the obvious missing equipment, or he just suffers with what's on hand. It's all frustrating, time-consuming and expensive. And it can be avoided.

All workbenches are designed to do a finite number of things in a woodworking shop. And there are a finite number of vises and devices to choose from. So if you can make a list of all the basic tasks you expect to perform on your bench and then match those tasks to the bench equipment made to accomplish that task, you can come close to getting a good design the first time, even if you are an inexperienced woodworker.

It might not be a perfect process. For example, if you never plan on hand-dovetailing a drawer, I would argue that you shouldn't bother with a shoulder vise. Dovetailing is the task that the shoulder vise

---

"You will find something more in woods than in books. Trees and stones will teach you that which you can never learn from masters."

— Saint Bernard, (1090 - 1153), French abbot

THE IRON AGE MEETS THE POST-INDUSTRIAL: I can think of no better way to secure work in the middle of my bench than a holdfast or hold-down. Traditional methods work well in tandem with modern tools.

A 350-POUND FOUR-FOOTED CLAMP: A twin-screw, tail or wagon vise is effective for assembly and disassembly. In early shops, when clamps were less ubiquitous, some benches were designed for clamping.

excels at. So you might build a bench with a small quick-release face vise instead. But after a few years of working with wood you might change your mind about dovetailing. So you have to be a bit flexible in choosing the woodworking tasks that will be performed on your bench. Next year, you are going to be a different woodworker.

What follows is the soul of this book. It is a list of the common tasks performed on a bench and the devices that can accomplish those tasks. There also is a fair amount of my opinion about how suitable each device is at accomplishing that task – I think a twin-screw vise is better for dovetailing than a quick-release face vise, for example.

A word of warning: I use both hand tools and power tools in my shop, and so my opinions on workholding devices are colored by my blended approach. I like old techniques (such as holdfasts) to secure modern-style work (for pattern routing).

Once you make a list of all the tasks you'll be doing, you'll see your choice of vises narrow. And then you can see a bench take shape in your mind that makes sense to your pocketbook and prepares you for the future and the skills you will acquire. In fact, the goal of this book is to help you envision and build a workbench that will be difficult to outgrow. So get some paper and a pencil.

ASSEMBLING & DISASSEMBLING JOINTS
First Choice: Tail Vise
Many woodworkers forget that vises are clamps that are effective for assembling and disassembling things. If you need to take apart frame assemblies, such as doors, windows or frame chairs, a tail vise is ideal. Raise the dogs up, place the work over the dogs and unscrew the vise. The dogs grip the work and pull it apart gently.

You also can use this function to take apart assemblies that you knocked together without glue but that have joints that are too tight to yank apart. (So you don't need spreader clamps.) It also works well for assembling a joint without glue to test the fit.

Second Choice: Wagon Vise
The wagon vise is good at assembly and disassembly, but it usually has fewer locations for dogs. It's almost a tie for first with the tail vise.

Third Choice: Wonder Dogs
These work OK for assembly and disassembly, but you sometimes have to do a lot more fiddling with them because the Wonder Dog has a small bearing surface that can be difficult to secure on a round chair leg, for example. You can screw a clamping caul to the dog that will solve most problems, but that's an extra headache the above choices won't give you.

Fourth Choice: Face Vise or Twin-screw Vise
You can use a face vise for these functions if it is equipped with a dog that is in line with a row of dog holes. The quick-release varieties of the vise won't help you with disassembly – moving the screw out disengages it and the jaw slides free. So it won't work. If you want to try a twin-screw vise for disassembling things, it's doable if the vise has dogs and the vise is not a quick-release unit.

BEFORE THE VERITAS: This hold-down, most often associated with Record, was the hold-down of choice in the early 20th century. You need a metal collar set into the bench to make it work.

ANOTHER HOLD DOWN: Some hold-downs used a screw; this one from the Cincinnati Tool Co. uses a lever. Note that this one also requires a collar that is let into the top of your workbench.

DIRT-SIMPLE SOLUTION: A planing stop can be as simple as a stick mortised into the benchtop. Here are some other ways to set up an adjustable planing stop on your bench: drive a couple screws into your benchtop, screw a deadbolt door lock to the end of the bench, clamp a piece of scrap to the benchtop.

ANY WIDTH, ANY HEIGHT: This is a fancy planing stop on the end of one of my benches at home. It took about an hour to build and attach. The star knobs release the stop so it can move up and down (and even left and right). The secret? The bolts attached to the knobs are riding in a piece of aluminum T-track in the end of the bench (top). Sandpaper is stuck on the inside face of the stop to ensure the stop moves only when you want it to. Turn the knobs and the stop stays put.

FACE PLANING NARROW BOARDS (8" WIDE OR LESS) WITH THE GRAIN

First Choice: Planing Stops

The simplest and best solution for planing the faces of narrow boards is to simply butt one end of the board against a planing stop and go to work. Gravity and the downward force of the tool keep the work flat on the bench. The forward motion of the tool keeps it in place against the planing stop. There's no clamping and unclamping.

Once you start figuring out how to control longer and wider stock against a single-point planing stop, your planing speed will increase. Why? There's no need to clamp and reclamp boards, changing your setup every time you plane a board of a different length. Planing stops, once mastered, are a joy. As you learn to control your stock, you can use the single-point stop with a holdfast and scrap wood batten or doe's foot to keep the tail end of the board from whipping around. You'll also learn to skew the plane during the cut to take advantage of the side support from the batten.

There are many styles of stops. The historical type is a single wooden post that is friction-fit into the benchtop and adjusted up and down with mallet taps. Another type of planing stop is as wide as the benchtop. Those two types of stops are common, but there are plenty of uncommon ones. Some adjust up and down. Some are fixed. Some clamp into a face vise. Some attach to the bench. Some drop into dog holes. Some lurk below the top and can be adjusted up and down with a screwdriver or with some fiddling below the bench.

Need a recommendation? I like the kind that are wide, built into the end of the bench and adjust up and down. These can deal with stock that's thin and thick, narrow and wide, including most panels. (Panels are difficult or impossible to balance against a single narrow stop in my experience.)

My second choice for a stop is a stop that clamps in a face vise and spans the width of the benchtop.

Second Choice: Wagon Vise or Tail Vise

Many woodworkers use a wagon vise or tail vise to secure boards when planing with the grain or sanding. There are some advantages: Clamping the work between dogs requires less skill to keep the stock under control as you work. The dogs keep the work put and you can focus more on the work. But here are the downsides: Every time you plane a board that's a different length, you need to rearrange the dogs. Plus, add to that the extra step of opening and closing the vise and the minutes accumulate. Also, you do need to be careful about how

PLANING AT THE OTHER END: One of the odd things about using a wagon or tail vise for planing is that it moves the work to the right end of the bench. Most of the action on a bench occurs at the left end – the right end is typically where assembly takes place. With some practice, you will get used to planing at the right end of your bench.

A SECOND BENCHTOP: A planing board perches on top of your bench (or any bench), allowing you to have a flat surface uninterrupted by a tool tray or the fact that the top of your bench might not be flat enough for precision planing.

DOGS DO ROAM: One of the best things about Wonder Dogs is that you can set them between two holes anywhere on your benchtop.

THE RIGHT AMOUNT OF PRESSURE: When planing or belt-sanding across a panel, you don't want the panel slipping out of the dogs. And you also don't want to bow the stock by using too much pressure. So some woodworkers use metal dogs that have a toothed surface. Be wary when using this setup because your tools can be damaged.

much pressure you apply with the vise. Too much and your work will bow off the bench. Even a slight bow is bad news. And it doesn't take much pressure to bow $^{3}/_{4}$"-thick stock, especially narrow stuff.

Third Choice: Planing Boards

Planing boards (sometimes called planing trays) are a decent third choice in my book. They allow you to plane narrow stock and wide stock with the grain and (as noted in the next section) they are useful for planing across the grain with panels or assembled door frames. In fact, I find planing trays quite excellent if I'm traveling to a place where I'm not sure what the workbench will be like because they handle many typical planing situations. However, they do have downsides. The number one disadvantage is you have to make a sizable planing board for it to be useful (24" x 50" is good), and that's quite a thing to store or set aside when not in use.

Fourth Choice: Wonder Dogs

Wonder Dogs have all the advantages and disadvantages of a tail vise, with one additional disadvantage: Planing thin stock requires extra measures to avoid striking the dog or its post with the body of your precious tools.

The supreme advantage of the Wonder Dog is that you can create a tail-vise-like setup anywhere on the bench, and retrofitting a bench with a Wonder Dog is about a thousand times easier than retrofitting it with a tail vise.

FACE PLANING ACROSS OR DIAGONAL TO THE GRAIN

First Choice: Doe's Foot & Holdfast

As I get older, I seem to like gizmos less. My current bench doesn't have a tail vise, and I have no plans to add one. I use a doe's foot, a holdfast and a planing stop. It's as fast to readjust as a tail vise. And it will never bow the work. I admit this is a radical choice.

THE SIMPLEST SOLUTION: The notched batten – or doe's foot – is a remarkable and simple appliance. Try it before you reject it.

EXTEND YOUR BENCHTOP: A piece or two of scrap that act as an outrigger can support a drawer or an entire cabinet. Note how the face vise works with the outrigger support to immobilize this cabinet while I trim its dovetails. Thicker outriggers are better than thin ones.

Second Choice: Tail Vise or Wagon Vise

When working across or diagonal to the grain, pinching your work between dogs is ideal. These particular vises pinch the work on the end grain as you move the tool across the width of the board, with little chance of the tool striking your bench hardware. Using wooden dogs (instead of metal ones) ensures that your tools are safe from damage. It's easier to replace a wooden dog that has suffered multiple indignities from a fore plane than it is to fix a fore plane that has one brief and fateful encounter with a steel bench dog. As mentioned earlier, the downside to both the tail vise and the wagon vise is that you can apply too much pressure and bow the work. This will make the work behave unpredictably under your tools.

Third Choice: Twin-screw or Quick-release Vise

If you place your twin-screw vise or quick-release vise on the end of your bench, it can be used like a tail vise to pinch the work between dogs. However, be advised that if you go this route, you should place the dog holes in your benchtop close together, let's say 4" apart or less. If you place them long distances apart you'll end up extending the vise quite a bit for some clamping situations. And that will leave a significant section of your work unsupported from below. So if you set it up correctly, these vise arrangements can work well.

BATTENS: This plate, which I stumbled on in a poorly footnoted book, shows battens in use on a bench. The two well-dressed gentlemen are pulling a board through a thicknessing machine (a precursor to the portable surface planer). The tool is wedged between battens that are held down by holdfasts.

GRAVITY IS SIMPLE, CHEAP, GRIPPY: I've thrown away every router pad that's come into our shop. I use a moving blanket, which we need for transporting furniture anyway. When they get dusty, we wash them.

SOFT AND LOW-TECH: If you have good dust collection on your sander, then you don't need to invest in a downdraft sanding station. You also don't need some fancy "sanding pad" (read: anti-slip pads for area rugs that have been repackaged and repriced). Get a moving blanket, which is great for many workshop tasks.

HOLD ANYTHING: Holdfasts and hold-downs are indispensable workshop servants, no matter what sort of work you do. They are like a clamp that has a bar that never gets in the way – it's buried in the benchtop.

Fourt Choice: Wonder Dogs

A Wonder Dog and a bench dog will do a fine job of securing your work for cross-grain planing – as long as you are dealing with stock that is thicker than $^5/_8$" and isn't supposed to end up thinner than $^5/_8$". If you need to work thin stock, it's fairly simple to rig up a few wooden shims between the work and the dogs to keep your tools away from the metal dogs in this set-up.

Fifth Choice: Planing Boards

A planing board can be used to work across the grain and diagonally to it. The stops of the planing board restrain the work with little effort from the user. There are some downsides, as mentioned above. A good planing board needs to be large and takes up a fair amount of space. Plus, it's not so good with rough stock, which needs to be shimmed from below to keep it stable while planing it cross-grain, diagonally or even with the grain. If you purchase wood that is already dressed (or if you dress it yourself with machinery, as I do) the planing board is great. Shimming is then infrequent, and the planing board takes care of holding the work in any orientation without bowing the stock as you might with the above solutions.

FACE PLANING ASSEMBLIES: CABINET SIDES, DRAWER SIDES, ETC.

First Choice: Any Face Vise, Plus Outrigger Support

Many woodworkers are loathe to plane or scrape an assembled cabinet or drawer. Too bad. That's when you really can control the flatness of the sides (for attaching moulding), trim face frames flush and fit drawers. Hands down, the best way to plane the faces of assembled boxes is to support them off the front edge of the benchtop with an outrigger support (usually a thick piece of stock affixed to the bench with clamps or holdfasts). The outrigger supports your work from below and the face vise holds it at the front corner so it stays put as you plane or scrape it. This is a far better strategy than clamping your project up on the benchtop because then your working surface will be too high to work easily.

BELT SANDING NARROW STOCK OR SMALL PANELS

First Choice: Tail Vise or Wagon Vise

Without a doubt, you need to restrain your work when belt sanding small pieces. While large tabletops and the sides of cabinets can be sanded on a blanket or carpet pad alone, smaller door panels or individual boards require restraint. And lots of it. I have seen (and have tried) what might be called a backstop. Essentially it is a wide planing stop that is placed on the outfeed side of a belt sander. From a handplaner's perspective, this seems a good idea at first. The circular motion of the sanding belt will push the work against the stop. Gravity and the weight of the tool will also help in holding things in place. In practice, however, this is ... iffy. It works only if you keep your 1,100 square-feet-per-minute tool aligned directly in line with the grain. Turn it at an angle and small pieces of unsecured work can go flying with astonishing results. So forget the backstop and restrain the work at front and behind when it's small. For that, a tail vise or wagon vise is ideal. As with planing, be sure not to use too much force when securing your work or you will bow it. Adding a pad or blanket under your work can also help your work stick to your benchtop.

ONE JIG, ONE JOB: One workhorse jig in our shop is designed for routing dados in case sides. You line up the notch in the fence with a mark on your work. Clamp the jig down. Rout your dado. No thinking required. I don't care for Swiss Army-style jigs. I tend to forget all the things they do after a year or so.

BISCUIT JOKE HERE: Holdfasts and hold-downs excel at applying clamping pressure exactly where you need it. This allows you to keep both hands on the tool, which results in far more accurate cuts.

Second Choice: Wonder Dogs

These work well with stock thicker than ⅝. Thin stock requires some extra jigging to avoid abrading the brass (usually just a couple pieces of scrap do the trick). Sanding a dog won't hurt the sanding belt too much, but it does throw some nice metallic dust everywhere.

RANDOM-ORBIT SANDING

First Choice: A Moving Blanket

My favorite way to restrain and protect my work when sanding with a random-orbit sander (or orbital sander or sanding block) is to place the work on a quilted moving blanket draped over the benchtop. Except for really small pieces of work, which don't lend themselves to power sanding, this is ideal. Downdraft sanding tables work just as well (if you have the cash for a big one), but I have had excellent results with a blanket and collecting the dust through the pad with a shop vacuum. Note that some sanders and vacuums are markedly better than others.

Here are some pointers: The eight-hole paper collects dust better than the five-hole paper. Nothing collects dust better than Mirka's Abranet system; this stuff is basically porous sandpaper and the dust is collected through the paper itself. It seems like alien technology when you use it for the first time.

Finally, you get what you pay for with dust collection. The high-end German sanders and vacuums from Festool and Fein do indeed work better than the consumer big-box stuff. These German tools are used in industry, where dust is not only a nuisance, it's a hazard to the health of the daily user.

ROUTING FACES OF BOARDS

First Choice: Holdfasts or Hold-Downs

This amuses me. When I need to do some pattern routing, rout profiles on an edge or rout dados and rabbets in a case side, I reach for my 17th-century holdfasts whenever possible. These work better than many clamping arrangements, no matter how deep the throats of your

clamps are. Holdfasts (and hold-downs) are ideal for routing because you are machining only small areas of your work, so it's easy to place the holdfasts out of the way of the tool. Remember to use a scrap between the holdfast and the work to protect it from bruising.

Second Choice: F-style Clamps

When a holdfast won't do, I secure the work with clamps to the benchtop. This is when a well-designed bench shines. If you have aprons supporting your top, your clamps will not be as useful. If your top is thin with a wide apron banding it, your clamps will sometimes balk at the task. But if you have a thick slab of a benchtop with no obstructions below, you will be rewarded by easy clamping setups for routing. My French-style bench is a workhorse for routing.

Third Choice: Specialized Jigs

There are tool guides and purpose-built jigs for working on faces of boards with a router. A common commercial one is an aluminum fence that grabs the edges of your work. The fence acts as a straight-edge guide for the router's base.

Fourth Choice: Wonder Dogs

If you bore an array of dog holes in your benchtop, you generally can create an environment where the Wonder Dog can thrive. With Wonder Dogs, you might have to do the work in a couple different setups when edge routing – because the Wonder Dog system restrains work on its edges. But you can restrain odd shapes (circles, ovals etc.).

Fifth Choice: Blankets

Generally, I don't trust router mats. They work with workpieces of a certain size. When the pads are new, they work with pretty small pieces of stock. As the pads become impregnated with dust, they lose their grip. And when they finally give up, that workpiece is going to take wing. If you like router mats, you also should know that they are exactly the same as inexpensive rubber carpet pads, which are used under area rugs on hardwood floors. There's one major difference: The

A STRAIGHTEDGE MARRIED A CLAMP: I would be grumpy if I had to give up my edge guide with integral clamps. I use a long one to break down plywood with a circular saw and a short one for biscuiting and routing case sides.

NOT GOING ANYWHERE: When chiseling out waste, immobilizing your work is key. And when chiseling out waste between dovetail joints, you want a clamp that is fast and firm. Holdfasts and hold-downs are the answer. They're faster than an F-style clamp.

price. Call it a router mat and the price goes up. When routing larger pieces of work, I use my moving blanket below the work. It always has the same amount of grippiness, no matter how dusty it is. And it protects the work from scratches.

BISCUIT OR DOMINOS

First Choice: Holdfasts

Just like with the router, I reach for my old-style holdfasts when using a plate joiner or Domino. This should come as no surprise. When you take the machine to the face of a board, you generally are working against some sort of fence that is secured to the face of the work. Holdfasts and hold-downs excel at applying downward force in a localized area. And if you have a dozen holes in your benchtop, you'll find that you can hold anything almost anywhere with holdfasts.

Second Choice: F-style Clamps

The modern option to holdfasts. They're limited by their throat capacity. However, if you have a bench that's uncluttered by aprons, these clamps work – especially at the corners and ends of your bench.

Third Choice: Specialized Jigs

If you do a lot of biscuit or Domino joinery, you're probably going to purchase a jig that combines a fence with edge clamps. This clever jig allows you to place the work flat on your bench and move the jig anywhere on the face of the work. The jig grabs the work. Gravity holds everything down. Most power tool users end up with one of these jigs because it can guide just about any power tool, from a router to a circular saw to a jigsaw.

DRILLING FACES

First Choice: Holdfasts or Clamps

When hand pressure isn't enough to hold the work, I resort to holdfasts or clamps to hold things down. I place a piece of scrap below the exit hole to avoid splintering, and I work perched off the edge of the benchtop to avoid boring the bench. These devices also excel at holding jigs on the work while boring shelf pin holes in carcase sides.

CHISELING FACES OF BOARDS

First Choice: Gravity

Whenever I'm popping out the waste between dovetails I put the arm holding my chisel on the work. That's enough.

Second Choice: Holdfasts

If I cannot use my body weight to restrain the work, I turn to my holdfasts. The same goes when I am roughing out details with a chisel, such as shaping the arm bow of a chair. Holdfasts and hold-downs apply pressure at one point, even in the middle of the bench.

Second Choice: F-style Clamps

This is my number three choice because these clamps are slower than holdfasts, plus I have to stoop to secure the clamps below the benchtop. I think we have only so much stooping in our lives before our backs decide to put a stop to it.

"Economical and rapid production is now a matter of eliminating the human factor as much as possible, a responsibility to be placed upon automatic machines."

— *The Wood Worker* (1921), a magazine for the trade, in an Advertisment for a Reynolds Automatic Screw Driving Machine

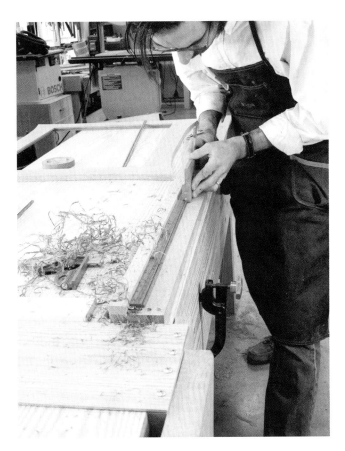

MAKE ANY MOULDING: Routing or planing small pieces is difficult and (occasionally) dangerous. A sticking board allows you to secure your work so that the tool – a router or plane – can work it. The force of the tool and its cutter help out with clamping here, whereas you are usually fighting the action of the cutter.

STICKING MOULDING

First Choice: Sticking Boards

A sticking board is a useful benchtop appliance if you use moulding planes. What's a sticking board? It's a long piece of scrap that holds your moulding (usually in a rabbet) at the front edge of your bench. The sticking board also has a stop at the end (sometimes both ends) that holds the moulding piece at the ends. You can secure the sticking board to the benchtop with clamps. My sticking board isn't that fancy. It's stopped at its end by my planing stop and braced against side pressure by my bench dogs.

Second Choice: Tail Vise or Wagon Vise

If the stock is wide and thick enough, I'll shape the profile directly on the benchtop between dogs. This works if the fence of the handplane isn't large (plow planes don't always do well with this approach). If you are moulding the edge of wide base moulding, the tail vise is an excellent solution. Depending on the work and the location of your tail vise you can even hang your work off the front edge of the benchtop, allowing you to use fenced planes.

Third Choice: Battens and Holdfasts

Set them up like an ersatz sticking board. Easy.

SCRAP GUIDES THE TOOL: Does this look familiar? Yup, it's the same setup I use with my biscuit joiner. Holdfasts secure the guides for your tool better than any other clamp.

CARVING & INLAY

First Choice: Holdfasts & Vises

I'm unqualified to discuss this topic with authority because I do little carving and inlay. In recent years, I've been doing more carving of furniture components and inlay, but still, I'm an amateur. So take this for what it's worth. For my carving efforts, I tend to work with a combination of holdfasts and dogs. The holdfasts hold the work down on the bench and I brace the work against a dog (two if I can manage) in the direction I'm thrusting with the tool. This works well with irregular shapes as you can wedge the work against a couple dogs and then find a way to secure everything with a holdfast or hold-down. The same goes for inlay, whether it's with a router plane or electric router. For carving legs (cabrioles, ball-and-claw feet) a patternmaker's vise is ideal because you can swing your work around. There also are vises dedicated to carving, especially when doing work in the round.

Second Choice: Wonder Dog

These guys work great for odd-shaped pieces and allow you to clamp objects with ease if you have an array of holes in your benchtop and a couple Wonder Dogs to supplement your regular dogs.

Third Choice: Tail Vise or Wagon Vise

This device works OK in some situations (carving a table apron). But working across the grain can sometimes make the work slip out from between the dogs (especially my beloved wooden dogs). You can use a batten and holdfast to keep the work in place. Or even a batten and an F-style clamp. If you're working on many like-shaped and like-sized pieces, this is a decent way to go.

Fourth Choice: F-style Clamps

These always seem to be an OK choice with workholding. Use them near the corners of your benchtop and you can get the work done, but you'll work slower because you'll be shifting things around, fiddling with clamps and the like to get things to work.

SUPER DOGS: It's tempting to clamp things more than necessary. When adjusting joinery, usually the force of the tool is all that is required to immobilize the work against some dogs or a stop.

TOO MANY ANGLES: Scraping isn't like planing because it's generally performed in more localized areas. And because of a special feature of a scraper – it can be used in almost any direction, regardless of grain direction – it gets used that way. And so working against a single planing stop isn't a good option. You need to pinch the work or constrain it against more than a single point (unless the piece or assembly has great mass).

HAND SAWING FACES OF BOARDS

First Choice: Bench Hooks

Two bench hooks and a backsaw handle most crosscutting applications that need to be precise. Coarse crosscuts with a handsaw are best handled on a sawbench. Why do you need two bench hooks? One holds the work and guides the saw. The other supports long stock on the benchtop during the cut. You can get away with one bench hook if its bed is ³/₄" thick and you have lots of ³/₄"-thick stock on hand (and who doesn't?). That scrap stock can provide the support you need.

Second Choice: Holdfasts or Hold-downs

Sometimes I need to saw against a guide, such as when hand sawing dados into a case side (sometimes with a stair saw). It's times like that where your bench hooks aren't going to do. You need to clamp the guide to your work and the benchtop. And that's when the holdfast and hold-downs shine. In fact, I turn to these devices first when sawing curved components. These devices can hold the work and your guide firmly enough that you can focus more on sawing and less on keeping your work braced with your off hand.

Third Choice: Tail Vise, Wagon Vise, Wonder Dogs

These are a distant third choice. The force of sawing tends to pull or push the work out of the grip of the dogs, unless you cinch the vise down, perhaps bowing the work.

Fourth Choice: F-style Clamps

And in honorable mention is the F-style clamp. Its reach is limited. It is slower than other solutions. But you can make it work in a pinch.

ADJUSTING JOINERY

First Choice: The Dogs Stand Alone

There are many small adjustments to your joints that need to be made to get things fitted properly. Shoulder planes adjust tenons and rabbets.

Bullnose planes adjust assembled casework. Chisels and rasps adjust anything. Before I clamp parts for a super-secure setup, I try to brace the work against two dogs (raised high off the benchtop) and work the tool into the dogs. This works great with shoulder planes and bullnose planes especially. I'll even brace assembled casework or frame assemblies against two dogs to clean out rabbets when I can. If the work is small, I might use a single planing stop. But whenever I reach the limits of my benchtop or my arms, I'll turn to choice number two.

Second Choice: Tail Vise, Wagon Vise or Wonder Dogs

Any of these three devices can pinch your work at the ends, leaving you free to step forward (during a lengthy cut to clean out a rabbet) or apply pressure in a selective area. Generally, the work has to be long or wide before I crank open the tail vise. One caution: I've seen people adjust their joints while gripping the workpiece in a face vise, something I try to avoid. Working with the piece unsupported from below can be problematic. And if you slip your tool may go crashing to the floor because there's no benchtop below to catch it. That said, if I had only a face vise, I would make do.

SCRAPING FACES

First Choice: Tail Vise, Wagon Vise or Wonder Dogs

At first blush it might seem that scraping requires the same workholding strategies as planing. But the two processes are different. When planing, I use the momentum of the tool and gravity to keep the work fixed. That doesn't work with a card scraper, which has less mass and no sole in front of its cutting edge. (If you're using a scraping plane, use the strategies for planing.) You must fix your work to scrape it in most cases. And the tail vise-type devices all work well for this.

ESSENTIAL EDGES: One failing of many workbenches is they don't do enough to help you stabilize a board on edge to work it with hand or power tools. Luckily, a simple design change or a modification can make most benches friendly to edge-work.

BIG BOY: I wondered why old wooden planing stops were so long. My first theory was that they would get chewed up with use. That's true, but a better theory is their length is an asset. Indeed, when you're planing stock that's 4" wide on-edge, you have lots of support from below.

Second Choice: A Planing Board or Stops Plus Battens

Either of these two workbench appliances are superior to a lone planing stop. Planing boards prevent the work from spinning when you begin work at one corner. Planing boards (despite their disadvantages) are likely the best second choice because you can easily move a piece of work to scrape across the grain. Or use battens and planing stops to fence in your boards to work them from any angle.

SCOOPING OUT CHAIR SEATS

First Choice: Scabbing on a Block

You can get fancy with your clamping setups and your seat blanks. Or you can screw a scrap length of 2x4 to the underside of your seat blank and clamp the sucker with whatever you have available: face vise, leg vise, Emmert or tail vise. This gives you complete access to the saddle of the seat and eliminates the risk of splitting the seat blank that comes with holdfasts and F-style clamps. This is the voice of experience here. Don't make it harder than it has to be. No one will care about three screw holes on the underside of a chair seat.

Second Choice: Wonder Dogs

If you have an array of holes in your benchtop, a pair of Wonder Dogs and a pair of regular (wonderless?) dogs, then clamping chair seats is fairly easy. The omni-directional nature of the Wonder Dog makes it great for shield-shaped seats and the like. Although you will occasionally hit a weird patch of grain and pull the blank up out of your clamping setup.

Third Choice: Holdfasts and Clamps

I mention these only to stress that they are slow, get in the way of your tools and are risky. Don't do it.

WORKING ON EDGES OF BOARDS AND ASSEMBLIES

This function of a workbench is often neglected – not only by the woodworker, but also by the commercial bench manufacturer and garden-variety bench designer. You need to work the edges of boards and doors, and sometimes the boards are too long to simply clamp into a face vise effectively (though some woodworkers do this).

This function of a bench isn't just a hand-tool concern. The next time you have to cut some hinge mortises into a door stile or trim solid-wood edging on a long shelf, consider the typical awkward clamping setup. Most traditional workbenches are designed to make it easy to clamp any edge at a comfortable height for sawing, routing, biscuiting, mortising, planing, whatever.

The number one feature in a bench that will make it good for working on edges is having the front legs of the workbench in the same plane as the front edge of the benchtop. Most commercial benches ignore this principle – perhaps because our eyes expect our workbenches to have the graceful overhang of a dining table or side table. Or maybe people have just forgotten how useful this design point really is. Luckily, it's an easy fix with most benches: Re-attach the base to the top so the legs are flush to the benchtop. Or, if you have a fancy bench with trestle ends, you can scab on some pieces to the legs that will create a clamping surface that is in line with the front edge of your benchtop. Or you can build (or retrofit) a sliding deadman into your workbench's design that will give you an adjustable clamping surface that is co-planar with the front of your bench. This is quite handy. All of these solutions can be considered and executed in just a few hours.

"Everything should be made as simple as possible, but not simpler."
— Albert Einstein (1879 - 1955)
scientist, mathematician, inventor

EASY CONSISTENCY: Need a bunch of spindles all the same size and ready for finishing in a hurry? Plane them as a group. Sometimes I'll clamp them together before I plane away, but usually that's not necessary. This is faster than planing them individually or hand-sanding the edges.

The other element missing from many modern workbenches is some way to support long work from below while you are working on the edge of a board. You can, in a pinch, work on the edge of a board with the following clever setup: Clamp one end of the long board in your face vise. Clamp the trailing edge in a handscrew clamp and clamp the handscrew to the benchtop. I know this works because I've done it many times. Handscrews can hold a tight grip that a big No. 8 bench plane cannot easily break.

But the handscrew support method is slow and is fighting gravity instead of harnessing it. A wooden peg below the work does wonders because you don't have to fiddle with clamps – gravity and your downward pressure do all the work.

But where do you place the holes for your pegs? In the legs? That's good. How about in a wide front apron? That's better. In a sliding deadman? Much better. In fact, a peg in a sliding deadman, a face vise and a bench with the legs flush to the front can help perform a lot of operations quickly that other (sometimes fancier) benches struggle with. And that particular operation is where to begin the list of devices designed for working on edges.

SO WRONG: I think Joseph Moxon got a lot of things right in his book on the early woodworking trade in England, but the twin-screw vise illustration is ridiculous. Moxon's text calls out the vise as movable, so my guess is the illustrator made a mistake.

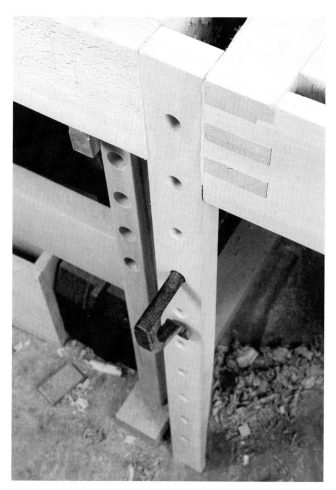

SOMEWHAT USELESS SLAVE: This is a slave block that's clamped into a tail vise. While it works well with long boards, it's not much help in clamping cabinet doors on edge.

PLANING THE EDGES OF NARROW STOCK

First Choice: Planing Stop

The planing stop and your benchtop are surprisingly effective at supporting and holding work that is 4" wide and narrower. Raise your planing stop up fairly high (mine goes up almost 6" with ease), butt your stock against the stop with the work on edge. Go at it. Gravity and your plane keep the stock immobile as you plane it. This is remarkably fast for dealing with many narrow components of different lengths because there is little (usually no) clamping involved.

Second Choice: Wide Planing Stop

When I need to plane several pieces to the same dimension, I lean heavily on this technique. Clamp a wide planing stop to your benchtop and butt all the boards you need to plane against the wide stop (don't forget to check their grain direction). If you're new to this technique, apply a clamp to the back end of the group of boards so they act like one big board. Now plane away across all the edges, treating them like they are one board. This works wonders and works fast. Keep the pieces clamped together as you flip all the pieces over to plane their other edges. Sometimes you can butt the clamp itself against the planing stop to save time.

NO SHOOTING BOARD REQUIRED: When shooting between dogs, I tend to place the plane on the far side of the work and pull it toward me and along the edge. This feels natural. You can place the plane on the side closest to you if your work and bench placement allow it. A flat and smooth benchtop assists in establishing a square and clean edge.

HELD FOR A HINGE: No matter if you use a router plane or a trim router to cut mortises for your hinges, proper support is critical. A scrap stabilizes the base of the tool.

Third Choice: Bird's Mouth (Wedging) Jigs

Many woodworkers end up using an old-style wedged-shaped planing stop that allows you to insert your work into the wedged jig and immediately plane away on the edge. I don't find the wedge particularly advantageous compared to simply working against a tall planing stop. But some woodworkers swear by it.

PLANING, SANDING OR SHAPING THE EDGES OF WIDE STOCK

First Choice: Any Face Vise Plus Support from Below

I know this sounds vague, but there are many solutions to this problem. Any face vise, from an Emmert to a leg vise, will pinch and immobilize the work. No matter what vise you choose, there's a critical point you should be aware of: You'll have better support if the rear jaw of the vise is flush with the front edge of the benchtop. The quick, easy and thoughtless way to mount a face vise is to simply bolt it on the benchtop without cutting a recess for the rear jaw. So the rear jaw is proud of the front edge of the benchtop. This makes it difficult to work on long edges with your face vise because it takes the front edge of your top out of the picture (without some shimming). By the way, if you are too lazy to cut a recess in your benchtop (or perhaps you like your benchtop too much to – gasp – cut it) may I suggest scabbing on a piece to the front edge of your benchtop to bring it in line with the rear jaw? The other part of this equation is the support from below for your work.

My number one preference is to have a sliding deadman that has an array of holes bored into it. This is a flexible and reliable way to put a peg right where you want it. There are, of course, other ways to go about this. Holes in the legs. A separate bench slave. A 2x4 clamped to the legs to act as a shelf to support the work. Some people clamp a slave block in the tail vise. The slave block is bored with a variety of holes. I know this looks like a capital idea at first, but it usually doesn't do jack when you are trying to support shorter boards or doors.

Second Choice: Tail Vise (Or Wagon Vise) With a Bench Plane

I first stumbled on this approach in an old tool catalog that was touting the tail vise as a great device for shooting edges directly on the benchtop. I tried it and it works. Place your work on top of a couple battens. Anything thicker than ¼" will do; it simply has to hold the work high enough to touch the iron. Clamp the work between the dogs. Now turn the handplane on its sidewall on the benchtop. I like to pull the plane toward me, though you can push in many situations as well. At times, the seemingly vestigial L-shaped outrigger on the tail vise will come in handy to support a long plane as it cantilevers off the benchtop when starting a cut. This shooting method requires a plane with an iron sharpened straight across, a sidewall that is square to the sole and a reasonably flat benchtop. What are the rewards for this extra fuss? It's easier for beginners to control a plane used like this than it is for beginners to master the act of balancing a plane in use on a narrow edge.

Third Choice: Wonder Dogs

Just like with the tail vise and wagon vise, the Wonder Dogs can be used for edge-planing a board on a benchtop.

Fourth Choice: Crochet

The classic old-school way to plane an edge uses no vises. I do it frequently, but it can require a bit more setup than using a face vise. A crochet is a wooden hook-like apparatus located on the front edge of your bench where the face vise goes. When you press the end of the work into the open mouth of the hook, its shape immobilizes the board. Support from below comes from holdfasts, pegs or a 2x4 employed as a shelf. This takes a bit of skill, though not much. If you cannot afford a face vise, you'll find a crochet a great companion. With one clamp or holdfast, you can even dovetail boards with it.

AT FIRST GLANCE: This commercial bench seems to offer a lot of functions packed into a small space. But it's still a quart short in my opinion. The 30"-long board in the face vise is the absolute maximum length I can handle when working on edges.

MORTISING FOR HINGE GAINS

First Choice: Face Vise & (Sometimes) Lower Support

The real trick with mortising for a hinge in a door (or face frame) is that you need something additional to balance the tool on as you work. This is true whether you use a router or a router plane. The door's stile alone doesn't offer enough support for the tool to ensure a good mortise. So in addition to securing the door, you need to secure a scrap next to it. Another strategy is to clamp the door stile and face frame stile together and mortise them simultaneously. This ensures accurate alignment between the two hinge gains. With so much going on, clamping can be a challenge. I like a face vise to hold the door and a support scrap at one corner. A clamp (usually a handscrew) holds the scrap to the door. I usually rest one of the wooden jaws of the handscrew on the benchtop if I can. And a peg in the sliding deadman supports the door from below. Another option is to clamp the door so it is 3/4" above the benchtop and to support your router or router plane using a piece of 3/4" scrap on your benchtop.

Second Choice: Face Vise and Clamp

With a small or lightweight door, you can sometimes work directly in a face vise or twin-screw. If the door is long you can clamp the unsupported corner to the front of the benchtop with a long bar clamp.

SAWING EDGES

First Choice: Face Vise

Most of the edge sawing on a workbench involves short cuts. Long cuts on edges and faces are best handled on a low sawbench. These short cuts are usually handled in a face vise. This can be notching the corners of a bottom piece to fit it around some posts. It can be slicing off the little bits of leftover tail scrap when dovetailing drawers. Cutting half-lap joints is another application. For deep notching cuts, I switch gears and use the clamping strategies for letting in hinges.

Second Choice: Bench Hook

A lot of edge sawing involves slicing the edge and face shoulders of tenons. The best way to do this is with a bench hook on the benchtop, as noted in the section above on sawing faces of boards.

Third Choice: Holdfasts

In some of the old engravings in books, it shows woodworkers sawing narrow boards on the benchtop with a holdfast keeping everything in place. I don't find myself drawn to this strategy much, perhaps because of the scale of my work. The engravings I saw (from Roubo's 18th-century texts) were illustrating a joiner's shop, where they were making large doors and sash windows for houses. I can see how a wide door rail wouldn't be easy to mess with on a bench hook.

WORKING ON ENDS OF BOARDS

For the most part, working the ends of boards involves cutting end grain to make joints: dovetails, tenons, rabbets, biscuits. Or it involves trimming that end grain so the finished joint is flush.

The end grain of a board is by far the most difficult to work. It resists planing, sanding, gluing, screwing, nailing and sawing. It, however, can be very accommodating to riving tools, such as a froe, wedge or hatchet, especially when the wood is green and the grain isn't interlocked. However, most operations that are associated with building cabinets bring out the worst behavior of end grain.

As a result of the unyielding nature of end grain, it must be clamped fast and worked with confidence and sharp tools. In general, I find that projects proceed more smoothly when I design and build them in a way that avoids working the end grain as much as possible.

This isn't a new strategy. It is, in fact, quite old. Furniture from the Golden Age of woodworking (the 18th century) shied away from visible joinery – through-dovetails, wedged and proud through-tenons and the like became popular at the beginning of the 20th century. Carcase dovetails were covered in moulding. Mitered joints and what we call breadboard ends also would hide end grain when possible. No matter what furniture-building strategy you employ, you can't avoid end grain entirely. So here are some strategies.

A DOVETAILER'S DELIGHT: If you are fond of cutting dovetails (or think that you will become that way), you would be hard-pressed to find a better vise for this operation than a shoulder vise. It's fast and effective for dovetailing drawer parts, less so for carcase pieces. However, there are always more drawers to dovetail than there are case sides.

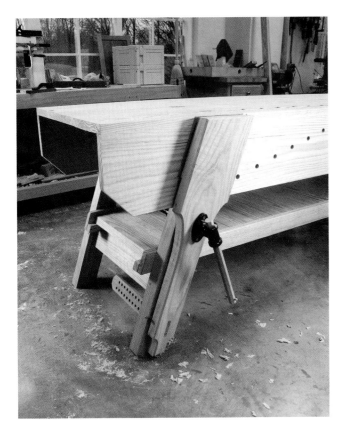

AN EFFECTIVE ANGLE: The angled leg vise allows you to clamp parts for dovetailing that are a bit wider and longer than a comparable leg vise that is pointing straight up. It's not as versatile as a shoulder vise, but if you are an occasional dovetailer (as opposed to a religious one) the angled leg vise is a good compromise.

DOVETAILING DRAWER PARTS

First Choice: Shoulder Vise

The shoulder vise excels at dovetailing parts for drawers. The screw of the vise can be positioned directly on the center of the board's width, which eliminates any chance of the jaws wracking or loosening their grip. There are no bars or screws to interfere with clamping. You can clamp a piece that has one end on the floor just as easily you can clamp very short work. Are there downsides? When it comes to drawer work, not really. Some woodworkers complain that the dog-leg section of the vise on the front of the bench requires them to lean forward more than they like, but I don't find that to be the case. In fact, I find the dogleg section of the vise an excellent place to brace myself as I work. The shoulder vise isn't perfect, but for dovetailing drawer-scale material, it's the cat's pajamas.

Second Choice: Twin-screw Vise

A close second for dovetailed drawers is the twin-screw vise or Moxon vise. For clamping drawer sides it excels in all the same ways that the shoulder vise does. Where it falls short is in the fact that it is a more complex mechanism. And in some designs when the screws operate independently of one another, there is a degree of subtlety required to make the vise work well, much like learning to operate traditional handscrew clamps. You have to learn where the pinch points are on the clamp and how to close everything up so it's clamping the work squarely without stressing the work or the threads of the vise.

Improve the Leg Vise

One of the biggest complaints about leg vises is having to engage some sort of secondary mechanism to keep the jaw parallel as you advance it and to act as a pivot point when squeezing the work. I have a bar in my tail vise that is bored with a series of holes. By moving a steel pin into the correct hole I can control the parallelism of the jaw and set the jaw for different thicknesses. I'm so used to it that I don't think much about it and it has become part of the natural rhythm of my work.

However, if you don't like stooping, you won't like having to do this day after day.

One solution, which is presumably French, is called *Croix de St. Pierre*. I've seen it in action on a commercial leg vise and it is ingenious. It is, essentially, two flat pieces of steel that are joined by a hinge in the center, much like scissors, forming an X shape. At the top of the X, one end is attached to the bench; the other to the jaw of the vise. The two ends at the bottom run in grooves in the jaw and leg of the bench. The scissors action of the X keeps the jaws parallel as you work.

FIG. 243. THE CROIX DE ST. PIERRE.

Third Choice: Leg Vise

Leg vises can be excellent for dovetailing drawer parts, particularly when the vise is built so it is angled. The angle (typical is 20° off 90°) allows you to clamp fairly wide drawer sides (up to 8" wide) without the screw of the vise interfering with the work. Leg vises exert enor-

DESIGNED FOR DRAWERS: This space between the tail vise block and the benchtop is suitable for dovetailing drawer parts (within reason). The benchtop and vise block secure the work with a Western-style push saw. I've used it with a pullsaw, which seems like something that shouldn't work, but the side-to-side clamping can withstand the pulling action.

FACE IT: The face vise isn't my first choice for dovetailing drawers that have any significant width. Note the wracking of the jaws without the benefit of a vise block. Even with the vise block, you'll need to add another support mechanism (or two) when dealing with wide pieces.

mous pressure on the work (a good thing) but require more stooping to keep the vise's parallel guide in the right place. (Though there are mechanisms that can do this for you.) Leg vises are good for a shop that doesn't live or die by the dovetailed drawer and requires some more versatility for other clamping operations.

Fourth Choice: Tail Vise

The space between the benchtop and the vise block of a tail vise can be useful. For a year, I used this space anytime I needed to dovetail anything narrow. Drawer sides were the typical customer. The arrangement works rather well with Western push saws and fairly well with pullsaws. Place the work in that open space and tuck it against the corner of the benchtop. Close the vise on it. There. It's now supported on three sides and is automatically at 90° to the floor. Your width capacity is limited by the maximum opening of your tail vise. For an added grip, some woodworkers will line the jaws of the vise block and end grain of the benchtop with felt or leather.

Fifth Choice: Quick-release Face Vise

Sorry, but these vises are a poor choice for dovetailing drawers. The vise's parallel bars crowd out the drawer stock from the center of the vise, which is exactly where the vise has the most power. And when closed down on one side only, the vise's jaws wrack – and badly. You can compensate with a shop-made vise block, which is in essence a stepped wedge. Place the vise block on the outside corner and the drawer side you plan to victimize in the other corner of the vise. Make sure the thickness of the vise block matches that of the workpiece. Close the vise and the work should be clamped more firmly than if you skipped the vise block. This approach is, of course, extra work. And make sure you come up with some trick to keep the vise block from swan diving to the floor when you release the tension on the vise. I pierced my vise block with a 3/4"-diameter dowel. When the pressure is released on the vise, the block merely swings at the top of the jaws of the face vise, waiting for its next assignment. With a wide drawer side, you might have to pull out all your tricks: face vise, vise block and a bar clamp across the benchtop to position everything and hold it immobile.

Sixth Choice: Crochet and Holdfast/Clamp

This technique works surprisingly well. The only reason it is at the bottom of this list is that the crochet and leg arrangement necessary for it to work are not common in this age. Here are the basic steps: Wedge one edge of the drawer side into the crochet and then clamp the face of the board near the opposite edge with a holdfast or bar clamp. The holdfast or bar clamp holds the work against the front of the benchtop and the leg, which adds stability. Because there are no bench screws involved, your workpiece can go clear to the floor. You are limited only by the position of your crochet and the holes in your legs for a holdfast. I have found that this setup works well for either Western saws or pullsaws. Its main downside is it's slower than the fancy setups detailed above.

DOVETAILING CARCASE COMPONENTS

First Choice: Twin-screw or Moxon Vise

If you can get your twin-screw vise to clamp boards 24" wide, then this setup is the bee's knees. It is the simplest one-stop-shopping way to clamp a wide case side that I know of. The downside to any twin-screw vise, as mentioned before, is that once you reach its limit, that's

SIMPLE: You can dovetail just about any piece of casework with a cro-chet plus a clamp or holdfast. It's not as fast as the more complex solu-tions, but it does require little money to get the bench up and running. This set-up also works when hand-sawing tenons cheeks.

GIVING YOU A LEG DOWN: With the leg flush to the benchtop's front edge, it can be employed to support your work from below. Either a clamp, peg or a holdfast will do the trick. If you use hold-downs in your legs, space the holes so you get complete coverage. This is based on the throat of the hold-down. If your hold-down has an 8" throat, then space the holes 8" or less.

usually all you can do with it. In contrast, other vises can be tricked or tweaked to deal with wider stock. In my opinion, the ideal twin-screw vise for carcase dovetailing is with the vise employed as a face vise or as a removable vise that can be stored away. Center the jaws over the left leg (if you are a right-hander). Make sure the leg is flush to the benchtop's front edge. Bore holes in the leg for a holdfast or simple wooden peg to support the work from below. Now go to town with a dovetail saw.

Second Choice: Shoulder Vise – Plus a Clamp

Using the shoulder vise with a bar clamp is the next best way to dovetail a carcase side. The shoulder vise holds one side of the board; the bar clamp holds the other side. All of these setups that involve a vise plus a clamp have some advantages and frustrations. The main advantage is that you can accommodate a board of almost any width. The other advantage is that the approach works with a wide variety of face vises and the shoulder vise. The disadvantage is that clamping and releasing your work can be a bit awkward with large case sides.

If you cannot support the work from below, you can sometimes drop the work to the ground as you release the clamp or the vise. For a typical case side, you can usually use your foot to support the work from below as you release the pressure. The reason the shoulder vise and clamp combination is my second choice (as opposed to my third or fourth) is because you don't have any vise screws that obstruct your work or vise blocks that you have to manage as you apply vise pres-sure. So things aren't flopping around as much.

Third Choice: Leg Vise or Face Vise – Plus a Clamp

The leg vise is my next choice for dovetailing case sides because you can clamp one side of the work all the way down the leg of the workbench. That adds stability during sawing. Once again, you have to worry about keeping your work under control as you release the pressure on the vise or clamp. A wooden peg or your foot can usually keep things in check. You do have to steer your work clear of the vise screw in the leg vise – and sometimes you'll need a vise block to keep the vise from wracking.

TENONS ANYTIME: Most any vise can handle your work when cutting tenons by hand (or when simply undercutting their shoulders).

TWO-DOG DAYS: With the assistance of two dogs (round or square), you can adjust both the shoulders and cheeks of a tenon. You can quickly move the work onto either side of the dogs for pushing or pulling a tool against the dogs.

A CUT BELOW: When undercutting the shoulders of a tenon (as shown above, beneath the side of the chisel), work with the tenon upright so you can see your work clearly.

If you don't have a leg vise, the quick-release face vise and a clamp can do the same job, but you won't always have the assistance of the workbench's leg (like you will with the leg vise). And I really recommend a vise block when clamping only one end with a quick-release face vise. The wracking isn't good for your vise or your ability to keep your grip.

Fourth Choice: Crochet Plus a Clamp or a Holdfast

As mentioned in the section on dovetailing drawers, this clamping approach works well. However, with case sides, it's unlikely that you'll be able to use a holdfast to clamp the free edge. You're probably going to need a bar clamp. I've also had good luck using my sliding deadman as part of the arrangement: One edge of the board goes into the holdfast, the other gets clamped to the deadman, up near the top of the board is best. This isn't the most stable arrangement for serious sawing – I usually prefer a bar clamp across the benchtop.

Fifth Choice: Holdfasts or Clamps against Benchtop

It's also possible to use two bar clamps across the benchtop to secure the work. I like to do this in front of one leg of the workbench (assuming the leg is flush to the benchtop). If you've bored holes in your leg, you can stick a peg or holdfast in a hole to support the work from below. Once you start supporting from below like this, you'll see the advantage. Promise.

CUTTING TENONS OR DOVETAIL SOCKETS/TAILS ON ENDS

First Choice: Face Vise, Shoulder Vise or Leg Vise

Securing your work for cutting tenons is much less trying than for dovetailing. When I cut tenons by hand, I use the traditional technique: I clamp the work at an angle so I can see two faces of the work at the same time and advance on both lines. Then I turn the work around, place it upright, and finish the cut.

"I will not give away my hard-earned skills to a machine. It's a bit like robbery with violence, for (machines are) not only intended to diminish my bank balance, but also to steal my power."

— John Brown, Welsh stick chairmaker and author

SHOOTING THE WORKS: A simple shooting board (plywood ones stay flat for a long time) can help plane the end grain of a board in a predictable fashion. When choosing a plane for shooting, I pick the one with the most mass and a keen iron that's sharpened straight across – no curve.

This technique makes sawing tenons easier and clamping is easy, too. That's because you don't have to worry as much about the vise's screws because you are clamping the workpiece at an angle. Ditto for the vise blocks; you generally don't need them. Clamping the work at an angle spreads the work out over more of the vise's jaws, reducing the urge of the vise to wrack. Add to that the fact that the stock for your tenon is generally narrow and you'll see that there are many good ways to get this done. Any face vise, shoulder vise or leg vise is up to the job.

As you get into tenoning wider stock you have two choices. You can work with a vise that has wide jaws (such as a leg vise or shoulder vise) or you can treat the joint more like a big rabbet and do it flat on the benchtop using planes and chisels to remove the bulk of the waste. Sometimes the approach you use is dictated by the width of the work and sometimes by the length (think breadboard tenons on a tabletop). When you start working flat on the benchtop for tenoning, clamps and holdfasts are generally the order of the day.

Second Choice: Tail Vise
(Between the Vise Block and Benchtop)
I mention this technique only so that you'll think about that clamping surface between the tail vise and your benchtop. It's useful, though not so much for tenoning. You can indeed clamp narrow bits of wood at an angle appropriate for tenoning: Tip the top of the stock away from you and the bottom of the stock will stick out between your legs. But you'll quickly run out of clamping power as the stock gets wider.

ADJUSTING TENON SHOULDERS
First Choice: Against Dogs or a Planing Stop
I prefer to adjust the shoulders (and cheeks) of tenons with the work flat on the bench, except when the work involves a chisel or other two-handed tool (a rasp, chisel or file). In general, try to work with the stock braced against something stout: two dogs, a planing stop, a bench hook. This way, the progress of your shoulder plane is

clearly visible when the work is flat, as is your knife line or pencil line. Working this way prevents you from stooping to see your line, which is what happens when you secure the work upright in a vise. It's also faster to rely on gravity and the force of the tool to hold it in place than of a vise's screws.

Second Choice: Face Vise, Shoulder Vise or Twin-screw Vise
When chiseling shoulders, a vise is best. You are generally working with the tool in a vertical position and you are generally undercutting your shoulders to get a tight fit at the shoulder (you dirty cheater). Having the work upright in a vise allows you to see the cut as it progresses and allows you to use two hands to control your chisel.

Third Choice: Tail Vise
Again, the opening between your tail vise's jaw and the benchtop can be put to good use. And clamping your work for paring the shoulders is an ideal use for this part of your bench.

Fourth Choice: Holdfasts or Clamps
If your work is very wide, then it usually has to be humped up onto the benchtop, secured with holdfasts or clamps and then worked with a shoulder plane or chisels.

BISCUITING ENDS (AND FACES)
First Choice: Benchtop and Stops
A good bench can be an asset to your biscuit joiner. One of the hardest cuts to make with this useful tool is to cut biscuit slots into end grain. When this cut is made using the tool's fence alone, there is a common tendency to tip the tool a bit and produce a cut that is not angled just right. The same problem occurs (and is even worse) when biscuiting face grain at the ends of boards. There just isn't much meat there to balance your tool on. When I biscuit end grain (typically a shelf side), I'll lay it flat on my benchtop and butt one end against my wide planing stop. Then I lay the biscuit joiner flat on my benchtop and lower the fence so it touches the face of the work. Some people skip this step, which is fine. I don't. I'd rather have the extra layer of aluminum between me and that spinning carbide blade. Then I push the tool against the other end of the board and cut my slots. No clamps whatsoever. I'll use the same approach on the benchtop when biscuiting faces. I remove or retract the biscuit joiner's fence and work with it upright on the benchtop. I'll clamp a fence to the work to position the tool (using holdfasts) and then use a piece of scrap that is the same thickness as my stock to support the cantilevered part of the tool. This works well and involves a minimum of clamping.

"It is a curious and sad fact that although most machines are developed not to cheapen quality but to lessen cost, this is precisely what usually happens."

— Graham Blackburn, *Traditional Woodworking Handtools*

SHOOTING WITHOUT A SHOOTING BOARD: You can clamp your work between your bench dogs to shoot the ends – as long as your benchtop is flat. Be sure to work the outfeed side a bit before working the full edge. This will help prevent the end grain from breaking out on one edge of the board.

HANGING OUT: By using a scrap clamped to the benchtop, you can plane end grain at a comfortable height. Secure one corner of the assembly in a face vise so you can work the end grain on the assembly in a quick and aggressive manner.

PLANING END GRAIN OF BOARDS NARROW AND WIDE

First Choice: Shooting Boards

In general, planing end grain is even harder than sawing it. You need sharp tools, and moistening the end grain with alcohol also helps the job. The most accurate way to plane end grain so it is square to the faces is to use a shooting board. This simple workshop appliance (usually three pieces of wood) holds the work as you plane the ends. It takes a little practice to master the shooting board, but the rewards are substantial. Even if you are a die-hard power-tool user, a shooting board can do things that no power tool can. Exhibit A: Reduce boards in length in .001" increments. When I'm fitting muntins and mullions in a divided-light door, or fitting a shelf in dados, shooting boards are quite useful. Shooting boards generally hook over the front edge of your benchtop, so you don't really have to worry much about securing them. Some woodworkers clamp the hook in their face vise.

I consider a shooting board essential bench equipment for every home shop woodworker. It beats the snot out of trying to plane long stretches of end grain freehand. There are also a wide variety of shooting boards for miters, bevels and moulding. They are good for specialty work. Make a simple shooting board first and you'll probably end up making a few more in short order.

Second Choice: Bench Hook

If you won't build a shooting board, you can use a bench hook to do the same job on small bits of wood. If your work is long, you'll also need something to support the work that hangs over your bench, otherwise, say goodbye to that square cut you were trying to get.

Third Choice: Tail Vise

If the stock isn't too long, you can lay it down on a thin bit of scrap and pinch it between the dogs of your tail vise. Then you can shoot the ends of the board with a plane that you slide on its side on the benchtop. Again, don't forget that you need a flat benchtop for this to work. This works quite well for wide boards that aren't too long. You can even shoot the end of the case side for a base cabinet this way if you pull your bench away from the wall.

Fourth Choice: Face Vise, Shoulder Vise or Twin-screw Vise

Yes, you can plane end grain freehand, and sometimes it's the only way to accomplish a task. The traditional vises (sometimes accompanied by a bar clamp) can secure your work for most of these jobs. If you can, support your work from below; planing end grain generally requires a lot of downward pressure.

PLANING END GRAIN OF ASSEMBLED CORNER JOINTS OR ASSEMBLED CASEWORK

First Choice: Cantilevered Platform Plus a Vise

Working on assembled furniture projects with planes, chisels or sanders seems daunting at first because of the size of the work. But there are tricks that can help. When working on assembled pieces (just like when you're working on individual boards) there are three goals: Get the surface you want to work on to a height that is comfortable for you. Two: Support the surface from below so it doesn't flex under pressure from the tool. Three: Prevent the assembly from wracking and self-destructing because of the pressure from the tool. Lots of woodworkers try to adjust themselves more than they adjust the work. They work over their heads. They stand on stools. They work on the floor or on their knees.

"To the very last, he [Napoleon] had a kind of idea; that, namely, of 'La carrière ouverte aux talents,' The tools to him that can handle them."

— Thomas Carlyle (1795-1881) Scottish-born historian and essayist Source: "Sir Walter Scott" *London and Westminster Review,* 1838)

Meet the Moxon Vise, A Useful Bench Accessory

Early French and English books on woodworking sometimes showed a "double-screw" vise, which is essentially a portable twin-screw vise (or an overgrown handscrew).

Joseph Moxon discussed this vise in his landmark book on joinery "Mechanick's Exercises" (1768), but the illustration was so odd that most modern woodworkers have assumed that the back jaw of the vise was somehow threaded to the front of the benchtop – a weird arrangement to be sure.

However a close reading of Moxon's text indicates that his double-screw is a portable vise that can be used anywhere on the benchtop or can be secured to the edge of the bench.

Many modern woodworkers now use this vise for dovetailing and allow 24" between centers so one can dovetail a carcase side. But even a small double-screw can be useful for woodworkers – even those who don't dovetail.

Woodworkers Peter Follansbee and Jennie Alexander, who study 17th-century joinery, use this vise to secure work on edge so they can plane it, plow it, mortise it or rabbet it. They clamp the double-screw to the end of the work and push the front of the work against a planing stop.

You also can use the vise for small riving chores. When Follansbee has to rive off the cheeks of a tenon, he clamps it in his double-screw on the benchtop and peels off the tenon cheeks.

I have built a number of these vises in a variety of sizes and using different kinds of screws. The first ones I made were using a wooden threadbox and tap to make the screws. This worked quite well, though finding a working threadbox can be a challenge at times. I have also built a few of them using Acme-threaded rod and nuts from an industrial supply house.

In recent years, several commercial models and kits have shown up that use metal screws and wheels or handles.

No matter how you build one, once you have used one for dovetailing, you are spoiled. The vise raises the work off your benchtop so you aren't stooping over it while sawing.

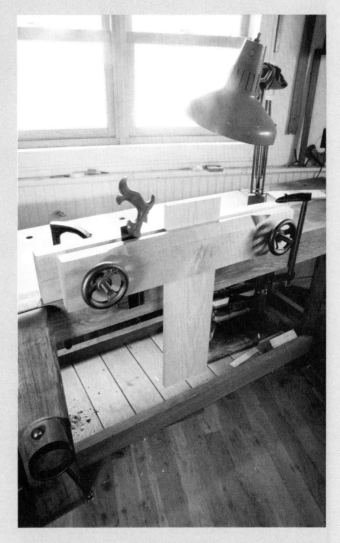

BIG WOODEN CLAMP: The so-called Moxon vise is outstanding for dovetailing wide case sides (and small components). And when you are done dovetailing, you can put the vise away.

There are other options (usually). Because of the open-frame nature of casework, you can use this to your advantage with some assemblies. This requires a strategy and some cleverness. First, the strategy: Build the outside of the carcase. Work that shell until it's ready to finish. Then the open carcase can be supported on a cantilevered platform off the workbench and clamped to the bench in some manner. Or you can sleeve the carcase right onto some benchtops. This allows you to plane, scrape or sand the sides of the case (and even perhaps the top and bottom – though those might not need much attention in a cabinet). Then you can prepare the interior components

as flat boards and fit them into the carcase. In the end, this allows you to easily work surfaces that will become difficult to work later on.

Note that this strategy might need to be altered for the scale of the piece. Really large cabinets might require their interior pieces fitted before you work the outside because you are going to have to lay the carcase on its sides on your shop floor (or on planks) to work them. And the interior pieces will stiffen the case. Drawers are one assembly that is best worked as a shell without the bottom in place: You can work them easily from all sides with the work on a cantilevered platform. If you have the bottom in the drawer already, use the strategy outlined below.

Second Choice: Face Vise Plus a Sliding Deadman

For narrow assemblies, drawers and doors mostly, you can work the ends (and faces) by clamping one corner in a vise and supporting the work from below with a sliding deadman alone. If you really need to stiffen things up for your work, you can clamp the assembly across the benchtop as well.

How to Design Your Bench

Boards (and flat assemblies — such as doors) have three kinds of surfaces: faces, edges and ends. So when you design your workbench, you should begin with the goal of building one that will accomplish at least those tasks with the tools you now use — or plan to use.

You also will be working on the end grain, face grain and edge grain of assembled boxes, so you need to make sure that you can accommodate some of this activity as well.

So you are sitting there with a blank sheet of paper, or a blank computer screen, as you design your bench. It's tough to make a first sketch, a first design. So let's do a warm-up exercise. I highly recommend it because it points out why building your own workbench — instead of purchasing one — is worthwhile. Let's pick apart some typical commercial workbenches, plus a 19th century craftsman-built bench and a couple other designs, using our guidelines and see how these benches measure up.

The 1882 Workbench from *Carpentry and Building* Magazine

This bench is a complete success, though it's more complex than necessary. The plan was submitted to *Carpentry and Building* magazine by W.A.Y. of Pierce's Landing, Pennsylvania, and was published in the August 1882 edition. Here are its vitals: 10' 3" long, 33" high, 18" deep (plus a 9"-wide tool tray at the rear). The 4"-thick top is made of alternating strips of walnut and ash (flashy!). The legs are thick: The vise leg is 4" x 5". The other legs are 3" x 5". All the legs are mortised into the top.

The leg vise and sliding deadman allow you to work on edges of boards or panels. The tail vise and dogs allow you to work on faces. The jack-leg leg vise (and the sliding deadman) allow you to work on ends of boards with ease. There are no aprons to impede clamping.

Carpenters' and Cabinet-makers' Bench.—Sketch Accompanying the Communication From W. A. Y.

1882 BENCH: This bench was featured in the August 1882 edition of *Carpentry and Building* magazine. Note the offset and jack-legged leg vise. This bench is more than 10' long, 33" high and 18" deep (with a 9"-wide tool tray at the back). The top is 4" thick. This bench is capable of all common workshop tasks.

EVERYTHING YOU NEED (EXCEPT A PLACE TO WORK): The H.S. & Co. No. 25A is highly prized by tool collectors, but it shouldn't be the bench of your dreams. Look past the included shiny objects to see that inside this bench beats the heart of a kitchen cabinet.

The bench is quite long and not too deep. I am hard-pressed to find anything to criticize except for the tool tray (a personal preference).

Hammacher, Schlemmer's Workbench

Now let's pick on a classic from Hammacher, Schlemmer & Co. — it's actually a more difficult assignment. While this company is still in business, the closest thing it sells to a workbench these days is a portable air hockey game. So a little criticism of its offerings of last century are unlikely to hurt sales of its laser-guided pool cue (item 72641, $59.95).

The Manual Training Outfit 25A looks like a swanky setup for $65. In addition to the maple workbench with a face vise and tail vise, you get 26 high-quality tools, including a Stanley No. 3 smoothing plane, a Disston 22" panel saw and a Millers Falls No. 323 bit brace with an 8" sweep. Sweet. Sign me up.

Or perhaps not. Let's talk about the length of that benchtop. Though the catalog doesn't call it out, it's easy to figure by using the Disston 22" saw for scale. My guess puts the benchtop at 56" long. That's too short for traditional casework. Though most individual parts in a cabinet will be 48" long and shorter, mouldings and assembled projects would quickly get out of hand for this bench.

NOT QUITE ROMAN; NOT QUITE RIGHT: This is one of the assembly benches in our workshop, but it's almost identical to my first workbench in our shop. This is basically what Roman workbenches looked like – except the legs were tenoned into the top.

MAKESHIFT AND SHIFTY: This is a temporary bench in the magazine's shop. It looks a lot like my first bench, without the fancy roll-around drawers below. This bench is tricky to use with hand tools.

On the plus side, the legs appear flush with the front edge of the top. Score one for the Hammacher. But the bail pulls on the three overlay drawers look like they might interfere with clamping things on edge. Speaking of that, where will you clamp a cabinet door when mortising its edge? There's a big storage cabinet below the benchtop – with no system of pegs or a deadman to support items from below.

In a pinch, you could pull out the drawers partially and hope they would be situated to lend a hand. And for many assemblies, you would be able to make do. But it wouldn't be ideal. And speaking of the cabinets below this bench, the storage is welcome, but be aware of what you are giving up: Room to clamp. The bench has a nice little cubby below the benchtop and cabinet box, but trust me, you ain't getting an F-style clamp there unless you stick the clamp's bar up in the air as you cinch it down. That cubby was designed to allow the benchdogs to slip fully into their holes, and perhaps to allow a few more tools to be stored under there.

If this were my bench, I'd make a slave block that would clamp in the tail vise and run it to the floor. I'd bore it with ³/₄" holes every couple inches and make a peg that could be used to support longer stock. Plus, I'd work on the edges of narrow boards on the benchtop, between dogs. Those strategies would cover most of the problems.

So all in all, the bench isn't designed for working on edges of boards and assemblies. I've seen worse than this, however, and the workbench could be made to work with shorter pieces.

Let's look at working on the faces of boards. Again, the top isn't long enough and will interfere with what should be routine tasks. (This bench needs to be almost twice as long in my book.)

There's a nice-looking face vise mounted in the end vise position on the right side of the bench. There's a dog that lines up with a row of dog holes (I count nine) located no more than 2" in from the front edge of the benchtop. This row of dogs is a bit too close to the front edge in my opinion. The bench is easier to laminate this way in a factory, but a bit of a pain to use. If you moved the dog holes so they were 4" in from the front edge that would be much better. It would put the dog in the vise in line with the vise's screw, producing less racking pressure on the vise, and it would allow you to grip the centerpoint of an 8"-wide board, which is nice. As the vise is now, it would wrack a

bit and you'd have to add pressure to keep the work secure, and that added pressure could cause you some bowing in your stock.

Other issues for dealing with faces of boards: There is no planing stop listed or shown. You'd need to add one or make one (or get out the random-orbit sander – always an option). There are no holdfast holes. And just drilling some would be no good because of the kitchen cabinet that lurks below. There are some commercial plastic holdfasts that might work with this bench, but there is no guarantee. In fact, securing things using downward clamp pressure would be limited with this bench setup. You could apply a clamp at the ends of the bench, and you could get an F-style clamp on that front edge if you used it with the bar of the clamp sticking up in the air (never fun) and put the clamp head in the cubby space.

For working on the ends of boards (planing, sanding, tenoning and dovetailing) the iron quick-release face vise is a pretty good choice for a commercial bench. You would need to make a simple vise block to keep the vise from wracking. And you'd want a bar clamp to work in conjunction with the vise when sawing on wide boards.

So what is this bench good for? It has a good deal of tool storage: the drawers and door below, a tool tray and a tool rack on the back edge. It's OK for working on edges of boards, somewhat limited for working on faces and OK for working on ends. All in all, the bench is a bit of a compromise and is really just too small for most work.

But in a power-tool workshop this bench would be fine. You'd be a bit miffed when trying to clamp some things to the bench for routing and the like, but all-in-all you wouldn't complain too much. I should know. This bench is much like a workbench I built for *Popular Woodworking* magazine that was designed to work as an outfeed table to a table saw, offer tool storage and handle the occasional handwork task. At that, the bench performed (and still performs) quite well.

An Unintentional Roman-style Workbench

Admittedly, I do a fair amount of handwork in conjunction with my machinery and hand-held power tools. And my power-tool-only friends tend to roll their eyes when I start waxing on about workbench designs. Their contention is I'm too fussy, that all most North Americans really need is a flat-panel door, a couple sawhorses and

POWER-TOOL WORKBENCH: This design, which we still use in our shop, is compact, stores a bunch of stuff, but is miserable for working on edges of long boards. My original plan was to use the dog holes on the front edge of the top plus the drawers. That was lame.

some kind of vise. Then you can take the money you saved by not building a traditional bench and buy another plunge router.

My first workbench at the magazine was just such a workbench. The benchtop was a solid-core veneered walnut door that was almost 2" thick. These 1920s-era doors were the cafeteria doors to our Art Deco building, which had begun its life as a Coca-Cola bottling plant. The slabs were heavy and stable and pretty.

The base was a set of sawhorses made from poplar 2x4s and a plastic kit that allowed you to make the sawhorses without many angle cuts. The vise was a nice Wilton quick-release vise that I had installed in the tail vise position. Its placement was a tough choice – I had only one vise and no other vise hardware.

I screwed the door to the sawhorses and bolted the vise to the door. I built it before lunch and was working on it that afternoon. Years after building that bench, I was struck by how much it resembled early Roman workbenches shown in frescos. The only differences between my bench and the Roman version were that I screwed the base and

top together and the Romans tenoned the legs into the top. Also, they didn't have a quick-release Wilton vise. Of that, I am sure.

So let's take this workbench and see how it would do in a workshop that required little handwork.

First, the good points. This bench was fantastic as a clamping surface. Its wide open area under the benchtop allowed me to clamp anything anywhere. I clamped a lot of router templates to that bench, plus stuff that needed biscuiting and drilling. I could assemble things directly on the benchtop because I could clamp pieces and assemblies to the benchtop, giving me extra support.

The quick-release vise (in the end-vise position) was good for a little bit of handwork. I could hold things for block planing and sawing. And because the bench was up against the shop wall, all the forces involved kept the bench stable during these operations.

The benchtop was long (more than 6') and wide enough (about 24") for woodworking. With a moving blanket spread out on the benchtop, it was an excellent place to sand. The top was a laminated structure and never went much out of true. I would flatten it up mostly to remove the glue and stain that had absorbed into the thick walnut veneer. And it was inexpensive, an excellent bonus for a young journalist with a family. All-in-all, I had no complaints until I started incorporating more handwork into my projects and couldn't always use the benches of the other editors.

That was the beginning of the end for that bench.

For planing faces of boards, I bored some holes in the benchtop in line with the dog on the vise that was in the tail vise position. This allowed me to clamp long boards between dogs, but the bench was too lightweight for heavy planing forces. While planing along the length of a board, the bench would creep left toward the drill press table. So working on faces by hand was difficult with that bench.

Because of the open nature of the top, I had no problems clamping stuff for chiseling and sawing. My real problems came when trying to work on edges of boards.

Except for the narrow stock I could clamp between dogs or in the vise, the bench was worthless for working on edges. When I had to mortise a door stile for a hinge or a mortise lock, I was out of luck. I had to move to someone else's bench. This was enough of a pain in the neck that I started using non-mortise hinges. That's a workaround, but not always a good one. Changing your furniture designs based on your bench isn't fun.

HOLTZAPFFEL'S BENCH: This is one of my favorite bench designs and is from Charles Holtzapffel's *Construction, Action and Application of Cutting Tools.* It has demerits (of course), but is a fair design.

"Work thou for pleasure — paint or sing or carve The thing thou lovest, though the body starve — Who works for glory misses oft the goal; Who works for money coins his very soul. Work for the work's sake, then, and it may be That these things shall be added unto thee."

— Kenyon Cox (1856 - 1919)
American academic, painter

ALSO APPEALING: Shaker-style workbenches, such as this one built by Stephen Fee, have an indescribable appeal. Unlike some benches with cabinets below, this one will allow you to work on the edges of boards with ease. Clamps and holdfasts aren't going to work as well, however.

Working on ends of boards was quite difficult. I could cut tenons in the vise and plane and sand small pieces, but dovetailing almost anything was an exercise in frustration. I tried everything.

It quickly became apparent that the bench that was perfect for me when I was a power-tool woodworker was holding me back as I introduced hand tools into my work. As a bench for any significant amount of handwork, it was a disaster.

So this raises a question: Are there benches just for handwork and benches just for power-tool work? I don't think that's how it works. While a Spartan bench will be fine for power-tool-only woodworking, a good hand-tool workbench will be excellent for both hand- and power-tool tasks. All of the attributes that go into a good traditional workbench also make the bench ideally suited for power-tool activity.

So even if you are a menace to the power-tool grid in your town, there is a good reason to build a traditional bench. It will handle power-tool tasks with great aplomb, and it will wait patiently as you decide if you want to incorporate more hand tools into your work. When you do (most home woodworkers make this move if they stick with the craft), then you will find your bench is ready to help you jump-start into handtools.

CARPENTER'S WORKBENCH: This bench from *Audels Carpenters and Builders Guide* (the 1947 edition) is designed to be knocked together on a home construction site. Note its resemblance to the English Workbench in this book and how it manages to sneak in tool storage.

A Power-tool Workbench

Several years ago I built a bench that attempted to bridge the gap between a traditional hand-tool bench and a power-tool slab on horses. It's a decent bench, but has some flaws.

On the good side, it works magnificently as an outfeed table for a cabinet saw. It stores a shop's worth of hand tools and is great for dovetailing and basic planing chores. The twin-screw tail vise is capable of a great many tasks and I've clamped some odd objects with that setup.

But the bench has its limits, and by now you should be able to pick these out with your eyes barely open. The bench is too short for working long stock. It doesn't handle planing the edges of boards well once they reach a certain width and length. The drawers below do help lend some support below the stock, but there's only so much they can do. Plus, there's just barely enough clearance under the top to put in an F-style clamp.

In the end, I give my own effort a *B*. We still use this bench, however, so don't write it off entirely.

Charles Holtzapffel's Bench

Though I like a functional bench more than a flashy one, I'm not immune to the wiles of a well-proportioned piece of work. One of the workbenches shown in Charles Holtzapffel's *Construction, Action and Application of Cutting Tools* (1875) has always charmed me with its stout looks and flashy features.

In some ways it looks like a typical 18th-century woodworking bench. The twin-screw vise in the face vise position is an excellent choice. The legs are flush to the front of the bench. There's a tail vise in the end vise position (with a sinuous outrigger support arm).

But the design has some things I'd change. Though one of the legs is bored for a peg to support long stock, I think this bench would be a pain for working on the long edges of doors. The twin-screw vise would probably help you hold most drawer parts and assembled drawers, but assembled doors would be a challenge. Plus there's the drawer, which impedes clamping to the benchtop. And the tool tray, which will attract a mess. I'm not too crazy about either of those features on a workbench.

But there is something about this bench that I like. I've built a few that were modified from the original 19th-century design and they worked quite well.

So as you stare at that blank sheet of paper, don't be afraid to dream about the kind of woodworker you might become. Dissect a few commercial workbenches that you find in the catalogs. Decide for yourself what sort of features appeal to your budget, your mechanical inclination and your patience. Then let the pencil (and eraser) loose on your page.

"A boat is not a boat unless it's in the water."

— John Gardner, founder
of Mystic Seaport's boatbuilding program

A FRENCH BENCH AT WORK: This plate, from one of Roubo's volumes, illustrates the basic French bench during the 18th century, which changed little up into the 20th century.

Chapter Four

About the Benches in this Book

In this book, there are plans for four benches that (as drawn) are good for both power- and hand-tool work. What I like about these workbenches is that they take different paths to arrive at the same result: a bench that can accommodate a full range of woodworking operations.

Each bench can be fitted to take a variety of workholding devices. If you don't like a wagon vise, then use a tail vise or a Wonder Dog system. If the leg vise looks too archaic to your modern eyes, then you can use just about any other face vise in that spot, from a Far East quick-release vise to a vintage Emmert.

I refer to these benches as English and French, but those names are imprecise. The heritage of each bench is pretty mongrel, which is true of most workbenches, methods of work and woodworkers. The two French benches are drawn from André-Jacob Roubo's enormous *L'Art du menuisier* (*The Art of the Woodworker*, 1769-1775). However, some of the bits and pieces of this bench show up on so-called German workbenches.

The English benches are adapted from Peter Nicholson's *Mechanic's Companion* (1831). This style of bench pokes its head up in a number of books during the next 100 years in Great Britain and the United States, and then the design all but disappears.

The Dominant Continent

Both the English and French bench are now hardly a blip on the radar screen compared to what most woodworking catalogs call the continental bench, shown on the next page. The continental style of workbench shows up everywhere and seems to have a German and Scandinavian pedigree. It was popularized in the 20th century in the United States by the Ulmia workbench, a company that has a rich past of supplying woodworking equipment but an uncertain future.

The anatomy of a continental workbench is important to know so you can see why the French and English versions are different.

- The continental bench is generally built on a trestle-style frame with sled feet. The benchtop frequently has a skirt that encloses it on all four sides — and these skirt pieces can be bolted on, finger-jointed or dovetailed at the corners. This detail makes construction more complicated than a simple slab top.
- The benchtop is usually pierced by a row of square holes for bench dogs. And these holes are angled and shaped to conceal the bench dogs when not in use. Sometimes there is a round hole or two in

the top to accept a holdfast. The bench can have a tool tray at the rear, though that's not a given.
- The face vise on the left corner of the workbench is typically a face vise with a single vise screw or there's a shoulder vise at that location, for those woodworkers who do a lot of dovetailing. The shoulder vise (as mentioned in earlier chapters) is an impressive bit of engineering and requires another leg be added to the trestle base to support the dogleg section of the shoulder vise.
- On the right side of the bench is typically a traditional tail-vise setup with an L-shaped jaw. The jaw is pierced with angled and square dog holes. If there's not a tail vise, there will usually be a wooden-jawed vise on the end of the bench that will act as a stand-in for the traditional tail vise. A few benches will put a twin-screw vise or single-screw vise on the end of the bench and rig it up with a couple dog holes in its wooden jaw to act as a tail vise.

This continental workbench is visually appealing, appears massive and seems — at first glance — to have everything you need to work wood. And if you do a limited amount of handwork, you'd be mostly right. I've worked on a fair number of these benches during the last 20 years, and they have their merits. But let's look at the bench from the wood's perspective for a minute. These benches can be great, but they can be frustrating at times, too.

In 2000, we brought a commercial continental workbench into our shop that was made in Eastern Europe. (The brand of the bench is meaningless because you cannot purchase it anymore.) From a distance, the bench was quite sexy. It had a wooden-jawed face vise on the left side of the bench and a tail vise on the right that was married to a line of dog holes on the top. The fit and finish of the bench was pretty good for the price.

So what was the problem? Like many continental workbenches, this one was not well-suited for working on the edges of wide boards or assemblies, such as doors or panels. Any time I needed to work on

"By all means read what the experts have to say. Just don't let it get in the way of your woodworking"

— John Brown (1932 – 2009)

CABINET AND PIANO-MAKERS' BENCHES

No. A

This has long been the standard Cabinet-makers' Bench. It is constructed throughout of the best selected maple, and is made in the most careful manner. Strong and rigid, it is, without question, the best Cabinet-makers' Bench made.

No. A. Cabinet-makers', 6 ft. 8 in. long; 2 ft. 1 in. wide; 2 ft 9 in. high; 7½ in. recess .... Each, $19.00

Our Piano-Makers' Bench "D" is the same in workmanship and material as the "A," but has a solid top (no recess).

No. D. Piano-makers', 6 ft. 8 in. long; 2 ft. 4 in. wide; 2 ft. 9 in. high ....Each, $24.00

See Discount Sheet

CABINET-MAKERS' BENCHES

No. B

Our "B" Bench is well made, strong and durable; all working parts are made of maple, excepting, of course, the screws, which are of well-seasoned hickory. It is a good, practical bench. Our "C" Bench is made on the same lines but somewhat smaller.

No. B. 6 ft. 8 in. long; 2 ft. wide; 2 ft. 9 in. high; 6½ in. recess..Each, $11.00

No. C. 5 ft. 8 in. long; 1 ft. 8 in. wide; 2 ft. 9 in. high; 7½ in. recess............................... " 10.75

See Discount Sheet

THE CONTINENTAL PERSUASION: This bench, usually called a European or continental workbench, is a popular style. When made properly, it's both massive and capable of most workholding chores. If you build one you might want to think about also building a bench slave to help support the ends of long boards.

the edge of a wide board I would clamp one end in the face vise and then I'd clamp the other end to the front edge of the benchtop. And then the fun would begin. No matter how firmly I'd clamp the piece, it would slip when I applied significant pressure to the work. Why? The beautiful and too-slick film finish on the bench.

I was reluctant to judge the bench harshly on this alone. After all, many woodworkers use a bench slave with their workbenches to prop up long pieces of work. But then I tried clamping things to the benchtop for pattern routing, and that's when I got my feathers ruffled. The benchtop looked massive, but it wasn't. The top was quite thin and was merely banded by a wide skirt board. So when I went to clamp stuff to the top with an F-style clamp, the pad of the clamp couldn't touch the underside of the top because of the skirt. So I would clamp stuff to the skirt; but that's not always ideal because sometimes you want to apply pressure in toward the center of the benchtop. I could sometimes use a parallel-jaw bar clamp to increase my reach, but other times I needed to reach more deeply into the benchtop.

The face vise wracked considerably, though that's not the fault of the design of the bench, merely the execution. So I made a vise block

for the face vise. When I went to cut dovetails on this bench, I would clamp narrow boards using the jaw of the tail vise on the right (this works well for drawer sides). But wider boards had to go into the face vise and required both a vise block and a hefty clamp across the top to make the work behave for the saw.

There is typically no planing stop on a continental workbench, especially the commercial ones. Some woodworkers, such as Frank Klausz, have added a planing stop to their designs. But other woodworkers either have to build a stop that clamps into the face vise, or they work between dogs using the tail vise. This dog-clamp-dog style of working gets time-consuming with the screw-in, screw-out action, especially if you have a fair number of boards that are different lengths. And I wish the bench were longer. The typical 6'-long bench has some limitations.

I gave the bench a pretty favorable write-up in *Popular Woodworking* magazine. That was before I had gotten frustrated with the way the top was made, the slick finish and the fact that the handy drawer blocked access to one key dog hole. A few months after the review appeared I wished that I could review the bench again to point out its flaws, but woodworking magazines typically don't do that.

MY ROUBO BENCH: I don't have a drop of French blood in my veins, but I am quite attached to this bench. Note the wide planing stop across the width of the benchtop and the sliding deadman. Those are non-French accessories, but they are effective for my work.

After that review, I resolved to design workbenches that were more useful, less expensive and easy to build. I attempted a number of strategies: a $175 workbench, a workbench for power-tool woodworkers, and a workbench that could be built in 24 hours (I built four of those). All these forms had their merits and are still in use today. And each bench inched me a little closer to the ideal. I turned away from the continental workbench, but I stayed on the same continent and dusted off my wife's high school French-to-English dictionary.

French Workbenches

The French workbench appears to be a simple design – almost too simple – for cabinetwork. One criticism of the design is that it is shown being used in a joiner's shop in Roubo's first volume – workmen are building doors and sash windows in the engraving. And so it must be designed to build only frame-like assemblies, oui? Non.

If you page through the other volumes of Roubo, you will see the same style of workbench being used for marquetry, carriage-building and garden-related woodwork. Other French books of the same era show a similarly massive workbench, particularly Denis Diderot's *L'Encyclopedie*, a collection of 71,181 articles on the state of the arts, sciences and trades in France between 1751 and 1772.

Let's first look at this style of bench from the original Roubo illustration. The French bench is – above everything – the most excellent three-dimensional clamping surface I have ever worked on. With a couple clamps, you can secure almost any size board or assembly for working on the faces, edges and ends. For working on the faces of boards and the edges of boards (up to a point), you can work against the planing stop. Working on panels with hand tools can be tricky, however. You can use holdfasts in conjunction with the planing stop or – if you have to work the entire face of the board – wedge the board against the planing stop and use a doe's foot to secure things.

As shown in the illustration at the beginning of this chapter, you work on the edges of panels and wide boards by using the crochet – the hook at the end of the bench. You wedge the board into the hook and secure the board to the legs or stretchers using a variety of methods. Holdfasts in the legs work sometimes. Or you can create a ledge for the work to perch on. The ledge can be a scrap of 2x4 that's clamped to the legs with holdfasts or modern clamps. Again, this works, but it involves some fiddling about that you might not want to do. There is, however, no cheaper substitute for a face vise than the crochet. Mine is made using scrap ash and two big lag bolts.

How about working on the ends of boards? In the stock configuration, you wedge the edge of the work into the crochet and secure the other end with a clamp or (if you are lucky) with a well-placed holdfast. You also can support your work from below with a holdfast or a clamp that presses the work to the gloriously wide leg.

So even in this simple form, the French bench can do a lot of things fairly well. I added a few details that make it quite a bit faster to use.

- Leg vise: Roubo shows leg vises in his book, so it's not a stretch of historical fact to add one to the left leg of the bench. The leg vise makes it faster to secure boards for working on their edges and ends. You can then omit the crochet or keep it because it's still useful, it's cheap to make and it's fun to use. One of the French benches in this book uses a parallel guide and metal vise screw. The other uses a wooden screw and no parallel guide, just like the 18th-century version.
- Sliding deadman: This is not in Roubo's book, but I love a sliding deadman. This device, which is flush to the front surface of the bench and pierced with holes, can support long boards and wide panels when working on edges. A deadman can also support your work from below when working on ends. I added a deadman to one of the French benches in this book.

ANOTHER ROUBO BENCH: In a later volume, Roubo shows off this so-called German workbench. It has two leg vises (one slides!), plus a tail vise and tool storage.

- Different kinds of planing stops: One of the benches has a simple wooden planing stop. The other uses a toothed metal stop, sometimes called a "bench hook."

  Metal stops can mark your work, especially when you use them properly, which is to push a board securely up against the metal teeth. They do help keep your stock under control, and they can be good if you build period reproductions, which generally hide the end grain with mouldings. The risk with a metal stop is that your planes will strike the metal if you make an error, and your iron or the sole of your handplane will get damaged. Let your work and your proclivity for living dangerously be your guide.
- Wagon vise: I added this gizmo in the end vise position of one of the French benches mostly to allow me to work across the grain of boards and assemblies without the hassle of moving around battens. Because my wagon vise was a retrofit, I used the round brass dogs from Veritas. These dogs can also faintly mark your work and be a hazard to cutting edges. I've had pretty good luck with them over the years and have yet to strike them with a plane. The dogs have gotten sanded on occasion.

As shown, these two French benches handle a wide variety of work. The major difference between the two benches is the materials and the top-to-leg joinery. One of the French benches is built with construction lumber and has simple blind tenons that pierce the benchtop. The other bench is built with French oak slabs from the 18th century and uses the super-sexy sliding-dovetail joint shown in Roubo's books. There are plusses and minuses to both designs, as you will see in the following chapters.

The English Efficiency Benches

When most people think of an English-style workbench, they usually think of what some people call the *strong table* workbench. It's an apronless table with four stout legs. Or it has a small apron as shown in the illustration above. Some people call this bench an Ian Kirby bench, after the modern English craftsman and author.

The bench's built-in workholding is generally quite simple – a face vise that is not at the far corner of the bench but is between the legs. Some benches even center the vise on the front edge of the benchtop.

A lot of workholding is done with accessories that clamp into the face vise, including the planing stop and a wide variety of gizmos (the English call them *appliances*) for shooting edges and ends of boards. I've worked on this style of workbench and find it lacking for working on edges as is. There are, of course, appliances for this. But it begins to feel a bit like a food processor as you are rummaging under the bench for the appliance that makes julienne fries.

Older English Benches

The English-style workbench I'm partial to was drawn in Peter Nicholson's book on carpentry and joinery. This is the bench you'll find the interpreters working on at Colonial Williamsburg, and it's a form that shows up even into the 20th century, especially in books on house carpentry. You'll never find anything like it for sale in the woodworking catalogs.

So let's look at this bench as Nicholson drew it and then discuss the two versions I made for this book. The most eye-catching aspect of Nicholson's bench is the wide front apron that is pierced with holes for pegs or holdfasts. This makes the bench ideal for working on the edges of boards and offers support anywhere along the bench's front.

MIDDLE ENGLISH: This bench is drawn by English cabinetmaker Charles Hayward and bridges the gap between the old English bench designs (with an apron) and the new ones (which eschew the apron).

The apron also helps turn the top into an effective torsion box, which allows you to use far less material to build your workbench (less than half, actually) than you would with a same-sized French bench. The top of Nicholson's bench is thin and gains rigidity from the aprons, the leg assemblies and three ribs under the top.

The aprons also allowed the joiner or carpenter to transform the space under the top into a tool crib. They would make one of the top slabs removable and build a box between the aprons that would hold the bench tools. Not only is this handy storage, but the tools add weight to the bench.

There's a face vise with a wooden jaw and a wooden screw. These vises are notorious for racking in use (just ask the interpreters the next time you are at Colonial Williamsburg), and so you'll need a vise block. The holes in the apron work with the face vise for working on both edges and ends when used in conjunction with a holdfast.

On the benchtop, there is a single planing stop, but other than that, the top is a wide expanse of nothing but wood. Like the so-called strong table workbench described above, you'll need appliances to make this bench effective for working on wide panels – that is the bench's biggest weakness in my book.

The Modern English Benches

My two English workbenches have probably been corrupted so much by other forms that the English would likely disavow them. On one design I angled the legs at 20°. This isn't to resist planing or wracking forces, but to allow the leg vise to clamp wider boards. Is it traditional and appropriate? I think so. Early English accounts show some benches with angled legs and benches with leg vises, though there is little doubt in my mind that the face vise Nicholson drew is the dominant form.

MODERN ENGLISH: Nothing says *English* like a wide front apron. This bench is similar to 19th-century English workbenches, but it has some modern adaptations, most notably a wagon vise in the end vise position.

OLD ENGLISH: You don't see this bench much in shops or modern woodworking texts. It disappeared during the 20th century and was replaced by the continental bench as the bench of choice.

I kept the single planing stop and have made a wide planing stop that clamps into my leg vise. However, my biggest historical transgression was the addition of the wagon vise. This is to get around building a planing tray for working on panels. In hindsight, building a planing tray is far simpler than adding a wagon vise, but the bench is what it is. I've also added some round holes to the benchtop for hold-downs or holdfasts.

So for working on boards' faces, I use the planing stop, the wide planing stop, the wagon vise and a hold-down. For working on long edges, I use the leg vise and the system of holes in the apron with a holdfast. For working on ends both wide and narrow, I use the leg vise in conjunction with a holdfast or hold-down in the apron.

The second English bench is simpler — no wagon vise or even face vise — but it is made to knockdown flat in about 10 minutes. I contend that the English bench is an ideal form for creating a knockdown bench that is great for a woodworker in an apartment or who has to put the bench away after each work session. Unlike other knockdown workbenches, this one isn't wobbly like most of the others I have encountered.

All four benches are what I like to call "open-architecture" work-benches in that they are easily modified to take any of the workholding devices available today. You can add a quick-release vise to any of the designs if you want to keep things simple. Or if you want to keep things truly simple, build one of these bench designs without any vises.

"Well, my standard formula was the better work you do, the more chance that you'll starve."

— James Krenov on teaching at the College of the Redwoods in an interview conducted by Oscar Fitzgerald in Fort Bragg, Calif., Aug. 12 and 13, 2004

ONCE COMMON: The wide front apron, angled legs and jack-legged leg vise are all unfamiliar to most modern woodworkers. However, about 200 years ago, each of these features could be found on benches for carpenters and joiners. These features disappeared as the continental bench became the preferred form.

Chapter Five

The English Workbench

The Ghost of a Bench: This workbench may not have been designed with the cabinetmaker in mind. It shows up in Peter Nicholson's *Mechanic's Companion* (1831). Accompanying this drawing is a short description of the bench in the section titled "Joinery." While modern woodworkers consider joinery to be a part of what we do to build furniture, joinery had a different meaning in the 18th and 19th centuries.

While carpenters built the framework of the house, it was the joiner who supplied the decorative surfaces inside: the windows, doors and mouldings that distinguish a simple barn from a home. It would be easy to think of joiners as the latter-day equivalent of the modern finish carpenter, but it's not quite that simple. Though modern-day finish carpenters are among the most highly skilled workers on a jobsite, joiners were called upon to do even more.

They typically would build sash windows, passageway doors and the wide variety of mouldings and fitments that would go into a house of that day. The tool kit of a joiner looked much like the toolkit of a cabinetmaker, with backsaws, joinery planes and moulding planes in strong evidence. But the tools had profiles that were intended to do house-scale work instead of furniture-scale.

So it should come as little surprise that Nicholson wrote that the typical bench for a joiner should be 10' to 12' in length, which is longer than most modern workbenches. This makes sense when you consider that long runs of mouldings had to be prepared for a house.

Other than that detail, much of the work that occurred on a joiner's bench would resemble work performed on the bench of a furniture maker. There are lots of mortise-and-tenon joints, rabbets, grooves and mouldings. Among the differences: The furniture maker would be cutting dovetails more often, though Nicholson discusses the dovetail saw as an essential tool for joiners in making drawers. The joiner would be making more mouldings than a furniture maker.

For the modern woodworker, I think that the distinction between the two benches and methods of work are insignificant. The joints and workholding challenges are similar. The tools are quite similar. And the wood is the same.

This bench shows up repeatedly in the 19th and early 20th centuries. In G. Forster's 1816 painting of an English woodworking shop and in manuals for carpentry, such as *The Amateur Carpenter and Builder* (1904), in plans offered by Stanley tools, in *Audels Carpenters and Builders Guide* (1947), and in Charles Hayward's *How to Make*

Woodwork Tools. But I have never seen this style of bench in an early woodworking catalog as a bench you can purchase. Instead, it is shown as a bench that you can build yourself.

Then, one day in the 20th century, it falls from favor.

After the middle of the 20th century, the joinery profession disappears. After World War II, houses are built differently. Windows and doors are manufactured. House carpenters work with small hand-held electrical tools, so the need for a jobsite workbench dissipates. The continental-style workbench, which has always been around, becomes ascendant.

Why Build This Bench?

When I stumbled upon this bench in an old book, it looked to me like the spiritual father of the plastic Black & Decker Workmate. The English bench seemed serviceable, but not serious. It seemed designed to be built quickly out of inexpensive materials — not something for a lifetime of service. But it was a dominant form among workbenches for more than a century. And the more I examined its particulars the more I was determined to build one and put it to work.

As I sat down to sketch a construction drawing, I had my laptop's CAD software at my left hand and Nicholson's book at the right. As I read Nicholson's description of the innards of the bench and tried to translate it into pixels, it became apparent that inside this old bench beats the heart of something modern: a torsion box.

"That's another thing the rural Welshman in me likes — that the tools and technology of the blacksmith aren't, or don't need to be anyway, terribly sophisticated. As with any craft or hobby, you can spend a fortune just getting set up, or you can spend next to nothing and get on with it."

— Don Weber, bodger, blacksmith, writer and teacher, from the article "The Magic of Iron & Fire," in *Popular Woodworking* magazine

HALF-ENGLISH: My English bench (top) is based on a bench from Peter Nicholson's *Mechanic's Companion*. And though the design is old, what's under those aprons is considered quite modern: a torsion box.

ONE LOAD, ONE BENCH: This trunk load of yellow pine is all I needed to build the English workbench. Once you get the materials, the next critical step is to treat it like you would any furniture-making wood.

Many pieces of contemporary furniture use a torsion-box construction to create an assembly that's rigid and lightweight. Essentially, the torsion box is like the wing of an old airplane or our own body cavities. The torsion box is made up of a number of stiff but thin ribs that are joined together and then covered in a lightweight, flexible and thin skin.

The ribs stiffen the exterior skins. And because the construction is mostly air, it's lightweight. When you see shelving units that are cantilevered off a wall and covered with heavy books, you're likely looking at a torsion-box construction.

"Between each pair of coupled legs, the length of the bench is generally divided into three or four equal parts," Nicholson wrote, "and transverse bearers fixed at the divisions to the side boards... for the purpose of supporting the top firmly, and keeping it from bending."

Yup, that's a torsion box. The beauty of the torsion-box construction is that it requires far less wood to create than the massive slab top of the French workbench. From a modern woodworking perspective, this is a big deal. While it was simpler in the 18th and 19th centuries to get a single slab top of massive proportions, today we are likely to make up our tops from some (sometimes many) narrower boards. The top for the French bench in this book required me to glue up 25 layers of boards. The English bench? Three boards and four edge joints (and a lot less glue, time and clamps).

Still another good reasons to build this bench: the wide aprons. This sounds counter-intuitive, but the wide aprons are an asset. Even though they restrict you from clamping stuff to the benchtop (to the point of being a fault) they make up for this defect in assisting whenever you want to work the edges of boards — which is a function that's sorely lacking on many modern and commercial benches. Once you use a bench that helps you work on edges, you'll wonder why other forms of benches have to make it so hard.

Begin With the Wood

This bench wants to be made out of construction-grade lumber. It was designed for carpenters and joiners, so making the bench out of purpleheart is a bit of a disconnect — like building a Shaker-style liquor cabinet. When you go to pick your lumber for this project, do not buy any 2x4s. It seems tempting to make the legs out of that size stock and "save" time with ripping. Resist the urge. All 2x4s are twisty, knotty lessons in frustration. They will work against you.

I've built a lot of benches out of dimensional stock, and I always get letters and phone calls from readers that go something like this: "Where did you get that primo pine?" I'll tell you: the home center. People don't believe me, but it's true. In fact, I don't even look that hard when I go to the home center. I usually pick off the top of the stack and cull enough material in about 40 minutes to make a bench.

In fact, the only time I've had trouble was when I was at the Home Depot near our office and there were only a couple boards in the lower rack. Naturally, I scaled the orange metal racks to open a new bunk of pine to pick through. They don't like it when you do this. They call the manager and yell at you.

So here's the trick: Stroll by the 2x4s and head directly for the 2x12s. If you have a full-size pickup, go to the 16-foot 2x12s. The widest and longest stuff will be the clearest and straightest. And usually it is also the driest. You want to use a species that contractors use to frame out a floor or a ceiling in your area. In the South, this can be

A MODERN CARPENTRY BENCH: This sawhorse setup is part of what doomed the English bench to obsolescence. With a circular saw, miter saw or crosscut handsaw, you can quickly get your boards to length. Then take them to the table saw for ripping.

Southern yellow pine. In the East, this can be fir. Out West, look for hemlock, fir or hem/fir (which can be either species). Avoid white pine or sugar pine – it's not as stiff, though it could be used in a pinch.

Pick out the boards carefully and use a moisture meter if you have one. You can use boards that are 17 percent moisture, but you will have to wait for them to come into equilibrium with your shop. Having some material that is wet (12 percent) and drier (9 percent) can be used to your advantage when building a bench. However, the really wet stuff takes its time in drying and delays your workbench – sometimes by a month or more.

When you get the stuff – and the old books called the wood *stuff* – the first order of business is to crosscut and rip the boards to slightly oversized chunks that will then sit until they get close to equilibrium in your shop.

Here's the funny thing about softwood. It has a reputation for warping, so we assume that it's one of those woods that moves a lot with the seasonal changes in humidity, such as red oak – a real mover and a shaker. This is not quite true. Softwoods such as yellow pine and fir move around and warp and twist as they reach equilibrium with their environment, but then they are fairly stable, much more than cherry, maple and red oak. But because softwoods come into our hands when wetter (fir is the soggiest in my experience), we think they are prone to considerable seasonal movement. It just isn't true. Most softwoods are incrediblly stable.

Because moisture moves in and out of wood through the end grain faster than it does through the face grain, your wood will achieve equilibrium much faster if you first crosscut it into smaller chunks. You still want pieces that are safe to pass through your machines, so try to shoot for chunks that are about 1" or 2" longer than your finished dimension.

As you choose your pieces, use your moisture meter (if you have one) to its best advantage. Choose the wetter boards to make the bench's legs. Choose the driest stock for the rails between the legs. The stock of middling wetness is fine for the aprons and the top. By segregating your boards, you can use their moisture content to assist

STICKERED FOR DRYING: Try to stack up your wood to allow air to flow around the end grain of your boards and through the face grain as well. This means you should separate the layers of your woodpile with stickers – thin strips of scrap.

your joinery. The mortise in the slightly wet leg will shrink onto the dry tenon on the rail. This will result in a tighter joint. With this approach, you'll be able to start working with your lumber as soon as the rails arrive at equilibrium with your workshop.

Now rip your stock so it is close to finished width. I usually shoot for ³/₄" oversized on the width. Why is this step important? While it won't significantly speed up the drying of your stock, it will allow you to squeeze a bit more thickness out of your boards. A 2x12 will cup considerably more when drying than a 4"-wide board. The smaller cup on the narrower board will be easier to machine flat.

Most dimensional lumber comes with at least one good straight edge, which you can use against your rip fence. If you don't have an edge that looks straight, it's safer to joint one long edge on your jointer before ripping it to size. This is, of course, easier after you've crosscut most of the pieces.

Now wait. Check your pile every week and mark the moisture content on each board so you can chart its progress. If you don't have a moisture meter, I'd wait three weeks and then use your sense of touch to guess how wet your boards are. The end grain of your wetter boards will feel cooler than the face grain. When the end grain and face grain feel similar in temperature, your boards are fairly dry. But usually, three to four weeks is enough time.

I know this sounds like a long time to wait, but you will be punished if you don't give the wood an opportunity to dry out a bit. It will warp after you machine it flat – I guarantee it.

JOINTING FOR PRECISION: I am fastidious about keeping my power jointer and planer in tune. Even so, I find that a jointer plane can make a flatter surface that is easier to glue up. Here's how: You want to first plane a slight hollow in the middle of the length of the board. Begin planing about 3" from the end and stop your plane 3" from the other end. Make three or four passes like this. Then make a pass along the entire length. Try it. It works.

CLAMP BOTH WAYS: By clamping each leg assembly across its width you'll line up the two layers, making for much less cleanup. You don't need to apply a lot of pressure, just enough to line up the two layers.

Laminate the Legs

While you could build the legs for this bench using 4x4 posts, I wouldn't recommend it. I tried that with one bench years ago. If you think 2x4s are gnarly, wait until you try the 4x4s. Instead, laminate the legs from two pieces. This has myriad advantages. One: Your wood will be clearer. Two: Making the giant notch for the front and rear apron of the bench is easy. You simply cut one layer shorter (and at a 20° angle) and then glue them up. Voilá: Instant angled notch.

So cut your leg stock close to finished size, perhaps ½" more than the finished length. You want a little extra left to trim at the feet and at the top. The dimensions provided are to make a bench that is about 35" high. So this is the time to scale things up or down.

Cut the 20° angle at the top of the shorter layer, but leave the rest of the ends square. You'll trim them at 20° after glue-up. Now straighten out your stock as best you can with your powered jointer, planer or your jointer plane.

If you glue up the legs with care you'll save headaches later in fitting them to the apron. Spread a consistent but thin layer of yellow glue on the surface of the short layer, line up the two ends of your two layers and clamp things up. If you are using a resinous wood such as Southern yellow pine, leave it in the clamps for five hours. The resins in this wood resist penetration by the water in the glue. As the glue dries, turn your attention to cutting the tenons on the rails.

Beefy Tenons; Deep Mortises

A traditional way to cut a mortise-and-tenon joint is to cut the mortises and then cut the tenons. If you cut your joints by machine, as I do, you can use the consistency of the machine cutters to reverse that process. Why would you do this? To reduce your layout chores. If you can use the actual tenons to lay out the mortises on your legs, you reduce the math in subtracting out the tenon's shoulders for each piece.

The price of this process is you have to first make one test mortise using your tooling so you can use that to test-fit your tenoning setup. The tenons are ⅝" thick on this bench. That's a bit thick by traditional standards. The rule of thirds would insist they be more like ⁷⁄₁₆" or so.

But because these rails go into very large legs, there is no chance that the legs will be weakened by these joints. Plus, quite honestly, my ⅝"-diameter Forstner bit is sharper than my ½" (I don't own a ⁷⁄₁₆" Forstner bit). So decide how big you want your joints and then bore a test mortise in some scrap using a Forstner bit and a drill press. Make a series of overlapping holes, then bore out the waste between the overlapping holes. Keep repeating this until the mortise is complete.

FIG. 217. ELEVATION OF BACK OF BENCH.

FIG. 218. ELEVATION OF FRONT OF BENCH.

FIG. 219. PLAN OF TOP OF BENCH.

GETTING CROSS: Many English bench designs use diagonal cross braces to add support.

TENONS WITH A DADO STACK: One nice thing about making tenons with a dado stack is you cut the shoulder and the cheek with one setup. You do need to keep firm downward pressure on the work, however. Note that I've raised my basket guard for this photo and the saw is off.

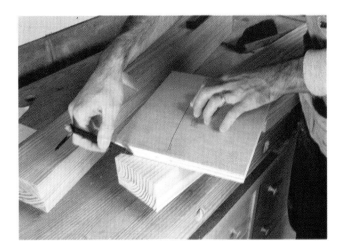

A STAND-IN FOR THE APRON: You don't want to lay out the top of the legs using a measurement – it can trip you up. Use a scrap that is cut to the same width as your aprons and use that to mark a line at the top of the leg. This will ensure you won't miss.

TEST-FITTING IN A TEST MORTISE: If your face cheeks need to be trimmed back you can raise the blades slightly, or use a rasp or shoulder plane to fit the tenon. I try to get as close as possible with the machines.

A TRICK FOR DEALING WITH THE ODD LEGS: Because of the shape of the laminated legs, they are a challenge to work on, whether that's planing, sanding or boring them. To remedy that problem, I took a piece of scrap from the project, cut a 20° angle on one end and applied some PSA sandpaper to the end. This little scrap supports the leg and holds on to the angled end grain of the leg. It's quite handy.

There is a variety of good ways to make tenons. If you are comfortable with your method, stick with it. I generally prefer a dado stack when working with large-scale stock such as this for two good reasons: the table saw has more guts than a router table for this operation. And the dado stack allows me to work with these long pieces flat on the table saw, which is easier than balancing a long heavy piece on end, as with other table saw methods.

I'll set up my dado stack with the maximum number of chippers my table saw will accommodate. I set the height of the blades to match the desired depth of my tenon's face shoulders. In this case, $^5/_{16}$". To set the length of the tenons, I use a fence on my saw's sliding table (a wooden fence attached to a miter gauge also suffices) with a stop to set the length of the tenons. Cut your face cheeks.

Then raise the dado blade to $^5/_8$" and cut the edge shoulders on all the tenons except for the edge shoulder at the top of the top rail. It needs to be larger: $1^1/_2$". Raise the dado blade to this height and trim the remaining edge shoulders of the top rails. The large shoulder ensures that the vulnerable end grain wall of your mortise will not self-destruct during fitting or assembly.

Dressing and Boring the Legs

Clean up the legs so they are straight and square and prepare to cut the 20° angle at the top and bottom of the legs. First you need to lay out the angle at the top of the legs. Take a scrap that is the same width as your apron piece and place it on the legs, up against the short layer. Trace the shape of the apron onto the legs and cut the top angled edge of each leg.

With the top edges trimmed, bundle your legs in pairs: one left pair, one right. Mark out the 20° angle on the foot of one of your legs and cut that to shape. Then use that first leg as a template to mark out the second. Trim the second leg identical to the first. Repeat this process with the other pair of legs.

REDUCING YOUR ERRORS: Remember: There are right legs and left legs. It's best to bundle them and mark their orientation in the finished bench to prevent mistakes. Here I'm lining up the angled laminations on a group of legs to confirm my marks line up before trimming the leg's mate.

THE TENON RULER: By using your tenons as a ruler you don't have to measure out the offset of the tenon's shoulder. Simply mark the location of the rail on your leg, then show the rail to that mark. Trace the shape on the leg. Bore a mortise there.

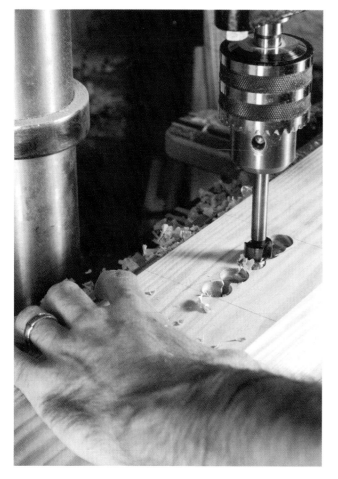

VERY BORING: When making mortises on the drill press, I never pare the mortise's walls with a chisel. That can introduce error. The only chisel work I do is with a corner chisel to square the rounded corners. To avoid paring walls, I bore the mortise over and over, removing waste all long its length until the Forstner bit can slide freely in the mortise left-to-right.

Now you can use the actual tenons to lay out the mortises on the legs. Bundle your leg assemblies and mark out the locations of the mortises on one leg and carry those marks over to the mating leg using a try square.

Boring the mortises is efficient on the drill press. Chuck a $^5/_8$" Forstner bit in your drill press and set the fence on your machine to bore along the center of your leg. The mortises are of two different depths, and these require two separate strategies.

The mortises for the lower rail are 2" deep and won't require any special consideration. They are just deep and blind mortises. Simply set the drill press to make the mortises $2^1/_8$" deep and go to town. However, the mortises for the top stretcher are a different story. They are through-mortises because you want to achieve the maximum length possible for the tenons on the top aprons. Remember: The leg is thinner up at the top than it is at the bottom.

You have two choices with these through-mortises at the top of the legs. You can bore them with your support block below (which is what I did) or you can turn the leg over and bore through the leg and into a larger piece of scrap. Either works.

There are other drill press chores at this point that you should tend to. If you are going to add a leg vise to the workbench, you need to bore a mortise and a hole in the front left leg. The $1^3/_8$"-diameter hole is for the vise screw. The mortise is for the parallel guide that assists the leg vise in applying tremendous force without racking.

Boring the hole for the vise screw is, of course, simple work. The through-mortise for the parallel guide takes a bit more layout to do correctly. This through-mortise is $^3/_4$" wide and 3" long. Mark it out on the face side of your leg using the construction drawing as a guide. Then transfer that same layout to the backside of the same leg.

Bore the mortise halfway through on the drill press, then flip the leg over (flip it end over end to keep the same reference surface against your drill press's fence). Then bore out the other side of the mortise so the two meet in the middle.

With all the boring at an end, you should clean out the corners of the joints, squaring them to fit the tenons. A corner chisel makes quick work of this operation. A stout firmer chisel can also do the job, but with more fiddling, layout and cutting.

A BLOCK BELOW: Rather than chewing up a piece of plywood to bore these through-mortises, I used my handy support block to keep the leg stable while boring the joint.

LESS MEASURING, MORE ACCURACY: If you tried to measure exactly where the bevel should be on the top of the top rails, you'd probably be off by a little. That's why it's best to mark out the angle when you get each end assembled, then rip the rails to their proper shape.

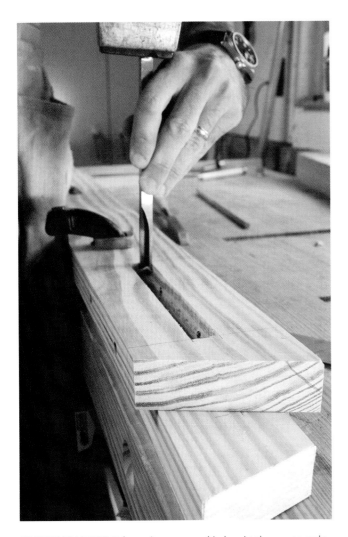

SQUARING HOLES: When using a corner chisel, resist the urge to make the cut with one big bite. There is more chance that the chisel will go off course or get stuck. Take two or three bites to get accurate results. Begin at the inside and work your way back into the corner with the last pass being right on your layout lines.

Fit all your joints. Examine the shoulders of your tenons for gaps and ensure that the tenons fit snug in their mortises. With the ends dry-assembled, letter all your joints so you can assemble them correctly with glue. Now mark out the angle on the top rails, using the top of the leg as the guide. Disassemble all the pieces, bevel your table saw's blade to 20° and rip the top rail to proper width at the saw. Assembly is next. Clean up all your rails and prepare them for finishing. Clean up the legs, too, though they'll require some more work after assembly as well.

Boring and the Drawboring

Whenever I build a project that requires an extra measure of stoutness (chairs and workbenches are prime examples) or use wood that is a little bit wet, I drawbore the joints for extra strength.

Drawboring is an old process that has fallen out of favor thanks to modern glues, modern kilns and piston-fit joints. But it's still a good trick to know and use. In essence, you bore a hole for a peg through your mortise. Then you assemble the joint and mark the hole's location on the tenon. Disassemble the joint and drill a hole through the tenon that is about $1/16"$ closer to the shoulder of the tenon than the mark. This $1/16"$ offset (or a bit stronger) is appropriate for heavy work such as this. Use a smaller offset for smaller work.

Then assemble the joint. If you own a drawbore pin – a tapered metal pin with a wooden handle that looks like a machinist's drift pin – you can test your assembly by twisting the pin into the assembled joints. The pin also slightly deforms the mortise and the tenon to ease the path of the peg. Glue up the joint (if desired) and drive an oak peg into the holes. If the joint is made correctly, no clamps are necessary.

Begin by boring $3/8"$-diameter holes through your mortises. You can drill these holes through the leg or stop them before they emerge on the other side. Drilling them through is the safer approach (more on this later). The centers of the holes are $5/8"$ in from the edge of the leg. I used two pegs in each joint for the top rail; and one peg in each joint for the bottom rail.

PREPARE FOR PEGS: Drill your initial bores with a brad-point bit. You can do this on a drill press, but a handheld drill is accurate for this job.

A BIT OFF: When you begin drawboring, you want to carefully measure everything out. After you do a couple dozen drawbores, you'll develop a feel for it and do it by eye. No measuring offsets or precision boring apparatus. These holes are through-holes, which is why I have the workpiece propped up on scrap.

ASSEMBLY: This is what assembly looks like. In the leg that's flat on the benchtop, I put glue in the mortises. Then I pushed the rails into their mortises. For the other leg that I'm positioning, I painted the mortise walls with glue, flipped the board over quickly and pushed it onto its tenons. A couple raps with a mallet and a block of scrap wood seats everything quickly before driving the pegs.

With all the holes bored in the mortises, assemble the joints and use your $^{3}/_{8}$" brad-point bit to transfer the locations of the centerpoints of each hole onto the tenons. Disassemble the joints and drill holes through the tenons that are $^{1}/_{16}$" closer to the shoulder than your layout lines indicate.

Reassemble everything and test your fits with a metal drawbore pin (if you own one). Then take some $^{3}/_{8}$"-diameter oak dowel stock and cut a bunch of pegs about 4" long. Whittle one end of each peg with a taper that resembles a sharpened pencil, but without the sharp writing tip. A strong (but fairly short) taper is the key to assembling this joint without disaster.

The taper allows the oak to snake through the offset holes without self-destructing as it slams into the tenon or far wall of the mortise. Using oak – as opposed to maple – ensures that the peg is more likely to bend rather than break when stressed by the structure of this joint.

One detail: The joinery purists will rive out their pegs from straight stock and create the pegs using a dowel plate. I've done this hundreds of times myself. It's gratifying and produces nearly indestructible pegs. But cutting the pegs from straight-cut, straight-grained oak dowels is also a good option. These dowels are cheap ($1 for 36") and really work with drawboring lightweight assemblies.

I glue my joints. If I'm using a yellow glue, I'll put a single clamp across the joint I'm drawboring. Because yellow glue can set up quickly (too quickly in a hot or dry shop) you want the shoulders of the tenon tight against the mortises before you drive the pegs. The clamp helps this. If I'm using liquid hide glue (another favorite of mine) I don't bother with a clamp because I have an open time with the glue that's as long as an hour.

Drive the pegs. Use a hammer or a mallet. When the peg starts to resist as it bends into the curve, keep tapping it firmly, even as your progress slows. As the peg passes through both components of the joint the peg will give up on its fight and eventually dive to the bottom of the hole. Or, if it is a short-grain, obstinate and brittle peg, it will bust apart no matter what coaxing you give it.

When this occurs, you have a couple options. If you drilled your holes through the mortises so they passed all the way through the legs, you're in luck. Simply get another peg and start driving it behind the first broken one. Usually the new one will push the old one out the exit hole. If the peg has splintered badly, you might have to resort to plan B: drilling out the hole through the assembled joint. This will remove the offset hole in the tenon, clear the hole of waste and allow you to reassemble the joint with a new peg. It won't be a drawbored, mechanical joint, but it also won't be firewood.

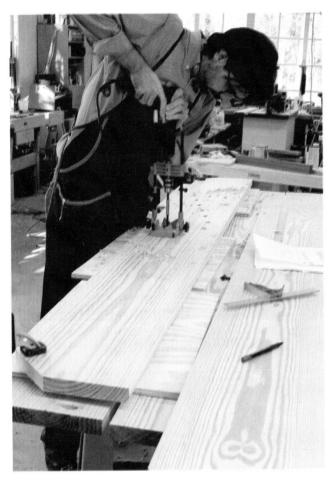

BENCHES ARE BORING: I'm always struck by how much accurate boring is required when building workbenches. This gizmo for my handheld drill helps keep my tool at 90° when making holes for dogs and the like. Typically, I'd drill these freehand, so don't feel compelled to rush out and buy one of these jigs. They're a bit flimsier than you want, and the depth stop for the plunging mechanism slips easily.

FAST FLUSHING: You could cut your tenon a little short so that you don't have to flush it up after assembling the legs. But because this is a critical joint, I decided to get the maximum amount of joinery surface, even if it added an extra step. Use mineral spirits or denatured alcohol to moisten the end grain before you trim it.

CLAMPING CORRECTLY: You don't need a lot of clamps for assembly. But you do need to place them strategically and apply pressure in a gradual fashion. First use the smaller clamps to snug up the apron to the wide flat surface of the leg assembly. But don't apply the death grip yet. Then clamp across the leg and the top of the apron as shown and apply steady pressure to bring the apron into place in the corner. Now snug things up.

With the pegs driven in place, you can saw or pare them flush with the legs and clean up your assemblies.

Aprons, and Getting the Bench on its Feet

The aprons are an essential part of the skeleton of this workbench. You want them as flat as can be so they'll attach easily to the leg assemblies. Working on 8'-long pieces of wood is a challenge. Add to the fact that these aprons are 11" wide, and you'll see that there's a challenge ahead.

Most importantly, make the inside face of the apron boards, which will attach to the legs, as flat as you can. It's actually easier to work on the exterior faces of the aprons after assembly. If you are having real difficulties with getting the inside faces flat, you can resort to working on just the two sections of each apron that will attach to the legs. When taken too far, this approach can introduce problems at assembly. But if you have a cup or bow of ⅛" or less, you'll be OK.

With the inside of the aprons flat, you also can clip the corners of the aprons as shown in the construction drawings. And then drill the ¾"-diameter holes in the front apron, again using the pattern in the construction drawings as a guide. While you can change this pattern of holes to suit you, be sure to watch where these holes make their exit inside the workbench. You can make some holes useless if they exit the apron and hit the leg assemblies.

UNDER THE HOOD: Here's what to look for as you glue the apron down. You want the wide surface of the apron to contact the leg assembly as well as possible. Wipe away any squeeze-out as you apply pressure so you can see if you have any gaps in the joints that need to be closed up.

CLAMP THE BACK: Once you have the first apron placed properly, the second one is easy. Check your joints for gaps as before and allow the glue to dry overnight before you begin pushing it around a lot.

BRING IN THE REINFORCEMENTS: Three screws through each leg will give you an extra measure of security. Though they are not mentioned in the old books, I decided to vote my own conscience here.

FAST FLUSH: While some woodworkers might choose a flush-cutting saw for this task, I think you'll find it too slow and too likely to wander in the cut – they are designed to trim dowels, not workbench legs. A cross-cut backsaw makes quick work of this task. Use your off hand to press the blade against the apron as you cut.

With the aprons ready for assembly, turn your attention to the leg assemblies. Use a square or wooden straightedge to examine the legs, particularly where the through-tenon on the top rail emerges from the leg. You want the tenon flush. Trim it with a block plane if necessary.

Assembly isn't difficult if you use gravity as an assistant. Clamp your leg assemblies to some low sawhorses so the apron lays on top of the leg assemblies, as shown in the photos. Position the leg assemblies so the apron drops exactly where you want it. The apron will require clamping in two directions. Use a few clamps to squeeze the apron onto the legs and one long clamp to pull the apron tight against the corner you formed by laminating the two leg pieces.

When the glue sets up after an hour, flip the bench onto its feet and glue the other apron in place using the same clamping setup. This time, gravity helps hold the apron in place. After you clamp up the second apron, check the assembly to ensure it is square. I use a length of twine to check the diagonals from corner to corner. If the assembly

is out of square, brace one of the two corners of the bench that is on the longer diagonal against a wall or something else stout. Shove a bit on the other corner on that diagonal. Check your work again.

Remove the clamps and then prepare to reinforce the joints with #10 x 2" screws. The apron and the legs are bonded in a cross-grain orientation. So there's a chance that the expansion and contraction of the apron could weaken the glue joint. Hence, the screws. First drill your pilot holes, then drill your clearance holes and the countersink. As you drill the clearance hole, rock the drill up and down a bit to make the hole oval shaped. This shape of clearance hole allows the screws to pivot a bit as the apron expands and contracts.

With the workbench's base assembled, you can flush up the top surfaces of the base to prepare it for the benchtop. My legs came out a tad taller than the aprons, as did the top rail. Luckily, it's easy to fix. Saw the tops of the legs flush to the apron, then waste away any excess material on the top rails with a rank-set jack plane.

PARALLELOGRAMS: The cleats are easy to install and clamp if both long edges are 20°. To do this, rip one long edge of a wide board to 20°, then move the fence toward the blade to rip free a parallelogram cleat.

WATCH THE GRAIN: Though this is shop furniture, you should compose the top so that the grain runs in the same direction throughout all the pieces. It's easy to do and is good practice for a dining table.

SAFE AND EASY: When you work with large stock, there are some operations that are best for hand tools because it would be tough to move the piece over your machines. This is one instance. A few well-placed strokes with a backsaw define the width of the notch for the vise.

Building the Top

Before you begin gluing up the top, glue in the cleats that will attach the end assemblies to the benchtop. I took some fall-off scrap pieces and ripped both long edges at 20°. Then I crosscut them to fit snugly between the legs and tight against the top rail. You can drill holes for the screws now, or you can wait. I waited.

The top is comprised of three 2x12s, though you can substitute other dimensions to get to the desired 27" width. Compose the top based on appearance and getting the grain of the three boards all aligned so that you can plane the entire top in one direction. When you have the boards aligned to your liking, mark a large triangle across the joints that will guide you as you glue up the top.

Now comes a decision: Do you want a wagon vise? If you do, now is the time to start making space in the top for the mechanism. If you have chosen to forego any sort of integral end vise, then you can proceed with gluing up the top and getting it flat.

If I were building this bench and was either intimidated by the wagon vise, or I thought it would be too much trouble, I'd definitely purchase a quick-release vise and mount it in the end-vise position. Then I would add a thick (a $2^{1}/_{2}$"-thick) wooden jaw to the movable jaw of the vise. This would give you many of the advantages of a tail vise and remove about 10 hours of work for you. If you decide to build the wagon vise, then congratulations. You are as determined as I.

Build the Wagon Vise

The first important step in building the wagon vise is to rip the benchtop board that goes at the front of your top into two pieces. With the required edge jointing and the saw kerf in this equation, try to get the front part of the board at 5" wide and the rear at 4" wide, perhaps a little more. Let's call this board the *dog board*.

With the dog board ripped in two, you can cut the notches on the ends that will create the opening for the movable wooden jaw of the vise. The notch on the rear dog board is $1^{5}/_{8}$" wide; the one on the front dog board is $2^{3}/_{8}$" wide. Both are 17" long. Cut the width of the notches with a handsaw and cut the length using your band saw.

To add a row of bench dogs to the bench, you need to beef up the thin top along the row of dogs. Then you'll cut the notches for all the dogs and re-assemble the two dog block sections into one unit. To double up the thickness, I used 2"-wide scraps that I cut to length so they would fit between the two leg assemblies of the bench. If you make the doubling any longer, you'll end up notching out your leg assemblies, which would be a pain.

Take each of these two strips of doubling and glue them to the dog blocks along the edge where these two pieces will eventually be glued together. Allow the glue to dry, then joint each of these surfaces and prepare to cut your dogs.

A bit of canine philosophy here: You will probably be able to squeeze about 6" to 7" of throw out of your vise screw for the wagon vise. However, it would be a mistake to space your dogs every 6" or so. That's too far a distance. While it seems to save time in the construction, it will drive you nuts for years in the future. Space your dogs with 3" between each hole. That will reduce the amount of turning you'll be doing to secure your work.

BALANCING ACT: Because you are working with a piece that is 8' long, it's a challenge to balance it on the saw and hold it in place during the cut. You are better served to have some sort of outboard support for your work. I used a portable stand.

ONE PIECE AT A TIME: The vise block is made by laminating several short pieces. First glue up two that will be milled with dog holes. Then glue up two more that will enclose the dog holes. After you cut the dogs, glue the two laminations together and then cut the block to final size – making sure that the dog holes in the vise block line up with the dog holes in the dog block.

CHECK YOUR WORK: After you rout the slight recess for the dog's head, place the dog in the hole and make sure there's enough space for it.

You want to size your holes to fit your dogs snugly. I purchased my wooden dogs from Lie-Nielsen Toolworks, and I based all of my holes off them. Wooden dogs hold most work quite well and won't damage your tools (you can add a thin layer of leather to a wooden dog to improve its grip). Metal dogs have tiny teeth on the faces (they look like a meat tenderizer). They grip the work particularly well when working cross-grain, but they do pose a hazard to cutting edges.

What's important about the dog holes is that they be angled by 2°. The holes in the dog block are angled toward the vise block. The holes in the vise block are tipped toward those in the dog block. Size your dog holes so that your dogs won't tip back significantly under pressure, and that a dog will stay in position (up or down) without coaxing. You don't want your dogs dropping into their holes (like prairie dogs) when left unattended.

You can mill these holes in a variety of ways. The best way I've ever seen is an aluminum routing template that is used with a big router equipped with a template guide and straight bit. If you are

going to build benches for a living, you can visit a machinist and get a template made or make your own with plywood.

I took a different route (or rout). I milled out the majority of the waste with a dado stack in a table saw and then finished up shaping the dog hole – adding the extra room for its head – with a routing template.

There are probably other good ways to do it, so you don't have to copy my method. It's based only on the tools I have in my shop. I own a small plunge router that doesn't have a template-guide adapter. And I have a gutsy table saw with a nice dado stack.

Lay out all the cuts for the dogs on your dog block. I used two pairs of dividers to do this. One was set for the size of the dog hole and the other was set for the spacing between each hole. Shade in your waste areas so you don't get confused at the saw.

Load up your table saw's arbor with as many wings and chippers as your saw can spin. Angle your miter gauge (or sliding table) to 2° and cut your dog holes. I merely lined up each cut by eye because each hole required two passes to make. Setting stops would be a pain.

With all the holes cut, angle your miter gauge 2° the other way and cut the two dog holes in the movable vise block.

Now make a router template that will cut the extra space for the head of the dogs. I made my template from some plywood scraps and used the dog itself as a pattern to trace around. I cut the shape on the band saw and refined the pattern with a rasp and sandpaper. Finally, I glued a small block onto the template that acted as a fence so I could clamp the pattern to my dog block.

The shape is routed out using a straight bit with a bearing on the top. My 1½ hp router wouldn't do this cut all in one pass. So I set the depth stop on my plunge router to cut at two depths: one where the bearing ran on the pattern, and the second where the bearing actually ran on what was cut before to make the final pass. It's a bit of a tricky setup that I boxed myself into. If I had to do it again, I would simply use a template guide and a straight bit.

Clamp the pattern and rout the shape. Then place a dog in the recess you have completed and make sure there's enough clearance. It's easier to fix now than when everything is assembled.

CAUTIOUS EDGE WORK: You want this joint to be strong because it will be regularly stressed. Take your time fitting the two pieces. Here I'm balancing one dog block on another and examining the seam for light.

Now you can glue the two dog blocks back together and then glue the completed unit to the other two boards for the top. As you are creating this edge joint between two dog blocks you need to be careful. Jointing the dog block that has the dog holes in it has consequences. Every pass you make with your jointer or jointer plane will tighten up the dog holes. This can be good or bad, depending on how tight or loose your dog holes are.

I jointed this dog block once, and then I simply worked its mate until I got the fit I wanted. When satisfied, glue up the two dog blocks by putting glue only on the edge with the dog holes. Don't overdo it or you'll have lots of unpleasant squeeze-out in your holes. Once the dog block is glued up, joint the edges of your other top boards and glue up the remainder of the top.

The top is essentially complete; now turn your attention to the bench and the guts that will make the vise work. The vise screw needs to be fastened to something that is stout – it will bear a good deal of the pressure from the vise when it is engaged. Although a properly used wagon vise shouldn't see extreme pressure, you can bet that it will be misused during its lifetime. It's better to make it stronger.

The end cap piece is the key to the vise. The vise screw mounts to it. And the end cap is attached to the workbench's aprons with dados, steel corner brackets and bolts. The first step to installing the end cap is to mill two dados across the aprons to accept the end cap. Whenever I want to mill dados in wide pieces, I turn to a straightedge guide and a router. The straightedge guide is essentially two pieces of wood

DADO AFTER ASSEMBLY: Don't try to do this process before assembly. You want the dados to be exactly in line with each other. The only way to ensure that is to rout them after the base is assembled.

attached at right angles. One piece sits tight against the apron; the other guides the router.

You'll need to make these 1¼"-wide x ½"-deep dados using a couple of overlapping passes. It's simple work. Simply mark out the location of the dados on each apron, place your guide in place and make the cut. Move the guide again and repeat.

Cut the end cap for the workbench and slide it into the dados in the aprons. It should stick out a bit at the bottom. It's best to cut it flush. So transfer the shape of the aprons at that point to the end grain of the end cap. This should be a 45° angle. Rip that edge to shape with a saw and clean up the work with a handplane.

BIG-BOY BRACKETS: With the vise flange in place, clamp the L-brackets where you want them and mark the locations for the bolts. Here's how I drilled these holes: From the inside of the bench, drill a ³⁄₃₂"-diameter hole through the center of each hole and through the wood. From the outside of the bench, drill a countersink using a bit that has more diameter than your washers. Place the center spur of the Forstner in the through-hole you just drilled. Drill a recess that's deep enough for the bolt head. Stop, then drill a hole for the bolt through the center of the recess you just drilled. The ³⁄₃₂"" hole will guide you throughout.

BOLTS ALL AROUND: Tighten up the bolts firmly on the end cap first, then tighten up the bolts to the apron. Note that I didn't bolt through the holes nearest the corner of the bracket. It didn't seem necessary. But check back with me in about 10 years for the real answer.

Before installing the end cap permanently, drill the hole through the end cap for the vise screw hardware. The vise hardware comes with a threaded flange that the screw travels through. You want to attach this piece correctly, and this is where I struggled like the dickens to make everything work. Here's the problem: You want the vise screw to be as close to your benchtop as possible because that arrangement will apply clamping force right where you want it. But you also want to put the vise screw in a place that is heavily reinforced so everything is stout.

In the name of stout, I schemed to reinforce the end cap with steel L-brackets. But the L-brackets forced me to move the vise screw hardware down lower than I liked. As I wrestled with this problem, I started searching the U.S. Patent Office's web site and found several plans for patented wagon vises that would be so simple (if they still existed). They all involved a metal frame that bolted to the underside of the benchtop and – in theory – would be stout and smooth. So if anybody out there is interested in manufacturing some vise hardware from expired patents, drop me a line.

So I drilled the hole in the end cap in the location shown in the construction drawings and then glued the end cap in place. Then I attached four L-brackets to the inside corners of the workbench with nuts, bolts and washers. It was stout all right, but would it work?

To find out, I had to get the top onto the base and complete the fiddly guts for the wagon vise. The top was still in two pieces. I needed to get each piece reasonably flat, get their edges jointed and glued up and then fixed onto the base itself.

When I get into a risky bit of work, my thoughts drift to the antique tool chest by my bench at home that has a tricky, sticky and unpredictable lock. Most days, I can open the chest with ease. I rotate the key. The cylinders turn. The lid lifts.

But every so often, the lock refuses to work. I rotate the key. The cylinders turn. The lid sticks. I curse and then repeat the process until the lid opens. However, a couple times during the last decade, no amount of fiddling would open the chest. And instead of reaching for a wrecking bar, I'd just walk away and come back to the chest later.

FIRST WORK ON THE BENCH: Flattening the underside of the top is fairly straightforward once you have the base constructed and leveled.

PRIMITIVE PLANING STOP: To hold the top while planing across its grain, I pushed it up against two screw heads that I had sticking out of the cleats that will be used to attach the top.

ALL THE CLAMPS: When you clamp the top to the base you want the top's edge to be flush or slightly proud of the front apron. The top is ½" wider than necessary, and I'll trim that off at the back later on.

RIBS MAKE IT STIFFER: The three transverse supports prevent the top from flexing. I attached these with screws (as shown). Then I got wise and replaced the screws with Miller Dowels.

Some days, I get that same uncertain feeling in my chest whenever I get ready to flatten and join boards that are long, wide or wild. Today was one of those days as I set out to flatten the top. The section of benchtop on deck this afternoon was 22" wide and 8' long. It was pretty flat, but it needed to be really flat to sit tight onto the base of the bench. Some days, it doesn't matter how skilled you are. Or how many times you've trued up a slab of wonky wood. Some days the wood wins and you exit the shop with your tail between your legs.

The first challenge when dealing with wide and long panels is finding a place to work on them. With this section of the top, the answer was simple. I placed it on the base itself and pushed it against the heads of a couple screws that I placed into the holes in the cleats that eventually will join the base to the top.

The ends were out of true and some quick work with a fore plane across the grain brought them into line with the center section of the top. A couple passes diagonally across the top with the fore plane got the surface flat enough to push it against the fence of our powered jointer.

Then-Senior Editor Glen Huey looked over as I was working the top and offered (sincerely, but with a twinkle in his eye) to put the top in his truck and run it through his wide-belt sander in his home shop.

I declined, saying that the exercise with the fore plane would allow me to justify drinking a second beer tonight after work. Glen smiled and nodded his head. All was going well, but edge-jointing the top piece was another tricky piece of work. It's another part of a project that can go wrong for no good reason. I jointed the edge. I jointed its mate and showed them to one another. I was shooting for a spring joint and I got one, but it was a little strong on one end of the top.

Undeterred, I straightened out the end with a few passes of a block plane. Within a few minutes the whole top was glued up and clamped with a tight seam all along the 8' top.

I had earned an extra beer, and the tool chest didn't win this round.

Glue it, Screw it and Hope

Attaching the top to the base is a challenge to do well. Here's the brief write up: Glue the front edge of the top to the front apron. Then attach the remainder of the top to the base using screws driven through the cleats. The screws nearest the front of the bench are in a simple,

straight hole. The remainder of the screws are in holes that have been slightly reamed out to an oblong shape. Note that for all the screws I also used a washer to limit how far the screw's head plunged into the work. This ensured that none of the screw tips would poke through the top when I planed it flat.

The net effect of this is to keep the front edge of the top fixed in relation to the apron and forces any seasonal expansion and contraction of the top to the back edge of the top, where it's not a nuisance.

What's difficult is getting that front edge seamlessly tight, especially if there's any bow or twist to the top (as there was with mine – it was cupped a bit). So before you attach the top, spend some time with a straightedge and a plane checking out the base and trying to level things up all around. Then lay the glue down on the front edge and clamp things up.

Once the glue is dry, flip the bench over onto a couple sawhorses. To complete the structural skeleton of the workbench, you should screw in three transverse supports to the underside of the top. These stiffen the top in lieu of a benchtop with great mass.

These transverse supports are spaced equally along the underside and are positioned so they don't cover up a dog hole. Notch each support to fit over the dog block on the underside of the top. Screw each to the top in a manner similar to attaching the base to the top. Drill a clearance hole for a screw at the front of the bench that's straight. The remaining three on each transverse support are slightly reamed out. You also can attach these supports with Miller Dowels. I know this

"Today's woodworking is left-brained. It is focused on machining wood like it was plastic or metal. Many woodworkers actually believe that a micrometer is a woodworking tool. Because of dust and noise, they dress up like they were going to work in a toxic waste dump."

— Michael Dunbar, *The Windsor Chronicles*, Spring 2004

WEST MEETS EAST: We tend to push our handplanes, but sometimes it's best to take a cue from the Japanese and pull them through the work. Here I've attached my vintage Stanley No. 386 jointer fence to my jointer plane and am pulling the whole rig toward me. This allowed great control, especially at this work height.

FIND THE BOTTOM: You want the dowels in your vise block to pierce the block right below the benchtop. Hold the vise block in position and scribe a line where the benchtop and vise block meet (top). Now you can drill a ⅝" hole through the block that's tangent to this line (bottom). Then drill a second stopped hole that's about 2" back of the first hole.

because I later pulled out the screws and drove in Miller Dowels. This step will ensure no metal ever protrudes through the top.

Now you can flip the bench on its aprons and trim the top flush to the aprons. I didn't have a lot to trim so I used a jointer plane with a fence. If you have more than ⅛" to remove, think about using a router that's armed with a straight bit and a pattern-cutting bearing. If you have a gross excess to remove, think circular saw and then router.

Finish up the Wagon Vise

I trimmed up the vise block to fit the slot in the benchtop and screwed the pad on the vise's hardware to the vise block. The way the wagon vise works is by having the vise block run in a couple tracks on the underside of the benchtop. The tracks are made by gluing up some scrap pieces to create two slots on either side of the vise block. Then you need something to run in these slots. I used a couple of ⅝"-diameter dowels that are friction-fit into the vise block and are removable.

The dowels captured in the track serve two functions: They keep the vise block from drooping when the vise is not engaged. And they prevent the vise block from riding up above the benchtop when you clamp something using the dogs. As a result, you want the dowels to

be right below the top. So position the vise block in its slot and mark out where the underside of the benchtop touches the vise block.

The next steps are easier to do with the bench upside down, so flip the sucker over. Push the dowels into the holes you just drilled in the vise block. Don't glue them in; when the vise requires adjustment or repair, you can just pull the dowels out and the vise block will lift out of the top of the bench.

The dowel that passes through the vise block only needs to protrude about 1" or so on the other side. And depending on how your brackets are bolted in you want to position the dowel so it doesn't bump into the bolts and nuts.

Now build the track for the dowels to run in. First you have to know how much open space to leave for the dowels. So with the dowels in position, close the vise all the way and mark the position of the forward dowel. Now unscrew the vise all the way and mark the position of the rear dowel. Now you know where to place the build-up blocks for the track.

The size of the build-up blocks is critical. Too thick and your vise will wobble and ride up and down. Too thin and your vise won't move. Shoot for a thickness that is a bit stronger than your dowels'

OPEN AND SHUT: The buildup blocks are just a hair thicker than the dowels. The less slop you have in the mechanism the better. These build-up blocks are just about to be glued and nailed in place.

READY TO WORK: Fit the strips that connect the build-up blocks. Don't attach them with glue because they might have to be removed someday. I tacked them down with a brad nail, then drove a single screw in at each attachment point. This construction allows you to disassemble things later if need be.

diameter. Glue and nail the four build-up blocks in place and then dig up some scrap for the pieces that will connect the build-up blocks.

The Leg Vise

After using a leg vise for a couple years on my French-style workbench, I was a convert. When it comes to choosing a face vise, I prefer it to an iron quick-release vise. The quick-release function of that vise is hype because most of your work with a vise on the front of your bench will be with a narrow range of thicknesses. (When a quick-release vise is in the end-vise position, however, that's another story.)

Making a leg vise is straightforward work and takes as much time as to install an iron quick-release vise. The first step is to drill a $1\frac{3}{8}$"-diameter hole in your leg for the vise's screw, and to hog out a through-mortise below that hole (mine was $\frac{3}{4}$"-wide and 3" long) for the vise's parallel guide. Position the vise's jaw on the leg and transfer the position of the hole and mortise to the jaw. Now install the threaded iron flange that comes with the vise screw. Install it on the inside face of the leg.

Measuring Shop Time

When I build furniture, I log the time I spend at each step in construction: 60 minutes on the top, 75 minutes to cut the mortises and tenons, 30 minutes to remake a munged-up apron.

The reason I keep this record is a bit of a mystery to me. I pitch it when I purge the shop of the shavings, scraps and screw-ups at the end of a project. But before I cast the log into the burn pile, I add up the minutes I've marked there and marvel at how few hours in my life are spent actually woodworking.

Now I don't like to get too philosophical about something so physical, but the hours I spend at woodworking are some of the best waking moments I have. And recently an acquaintance named Brian Welch passed on to me a passage from chapter 18 Henry David Thoreau's *Walden* that shook me good. Here it is:

"There was an artist in the city of Kouroo who was disposed to strive after perfection. One day it came into his mind to make a staff. Having considered that in an imperfect work time is an ingredient, but into a perfect work time does not enter, he said to himself, 'It shall be perfect in all respects, though I should do nothing else in my life.'

"He proceeded instantly to the forest for wood, being resolved that it should not be made of unsuitable material; and as he searched for and rejected stick after stick, his friends gradually deserted him, for they grew old in their works and died, but he grew not older by a moment. His singleness of purpose and resolution, and his elevated piety, endowed him, without his knowledge, with perennial youth. As he made no compromise with Time, Time kept out of his way, and only sighed at a distance because he could not overcome him. Before he had found a stock in all respects suitable the city of Kouroo was a hoary ruin, and he sat on one of its mounds to peel the stick. Before he had given it the proper shape the dynasty of the Candahars was at an end, and with the point of the stick he wrote the name of the last of that race in the sand, and then resumed his work.

"By the time he had smoothed and polished the staff Kalpa was no longer the pole-star; and ere he had put on the ferule and the head adorned with precious stones, Brahma had awoke and slumbered many times. But why do I stay to mention these things? When the finishing stroke was put to his work, it suddenly expanded before the eyes of the astonished artist into the fairest of all the creations of Brahma. He had made a new system in making a staff, a world with full and fair proportions; in which, though the old cities and dynasties had passed away, fairer and more glorious ones had taken their places. And now he saw by the heap of shavings still fresh at his feet, that, for him and his work, the former lapse of time had been an illusion, and that no more time had elapsed than is required for a single scintillation from the brain of Brahma to fall on and inflame the tinder of a mortal brain. The material was pure, and his art was pure; how could the result be other than wonderful?"

After reading this passage I got in my truck on my day off and braved the Christmas traffic to go to the office to do a little work on the leg vise for the English workbench. I logged only 75 minutes, but it was the best month of the entire day.

WEIRD PLACE FOR A FLANGE: From looking at the vise hardware, the manufacturers want you to install the flange the opposite of the way I'm doing it – the screw holes are nicely countersunk for that set-up. But you have to drill a much larger hole to install the flange that way, and that will weaken the leg. Install it the other way. It works just as well.

TRACE YOUR BENCH: Put the vise jaw on the leg and shift it around until it's right where it should be. Then trace around the leg, apron and top. Then trace the hole and the mortise in the leg. These marks will guide you as you shape the jaw.

WALK THE DOG: Use dividers to step off the locations of the holes in the parallel guide. I'd give up all of my digital measuring equipment before I gave up my dividers.

Drill the matching $1^3/8$" hole in the vise's jaw and bore out a through-mortise in the jaw. However, make this mortise a little narrower than the mortise in the leg: Mine was $^1/2$" wide and 2" long. I bored out the mortise on the drill press and squared up the corners with a chisel. Now you can shape the jaw as you see fit. I made mine resemble the shapes of leg vises from the 18th century (skinny at the floor; chunky at top). Do what you will, but I recommend the jaw be no narrower than the leg and that you keep the jaw as wide as possible near the workbench's apron.

Now work on the parallel guide. You will tenon and wedge it into the jaw – after you bore it with an array of $^3/8$"-diameter holes. The holes are for a metal pin that when positioned in a hole will pivot the vise's jaw against your work. Different holes are for different thicknesses. If this doesn't make sense to you at first, don't fret. It seemed odd to me at first glance as well. Once you get the thing together the light bulb will come on.

The holes are in two long rows and are spaced 1" apart. On the top row the holes begin 1" from the shoulder of the tenon. On the bottom row the holes start $1^1/2$" from the shoulder. Then I added one

more hole: It's centered between the two long rows and is $^1/2$" from the shoulder. This is the hole you'll be using the most – it's for clamping $^3/4$" material. Once you drill out the holes, countersink them to make the metal pin easier to insert. On the end of the parallel guide that isn't tenoned, I clipped the corners at 45°, just for looks.

The parallel guide should fit snugly but smoothly in the mortise you bored into the leg. The closer the fit, the smoother the action of the jaw. If you make it too tight, however, the jaw will hang up. This requires judgment on your part. Consider the expansion and contraction of the species of wood you choose for the parallel guide and what season it is when you are building. Then size the parallel guide so you will always have $^1/32$" of clearance above and below the guide. If you make it too tight, you can always adjust it later with a card scraper or some coarse sandpaper.

Now cut the tenon on the end of the parallel guide. You want the tenon to be longer than necessary so it protrudes about $^1/16$" from the jaw when the two are mated. As with the other tenons for this workbench, I cut this one using a dado stack on my table saw. Then I fit the tenon into the through-mortise using a shoulder plane.

TIGHT, THEN LOOSE: When fitting a through-tenon, you first want the fit to be snug. Then you'll widen the mortise on the exit-wound side into a trumpet-shape. That way when you wedge the tenon, it also will deform into a trumpet shape – locking it in for good.

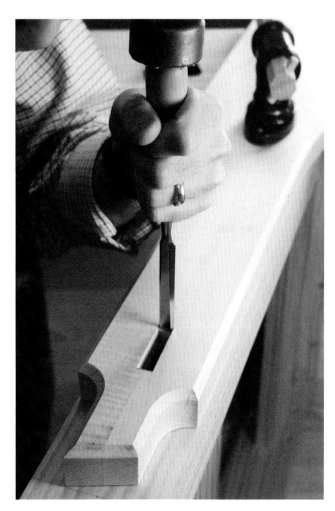

USE THE CHISEL GEOMETRY: You can make this harder than it is. Here's the easy way: Strike a line that's 1/16" beyond each end of the mortise. Then take a 1/2"-wide chisel and score the mortise wall up to the line (top). Then stand your chisel on end and drive it down (below). The geometry of the chisel's edge allows it to cut down a bit and then the chisel will be driven into the open mortise (where there's less resistance). This simple whack creates the perfect trumpet-shaped mortise for wedging.

Now you can shape the mortise to prepare it for the wedges. You want the mortise to be slightly longer on the exit side than it is on the side where the tenon is inserted. How much longer? That depends on the joint's size and how much abuse the tenon can take. For this joint, both components are durable (an ash jaw; a white oak parallel guide) but the joint itself is small. So I added 1/8" total – 1/16" of length on each end of the mortise.

To wedge the mortise you need wedges. I cut mine on the band saw by angling the tool's miter gauge to 7° and then ripping wedges from some white oak that was 1/2" thick, 1" long and as wide as I could find. Here's the trick: Trim one end of your wedge stock on the saw. Then flip the work over and slice off a wedge. This gives you a perfect wedge with a 14° angle.

Now you need to make cuts in the tenon for the wedges. Some books would have you saw kerfs down the tenon, perhaps even ending them with a little hole. Do not bother. I once tried all these techniques, which sounded smart at the time. Then I sawed apart the joints to see what happened inside.

I was shocked.

The little kerfs and little holes don't help close the inside of the joint. The tightest joints had tenons that had been split with a chisel – an old chairmaking trick I picked up at a Canadian class. So glue up the joint, then make two splits in the tenon using a 1/2"-wide chisel. Put a little glue in each split and drive in your wedges.

After your glue dries, trim the tenon flush with the jaw and install the assembled jaw into your leg. I like to glue a piece of leather to the jaw and the workbench itself to assist in clamping my work. You can do this now or wait until after you finish the bench (or until you've recovered from building this very large project).

Oh, and the pin that goes into the holes in the parallel guide? You can use a 3/8"-diameter dowel (use something stout). No matter how stout, there is a risk of snapping the sucker after some use. If you get tired of replacing the dowel, try using a 3/8"-diameter steel rod (a 5/16"-diameter O-ring keeps the rod in place in the angled piece.) That has worked great for me with other leg vises.

TAP, TAP AND WALK AWAY: Drive the wedges in with a hammer and listen to how the sound changes with each tap. The wedges will come to resist you. That's about the time you should stop driving them. OK, a couple more taps will be fine in this joint. It's solid.

WAX PAPER AND LEATHER: Real leather (not pleather) glues well to wood with simple yellow glue. Coat each skin with a thin but consistent film. Put them in place (one on the apron; the other on the vise jaw) with a sheet of wax paper between the pieces of leather and close the vise.

CUTTING IN: Mark the depth of each section of your mortise using tape, a permanent marker or both. When chopping with a mortise chisel, it's best to keep the bevel across the grain. If you mortise deeply with the bevel running along the grain, you likely will split your work. You can pare the long-grain walls of your mortise with the chisel after the mortise has been excavated, but chopping along the long grain is generally a no-no.

MESSY, BUT CORRECT: The mortise for the planing stop doesn't have to be pretty, but it should support the stop all around. Once you excavate the mortise, fit the stop and screw it down. If you did it correctly, the body of the stop should be a bit below the benchtop when the stop is all the way in the down position.

Planing Stops

I don't much care for the metal planing stops that rise up and down out of a recess in your workbench's top. The metal can damage your tools. And the manufacturing quality of these stops fits their price: The stops are cheap and so is their construction.

Nevertheless, I decided to install a couple metal stops in this bench in the interest of getting to know them better. They are not difficult to install, but it is a time-consuming process. Whoever designed the castings for these stops should have his or her head examined. The underside is quite complex, and it doesn't have to be.

The best way to install these is with a mortise chisel and a $3/4$" auger bit. First decide where you want the stops to go. I placed one directly in line with the square dog holes that go with my wagon vise. That way I can actually clamp some really long work between the vise's dog and the stop.

SHELF SUPPORTS: This is the heart of the shelf below the apron. I glued the cleat to the long shelf support. Then I cut the ends at a 20° angle to match the angle on the legs. (Ah symmetry!) Then I attached the shelf supports to the legs with glue and Miller Dowels. (Screws would be fine here, but I like wood more than metal.)

The second stop should be installed about 7" away from the first stop. Why? This allows you to work with a wide variety of materials. When you work against a single planing stop, there's a limit to how wide a board you can work until you end up flinging the work across the bench. For me, that limit is about a 6"-wide board. So a second planing stop that's 7" away from the first will allow me to plane wide boards without resorting to some other way to affix them for work.

Plus, I own an 8" power jointer, so the 7" spacing makes sense.

After choosing where to put them, place the stops upside down on your benchtop and trace around each with a marking knife. Go slow and use light pressure, especially when cutting with the grain. With both locations marked, use a ruler to determine where to put the ³/₄"-diameter hole that will house the spring-loaded basket of the stop. I drilled this hole with an auger bit and bit brace.

Now cut the remainder of the recess for the stop. Work from the center out to the edges. The center is the deepest point of your recess, plus, the hole you drilled allows the chips to escape the mortise.

The two critical points of the mortise are at the front (where the stop is screwed to the benchtop) and at the back, which has to resist typical planing forces. Here are a couple details about these stops to be aware of. One: The hinge of the stop is eccentric. You need to give a little more clearance at the rear for the hinge than you probably think. You'll know if you need more clearance; the stop won't open.

Also, the little pins that hold the basket that holds the spring are weak. Even a slight stress breaks them. You can replace those stops, or you can ensure that your ³/₄" hole is drilled to the correct depth to support the basket from below, making the pins vestigial.

With your mind on workholding, it's a good time to drill holes for holdfasts. It's easy to overdo and drill holes that you'll never use or (even worse) are in the wrong place. My recommendation: Start with four and ponder additional holes like you would a new body piercing.

Here's my philosophy on the four holes: The first hole is on the end of the bench where the two metal planing stops are and is 6" in from the back edge of the workbench. This hole does a lot of things, but its most important job is reinforcing a shop-made planing stop that clamps into your face vise. To drill the hole, position your stop

in your vise so it's clamped where you want it. Then drill a hole that's tangent to the stop and 6" from the bench's back edge.

The remainder of the holes are based on the reach of the holdfast. You want your holdfasts to reach all along the back edge of your bench with no dead spots. This allows you to clamp battens down anywhere along the back edge of the bench, which will support your work from the side.

The Veritas Hold Down has a reach of about 9", so I subtracted a bit from that reach and drilled my holes on 16" centers. All of the holes are 6" in from the back edge of the benchtop.

Adding a Shelf

At this point you can call it quits or build the shelf. Some woodworkers would be tempted to take a third course: adding a few drawers below to store essential shop equipment. Turning this bench into a cabinet could make it less useful. Drawers could interfere with your feet if placed low to the floor.

At the least, adding a bank of drawers will make it difficult – nay, impossible – for you to reach up under the top and push a dog up. A shelf, on the other hand, will allow you to keep your most-used tools at hand during a project. Your bench planes, for example, should camp out on the shelf as you work. Do this and you will find that you work a little more efficiently.

The shelf can be simpler than the one I show. You could screw a couple 2x4s on edge to a long piece of plywood that fits between the legs and let that assembly rest on the rails on the ends.

I opted for something more complex, stronger and interesting. All told, it requires you to buy three more 2x12 x 8' boards. For me, that cost was less than $35 – a bargain. First I created two L-shaped stretchers by gluing a 1¹/₄" x 1¹/₄" x 84" cleat to each long shelf support. This created a rabbet for the shelf boards.

With the cleat and shelf support assembled, attach these assemblies to the workbench. Rest the assemblies on the lower rails and glue them to the legs. I reinforced each joint with large Miller Dowels. Now turn your attention to the eight shelf pieces.

After surfacing your lumber, rip it to the maximum width possible and then make the tongue-and-groove joints on the board's edges. The tongue is ³/₈" x ³/₈". I made this joint on my table saw using a dado stack. First I cut the groove on one long edge of each board. Then I cut a matching tongue on each board's other edge.

After the boards have their joints cut, crosscut them to fit on the shelf supports. You want the fit to be snug.

If you are following the plans correctly, you should have more shelf than you need – the ends of the two outside pieces should stick out over the shelf supports. This is good. Center the eight shelves on the shelf supports and space them so there is a ¹/₈" gap between each shelf piece. I used a ruler snitched from a 12" combination square to offset the shelf pieces as I placed them.

"(T)hrough most of this age, the thinkers still made and the makers still thought."

— William Bryant Logan on 17th and 18th century shipbuilding; from *Oak: The Frame of Civilization* (Norton)

SLIDING INTO HOME: The shelves won't be glued, but you want the tongue-and-groove joints to fit closely but easily. Slide the shelf pieces in. Then remove them and number them so you can be sure to get them back in easily.

BEADS MAKE IT BURLY: My ³⁄₁₆" beading plane makes a tasteful bead. Remember that beading planes work like grooving planes: You start the cut on the far end of the work and work back toward the end vise, taking longer and longer strokes.

With the shelves in place, mark a cutline on the two outside shelf pieces so they will be inset 1¹⁄₄" from the ends of the shelf supports. Then rip the end pieces so they have a 20° bevel on one long edge.

Then prepare the shelf pieces for finishing. I cleaned them up with a jointer plane and then cut a ³⁄₁₆" bead on one long edge of each board on the grooved edge. This is both decorative and functional. The bead strengthens the corner and makes it look good.

Install the shelf pieces with Miller Dowels (one in the center of each end) or with a similarly placed screw. No need for glue. I used the Miller Dowels so that I could pop them loose if I ever needed to modify or repair something up in the body cavity of this bench.

Finishing

Break all the edges with sandpaper and then finish the bench. Please don't put a furniture-grade finish on your bench. A slick finish will allow your wood to scoot all over the place as you work. But I don't like letting the bench go nude either. It's too likely to absorb nastiness (glue stains, etc.) that could transfer to or scratch future workpieces.

There are a lot of fussy workbench finishes that ask you to heat stuff up, rub it in and work way too hard. Instead, buy some Danish oil (typically a mixture of boiled linseed oil and a little varnish). Rag on a couple coats and then go to work.

This finish is easy to apply and doesn't leave a film that can be cracked by beating on it. And the finish allows just enough protection against spills and stains to be helpful. When finishing furniture, I avoid these so-called Danish oils for projects that will see a lot of use, but a workbench is different. You are going to flatten the top regularly and refresh the finish, so an oil/varnish blend is ideal.

And Then to Work

I had a girlfriend in high school who had two unusual characteristics. Lynette was a drama major (not a recommended trait in girlfriends) and her father owned a sweet MG convertible. Whenever I would

go to her house for dinner, her father would be under the hood of the vehicle, wrench in hand, until the fried okra hit the dinner table.

The MG was always in need of something, and Lynette's dad had to do it himself. This was, after all, Arkansas. And anything that wasn't built in Detroit elicited stares from the townsfolk.

As I completed the English-style workbench I found that – like its British four-banger brethren – the bench needed tuning.

For example, I flattened the top one week, but it went a bit out of true the next. So I flattened it again. I also began wondering if the top was stiff enough to withstand heavy planing. The top has an almost imperceptible springy feel that gave me pause.

Perhaps the problem was that I was comparing this bench to the Roubo-style French bench. The top to that bench is almost 4" thick and is unyielding to all punishment. But that bench took twice as long to build and required three times the material. Clearly, I needed to take the English bench for more of a test drive.

As I began breaking in the bench, I found things about it that were nice. The angled leg vise is fantastic. The large front apron is excellent for supporting long and wide work. And I've been clamping stuff to the benchtop without trouble by using the wagon vise.

Bottom line: I go through this process with all my projects. I start with great optimism. After a series of highs and lows, I complete the project. I stand back, take a look and focus on its flaws. Then, after I put the project into use, I mellow. The flaws fade and I can see the project for what it is – somewhere between optimism and despair.

After some use, I found this to be true with this bench. The springiness I felt in the top was mostly a product of the fact that I was using a softwood. The top wasn't really deforming under pressure.

It was a happier ending than my relationship with Lynette (and her dad's MG). He sold the green convertible and Lynette dumped me for an officer of the drama club. But this bench stays in the picture.

English Workbench

NO.	PART	T	W	L	MATERIAL	NOTES
		SIZES (INCHES)				

☐ NO.	PART	SIZES (INCHES)			MATERIAL	NOTES
		T	W	L		
4	Legs, inside	1¼	4	38 *	Yellow pine	20° angle at ends
4	Legs, outside	1¼	4	25 *	Yellow pine	CTF, 20°
2	Top end rails	1¼	9	24½	Yellow pine	1¼" TBE
2	Bottom end rails	1¼	4	26	Yellow pine	2" TBE
3	Transverse supports	1¼	2	24½	Yellow pine	Notch over dog doubling
1	End cap	1¼	9¼	25½	Yellow pine	in ½" d. dado
2	Aprons	1¼	11	96	Yellow pine	
2	Top boards	1¼	9¼	96	Yellow pine	Trim the finished top to 27"
1	Top board (dog block)	1¼	4	96	Yellow pine	
1	Top board (dog block)	1¼	5	96	Yellow pine	
2	Dog doubling	1¼	2	56½	Yellow pine	
2	Attachment cleats	1¼	1½	22	Yellow pine	Attaches top to ends

Shelf

NO.	PART	SIZES (INCHES)			MATERIAL	NOTES
		T	W	L		
2	Long shelf supports	1¼	3½	84	Yellow pine	Trim ends at 20°
2	Cleats	1¼	1¼	84	Yellow pine	Trim ends at 20°
8	Shelf slats	1¼	11⅛ *	19½	Yellow pine	⅜" x ⅜" tongue on edge

Leg Vise

NO.	PART	SIZES (INCHES)			MATERIAL	NOTES
		T	W	L		
1	Leg vise jaw	2	8	38 *	Ash	Cut long, trim to fit
1	Parallel guide	⅝	3	16	Oak	½" x 2¾" x 2⅛" TOE
1	Vise handle	1	1	15	Ash	

Wagon Vise

NO.	PART	SIZES (INCHES)			MATERIAL	NOTES
		T	W	L		
1	Wagon vise block	4	5¼	7	Yellow pine	Laminated from 4 pieces
1	Through dowel	⅝ dia.		9	Yellow pine	Pierces vise block
1	Stopped dowel	⅝ dia.		4¼	Yellow pine	Stops in vise block
3	Build-up blocks	⅝	1¼	2	Yellow pine	Trim to clear brackets
1	Long build-up block	⅝	1¼	3½	Yellow pine	
2	Dowel track strips	⅝	1¼	14½	Yellow pine	Nail to build-up blocks
1	Vise handle	1¹⁄₁₆	1¹⁄₁₆	15	Ash	

KEY: TOE = tenon on one end; TBE = tenon, both ends; * = oversized, cut to fit

Fig. 1

A Joiner's Bench from George Ellis's *Modern Practical Joinery*.

THE NICHOLSON

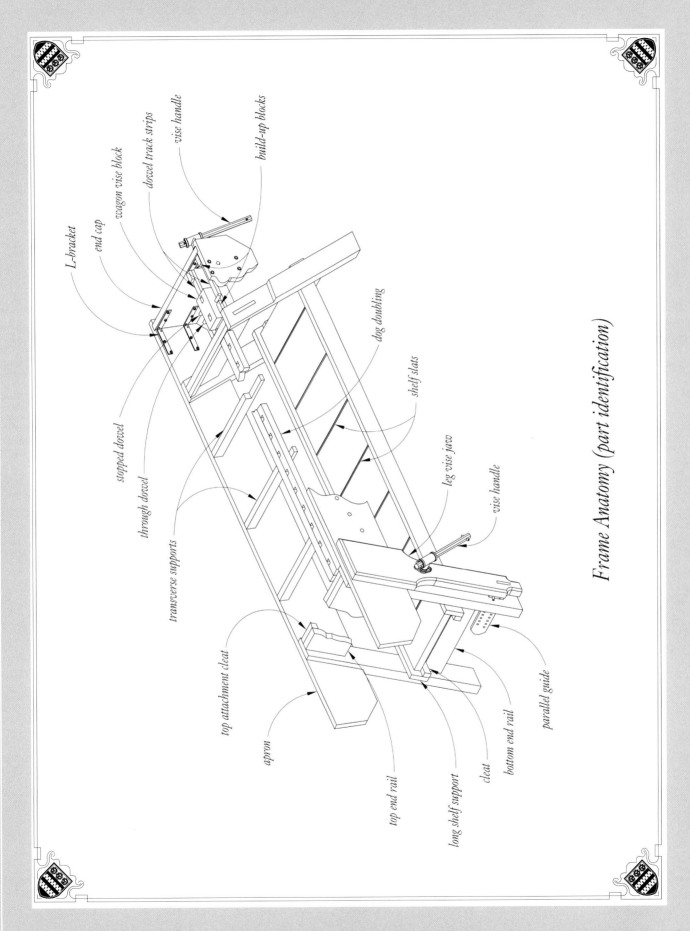

Frame Anatomy (part identification)

L-bracket

end cap

wagon vise block

dovetail track strips

vise handle

build-up blocks

dog doubling

shelf slats

stopped dovetail

through dovetail

transverse supports

leg vise jaw

vise handle

top attachment cleat

apron

parallel guide

top end rail

long shelf support

cleat

bottom end rail

Top View

Front View

Right Side

Left Side

Leg Vise
Arrangement

Handle

Leg Vise Jaw

Parallel
Guide

Vise Handle
(2 req'd)

15

1

1

3⁄8

2

Parallel Guide

3⁄4

45°

1½

1½

1½

¼ typ.

½

⅛ typ.

2¼

3

1

1 typ.

½

3½

5⁄8

1⁄16 typ.

½

2

16

upper curve profiles
1" sq. grid

R1⁄16

3⅛

lower curve detail

Leg Vise Jaw

Overall Length

37⅛

13³⁄16

15½

5⁵⁄16

8

20°

20°

2

½

20°

2⅛

4

2¾

4

Ø1³⁄8

12⅞

¾ chamfer

2

Leg Arrangement

Apron to End Cap
Groove Detail

Front Right Leg (opposite of shown)
Back Left Leg (opposite of shown)
Back Right Leg (as shown)

Front Left Leg

End Cap

- countersunk bolt hole size and locations to suit L-brackets

dia. to suit vise hardware

9½

25½

3⅛

2¾

1¼

45°

Shelf Slats
(8 Req'd)

⅜

⅜ typ.

⅜

⅜

⅝

⅝

1¼

¾

¹⁄₁₆ bead

19½

11⅞

Top Attachment Cleat
(2 Req'd)

1¼

22

1½

20°

Transverse Support
(3 Req'd)

24½

18¾

5¾

2

¼

Top End Rail

8½

1¼

⁵⁄₁₆

⅝

20°

24½

22

1¼

6

⁵⁄₁₆

Long Shelf Supports w/Cleats

84

20°

3½

2½

1¼

Bottom End Rail

26

22

2

1¼

⁵⁄₁₆

⅝

4

3⅜

⁵⁄₁₆

Dog Doubling
(2 Req'd - 1 as shown and 1 without dog holes)

56½

2⅜

2

⅞

1¼

8°

spacing to match dog holes in top board

Views of Wagon Vise with Top Boards Removed

Views of Wagon Vise From Underside of Bench

Dowel track strips

Build-up blocks

Stop dowel

Through dowel

Wagon vise block

Wagon Vise Arrangement

Wagon Vise Block

10-MINUTE BENCH: This bench takes about two days of shop time to build (if you stay focused), and when you are done you will have a workbench that takes only about 10 minutes to assemble and disassemble.

Chapter Six

The Knockdown Nicholson

Many knockdown workbenches I have encountered suffer from unfortunate compromises. Inexpensive commercial benches – most of which can be knocked down for shipping – use skimpy hardware and thin wooden components to reduce shipping weight and cost. The result is that the bench never feels sturdy, even when all its bolts are snugged. Plus, assembly usually takes a good hour or so.

These sorts of benches aren't ideal for someone who has to set up and break down a workbench between every building session.

Custom knockdown benches, on the other hand, are generally sturdier, but they are usually more complex than necessary and also take considerable time to set up and take apart.

In other words, most knockdown workbenches are designed to be taken apart only when you move your household. When I set out to design this bench, I took great pains to ensure three things:

1. When the bench was assembled, it would be as sturdy as a permanent bench.

2. The bench could be taken apart and put together by one person in about 10 minutes.

3. You would need only one tool to assemble and disassemble the entire bench.

The design you see here is an English-style workbench in its simplest form that is sized for an apartment or small shop at 6' long. It is made from construction lumber and uses the basic crochet and holdfasts for workholding. As a result, the lumber bill for this bench is only about $100. You'll need four 2x12x16's and one 1x10x8'.

I used yellow pine for this bench, but any heavy framing lumber will do, including fir, hemlock and even spruce.

The hardware is another $75. The supplies list uses high-quality hardware from McMaster-Carr; you could easily save money by doing a little shopping.

About the Hardware

The core of this workbench is the ductile iron mounting plates that are threaded to receive the cap screws. This hardware is easy to install and quite robust. (If you want it to be even more tank-like, use $\frac{1}{2}$" mounting plates and cap screws instead of the $\frac{3}{8}$". You will, however, have to pay a little more.)

I settled on using these ductile mounting plates after experimenting with less-expensive T-nuts in a variety of configurations and alloys.

NOT GOOD: I tried a variety of fasteners to make this bench. These die-cast T-nuts loved to self-destruct when over-tightened.

GOOD: The ductile mounting plates are easy to install and are durable enough for a workbench.

"The cabinet workbench is a blood brother of the plaid golf bag; there is no inherent reason why its owner should not do great things with the contents, yet he rarely does."

— Henry H. Saylor, "Tinkering With Tools"
Little, Brown, and Co. (1924)

FULL-FEATURED: Though this English bench breaks down into just a few easy-to-stow components, it is as stout and functional as a bench with fixed joinery.

None was tough enough to be used in a workbench. I consider the ³/₈" ductile mounting plates to be the minimum that you need. The only option is to step up to beefier hardware. Anything less will disappoint.

The rest of the hardware is standard off-the-rack stuff you'll find at any hardware store.

Begin with Good Wood

No matter where you buy your lumber, make sure it has acclimated to your shop before you begin construction. This workbench is made up of flat panels, so having wood that is dimensionally stable will make construction easier.

When I bring a new load of lumber into my shop, I cut it to rough length and sticker it. I have a moisture meter that tells me when the wood is at equilibrium. If you don't have a moisture meter, try to wait a couple weeks before starting to build the bench. Also, if the end grain of any board feels cooler to the touch than its neighbors', then that board is still wet-ish and is giving off moisture. So you might want to give that stick some more time to adjust.

This workbench is made up five major assemblies that bolt together: two end pieces, two aprons and a top. Each assembly needs some cutting and gluing. Let's start by building the legs.

Glued-up Legs

The joinery for this workbench is mostly glue, screws and a few notches. All those joints are in the two end assemblies. Each end assembly consists of two legs that are made by face-gluing two boards together. The act of gluing these two boards together creates a notch for the bench's apron.

FOUR LEGS GOOD: By gluing a shorter piece and a longer piece together you create a thick leg and the notch for the workbench's apron.

APRONS AT WORK: Here you can see the 2x12 apron glued to the 1x10 interior piece. The legs will then butt against the 1x10.

So begin making the end assemblies by gluing the 5½" leg parts together for each of the four legs. If you don't own clamps, you can screw these parts together with glue, then remove the screws after the glue has dried.

While the glue in the legs is drying, turn your attention to the aprons.

Laminated Aprons

Like the legs, the front and rear apron of the workbench is made by face-gluing two parts together to thicken the piece and to create notches for the other assemblies.

Each apron consists of a 2x12 glued to a smaller 1x10 piece. The 2x12 is the exterior of the workbench. The 1x10 makes notches for the legs.

The length of the 1x10 is the distance between the left legs of the bench and the right legs. In this 6' workbench, the 1x10 is 45" long. If you bench is longer, make these parts longer.

Glue and affix a 1x10 to its 2x12 – and make sure the smaller piece is centered on the length of the larger. I used glue and nails to put these parts together. Any combination of glue, screws and nails will do.

Once the aprons are assembled, you can then clip the corners of the aprons if you like. The 45° corners are cut 4" from the ends of each apron with a handsaw. I like the way the clipped corners look, but they do make the bench more difficult to pick up and move.

The next step is to use our hardware to bolt the legs and aprons together.

Hardware Install

Clamp a leg to one of the aprons, making sure the leg is snug against the notch created by the apron's 1x10. Now lay out and drill the counterbore for the washer and the clearance hole for the bolt's shaft. The clearance hole should go all the way through the apron and leg. The counterbore should be deep enough to hold the head of the bolt, the washer and the lock washer.

Now lock the leg and apron together with the hardware. Thread the bolt through a lock washer and then a washer. Push the bolt

How to Buy Construction Lumber for Workbenches

I use a lot of construction lumber in my projects – not only for workbenches but for furniture projects as well. If you carefully select your lumber you can end up with very nice wood for little money.

I don't buy it from a specialty lumberyard. I actually get it from my local home center. Here's how I go about it.

Now as much as I like my local independent hardware store, I end up visiting my home center about twice a week for odds and ends. No matter how much of a hurry I'm in that day, my first stop is the framing lumber. I don't always buy something, but I always watch the piles of 2 x 12s. And I look at the rack of lumber at the roof.

At my store, they usually have a Saturday-night cull. The employees pull all the junk from the racks that won't sell because it's too distorted or nasty. They band the culls and sell them for something real cheap. But I ignore the cull pile.

After they cull the racks they open up new bunks of fresh wood to replenish the racks that look skimpy. So Sunday morning is a great time to go to my home center.

I don't go every Sunday, but I am usually rewarded with beautiful, straight and clear 2 x 12s. And if the bunk has been sitting at the top of the rack for months, the stuff will be dry – between 5 and 7 percent moisture content instead of the typical 15 to 20 percent.

CLEAR FOR CONSTRUCTION: Your home center is a great source for workbench wood – once you figure out the pattern of how the lumber racks are replenished.

CAN'T MISS: By drilling these holes while the pieces are together, you ensure they will mate up again. (Note that this photo shows some of the die-cast hardware that failed.)

MOUNTING PLATES: Here is how the mounting plates look when they are installed. First you tighten the bolts, then you screw the mounting plate down. This way you can't miss.

through the clearance hole. Spin a ductile mounting plate onto the bolt on the other side.

Snug up the mounting plate, then tighten the nut with a socket wrench. Once both bolts are snugged up on the leg, you can permanently install the mounting plates with screws.

Repeat this process with the other three legs. When you are done you will have two aprons with their legs attached.

Beefy Benchtop

One of the downsides to many English workbenches is that the top is springy because it is thin or unsupported from below. The traditional solution was to add "bearers" under the benchtop.

These cross members ran between the front apron to the rear apron. And while they do make the benchtop stouter, I have never liked these tops as much as I like a thick French benchtop.

So this benchtop is a "Normandy" solution – a little bit of both French and English.

The top surface of the benchtop is made from 2x12s that have been edge-glued to create a flat panel. This benchtop is 22½" wide because it is made from two 2x12s. You can make it narrower if you like – an 18"- to 20"-wide bench is stable enough for handwork.

Glue up your two planks for your benchtop and cut the top to its finished width and length.

It might be tempting to glue on the second layer of 2x12s to make the benchtop its final thickness. Resist. It is much easier to attach the aprons, legs and thin top first. Then, once you finish building the end assemblies, you will know the exact size of this second top piece and exactly where it will go without measuring.

LEGS AND APRONS: With the legs and aprons bolted together you can glue up the parts for the benchtop.

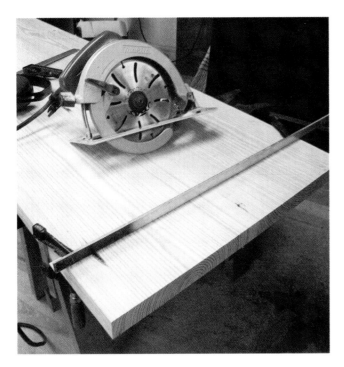

EASY & ACCURATE: I use aluminum angle pieces for winding sticks. I also use them as edge guides for my circular saw. Clamp the aluminum angle to your benchtop and make your cut – no fancy edge-clamping guides necessary.

Feet in the Air

This next step ensures that the end assemblies will be exactly the correct size for the width of your top. Assemble the bench upside down on some sawbenches. Clamp the aprons to the top and then push things around until the legs are square to the underside of the top and the aprons line up with the top all around.

Once you have everything clamped as you like it, you can fit the pieces for the end assemblies that go between the front legs and the back legs. There is a top mounting plate that is the same width as the legs, plus a top stretcher made from a 2x12 that fits between the front apron and the rear apron.

Cut these pieces to fit exactly. Then wedge the top plate pieces between the legs and screw the leg front plate to the legs.

With the front plates screwed to the legs you can take the bench apart and then glue and screw the top plates in place. Don't forget to glue the edge of the top plate to the face of the leg front plate. There is a lot of strength to be found there.

The last bit of work is to attach the lower stretchers to the legs. These stretchers are in a notch in each leg. I cut the notch with a handsaw and cleared out the waste with a chisel. Then screw and glue the lower stretchers into their notches.

Reassemble the bench's base so you can get the top complete.

LEG UP: With the bench temporarily assembled like this you can fit the pieces between the legs so they perfectly match the space available.

CAN'T MISS 2: With the top plate between the legs, you can put each stretcher on with screws (skip the glue because this is a cross-grain construction).

AN END, ASSEMBLED: I know this is a weird construction, but it works. And once you see it, you'll get it. Here you can see the finished end assembly with the lower stretcher ready for trimming and screwing.

FLAT MAKES FLAT: If your bench base is twisted, your benchtop will be twisted. It pays to get all the base bits in the same plane. Also note the glue blocks I added on the aprons.

BENCH, FLATTEN THYSELF: Traverse the underside of the benchtop with a jack plane to get the surface fairly true. Then finish up the job by taking out any twist in the benchtop with a jointer plane.

The Top (and Details)

With the base assembled, you should level out the top edges of the aprons and the end assemblies so they are coplanar — that's the first step toward getting a flat benchtop.

I dressed these parts with a jointer plane and block plane and checked my work with winding sticks and a straightedge.

Before you put the top on the base, I recommend one little addition at this stage. I attached glue blocks — for the lack of a better word — to the aprons so the end assemblies would be captured. You can see in the photo that I used an offcut from a 2x12 and oriented the grain sympathetically with the apron. This 5-minute upgrade makes the bench easier to assemble and a bit stouter.

Now you can flatten the underside of the benchtop by using the bench's base for support.

Put the benchtop on the base and plane the underside of the top flat with a jack plane — don't worry about flattening the top of the benchtop. A couple F-style clamps on the bench base will keep the top in place during this operation.

Test your benchtop by flipping it over and showing it to the workbench's base. When the two parts meet without any rocking, you are done. Clamp the benchtop in place with the work surface facing up. Now install the bolts, washers and mounting plates through the top and the top plate of the end assemblies. Do this in the same way you attached the legs to the aprons.

BORING FOR STRENGTH: I put three bolts through each assembly. This keeps things flat. Yellow pine doesn't tend to move much, so I allowed for only a little expansion and contraction by making my clearance holes a ¹⁄₁₆" bigger than the diameter of my bolts.

THE KING OF OVERKILL: After gluing and screwing the second benchtop piece in place I also clamped things together while the glue dried. I like a solid benchtop.

Now flip the assembled bench over. You now can see the precise hole where the interior benchtop piece should go. Glue up a panel using 2x12 material and cut it to fit that hole exactly. Glue and screw it to the underside of the benchtop. Then lift the workbench base off the benchtop and clamp the top pieces together for extra bonding power.

Holes and Holding

You just made a table. Now you need to make it a workbench. To do that you need to add three things: a crochet, a planing stop and holdfast holes. The holdfast holes will help restrain your work on the benchtop and front apron. The crochet is for edge planing. The planing stop is for lots of things. Let's make the holdfast holes first.

Make your holdfast holes match your holdfasts. Many commercial holdfasts today have ³⁄₄" shafts – but check your holdfasts before drilling.

To lay out the holdfast holes on the aprons, first draw two or three rectangles on the aprons between the positions of your bench legs. Two rectangles for a 6' bench; three for an 8' model.

Connect two corners of each rectangle with a diagonal line. Then use dividers to equally space six holes from corner to corner on the diagonal lines. Then divide the vertical ends of each rectangle into three using your dividers.

Drill ³⁄₄"-diameter through holes at each of these locations. These holes in the aprons are great for supporting work from below, especially when edge-planing or dovetailing.

Now lay out the holdfast holes on the benchtop. My preference is to have two rows of holdfast holes on the benchtop (you can always add more later). One row is about 4" from the back edge of the benchtop. These should be spaced every 10" to 14" depending on the reach of your holdfast. Then make another row of holdfasts that is about 6" in front of your back row. These should be spaced similarly, but these holes should be offset from the first row, as shown in the drawings and photos.

I also like to drill a holdfast hole that is ideally placed to hold stock down against my bench hook when crosscutting. The position of that hole depends on the size of your bench hook and where you like to saw.

Be sure to drill some holdfast holes in the legs – both to store holdfasts and to support large work, such as passageway doors.

APRON HOLES: Here I'm drawing the diagonal lines for the holdfast holes in the aprons. Many people use wooden pegs in the aprons instead of holdfasts. Both solutions defy gravity just fine.

SQUARE HOLE: This is a great first mortise for a beginning woodworker. Take your time in squaring up the walls.

The Planing Stop

The traditional planing stop is a workhorse. I push workpieces against it to saw them, plane them, stick moulding on them, you name it. The stop is a piece of dense wood (yellow pine is dense enough) that is friction-fit into a mortise in the benchtop.

First make the mortise, then make the planing stop to fit.

The mortise for the planing stop is right in front of the end assembly and typically 3" or so in from the front edge of the benchtop. This planing stop is 2½" x 2½" x 12" – a fairly traditional size.

Lay out the mortise on both faces of the benchtop. Then bore out most of the waste with a large-diameter bit. Finish the walls with a chisel. It pays to check the walls so they are perfectly square to the benchtop.

Then plane the planing stop until it is a tight fit in the mortise and it requires mallet blows to move it up and down.

Some planing stops also have a toothy metal bit in the middle that helps restrain your work. You can add that later if you like.

Le Crochet

For this workbench I decided to make a crochet that looks exactly like the one in Roubo's "l'Art du menuisier." But to be honest, I don't think the shape matters much. I've used a lot of different shapes and they all seem to work fine as long as they are vaguely "hook-shaped."

I made this crochet from some scraps left over from the workbench. I glued them together and then shaped them on the band saw, finishing them up with rasps.

I attached the crochet with two lag screws and one cap screw, which was backed by a ductile mounting plate. This allows me to remove the crochet from the apron. As you can see from the photos, the crochet slightly interferes with one of the cap screws through the apron. You can avoid this by altering the shape of your crochet or moving the hole for the cap screw.

A Shelf if you Like

I always like having a shelf below my bench to store bench planes and other assemblies. I haven't included the shelf in the calculation for buying materials, so you'll need some extra wood and screws to get the job done.

The shelf is simply a panel that rests on cleats that are glued and screwed to the lower stretchers of the end assemblies. You can also screw some battens to the underside (and/or top) of the shelf to help keep it flat.

The only thing holding the shelf in place is gravity.

And Finish

You don't want to make your bench too slippery, so I recommend little or no finish. You can use the oil/varnish/mineral spirits blend suggested elsewhere in the book, use boiled linseed alone or just leave it bare.

In the end, this really is a remarkably sturdy bench. Most people who use it cannot even tell that it is designed to be knocked down. It is only after they notice the cap screws in the benchtop that they suspect anything.

No Tail Vise? No Problem

If you cannot afford a tail vise – or aren't convinced you need one – you need to get to know the *le pied de biche*, which is French for "doe's foot." Benchmaker Richard Maguire introduced me to this appliance several years ago, and now I couldn't imagine life without it.

It's a thin piece of wood with a 45° bird's mouth cut into one end. Whack a holdfast against it and it will immobilize work for when you are planing across the grain. It's also fantastic for holding mouldings in place on the bench. I have several that are different lengths and widths. The one shown in the photo is made from Masonite (thanks Jennie Alexander, for that tip).

The doe's foot is described in *Roubo's l'Art du Menuisier* in plate 14, Fig. 17:

To trim [set right] the planks on their edges, you hold them along the length of the bench with holdfasts, or even when they are too short, you hold them at one end with a holdfast, and the other with a planing stop [figure 17], which is itself held on the workbench with a holdfast, and which you close against the end of the plank with strikes of the mallet. The planing stop is a piece of hard wood, at the end of which is made a triangular notch, in which enters the end of the planks, see figure 19.

MEET THE DOE'S FOOT: If you have a holdfast and a notched piece of wood you don't really need a tail vise.

THE HOOK: You can bolt your crochet on. Some early accounts indicate it was nailed on. You probably could get away with glue alone.

ANOTHER TRICK: People think English workbenches for joiners are a trick – until they see the benches for stairmakers.

Knockdown Nicholson

NO.	PART	SIZES (INCHES)			MATERIAL	NOTES
		T	W	L		
❏ 4	Long leg boards	1½	5½	32½	Yellow pine	
❏ 4	Short leg boards	1½	5½	21¼	Yellow pine	
❏ 2	Aprons, outside	1½	11¼	72	Yellow pine	
❏ 2	Aprons, inside	¾	10	45	Pine	
❏ 1	Benchtop, outside	1½	22½	72	Yellow pine	
❏ 1	Benchtop, inside	1½	18	45	Yellow pine	
❏ 2	Leg front plate	1½	11¼	19½	Yellow pine	
❏ 2	Top mounting plates	1½	5½	16½	Yellow pine	
❏ 2	Leg stretchers	1½	5½	22½	Yellow pine	
❏ 4	Glue blocks	1½	11¼	2½	Yellow pine	
❏ 1	Planing stop	2½	2½	12	Yellow pine	
❏ 1	Crochet	3	4	12⅜	Yellow pine	

Shelf

NO.	PART	SIZES (INCHES)			MATERIAL	NOTES
		T	W	L		
❏ 1	Long shelf	¾	16½	53	Yellow pine	
❏ 2	Shelf support	1	1	16½	Yellow pine	
❏ 3	Battens	1½	2	14½	Yellow pine	

Hardware

Ductile mounting plates for ⅜" x 16 threaded rod. You need 15. Available from McMaster-Carr, item 11445T1, $1.83/ea.

High-strength steel cap screws, ⅜" x 16 thread. You need 15. Available from McMaster-Carr, 92620A636, $9.75 for a pack of five.

Plain steel ⅜" flat washers. You need at least 15.

Plain steel split lock washers, ⅜". You need at least 15.

No. 10 x 1" slot-head screws (for attaching the mounting plates).

No. 8 x 2½" wood screws to assemble the ends.

No. 8 x 1¼" wood screws for attaching the interior apron bracing. You'll need about 20.

Gramercy Holdfasts. One pair. Available from Tools for Working Wood, $35.

*Prices correct at time of publication.

YE KNOCKDOWN NICHOLSON

Top View

Front View

Left Side

¾ dia. holes for holdfasts

22½

16

10¾

10

typ.

5

typ.

72

3

6

10¾

4

7¼

7¼

3

12¾

5¾

45

5½

1½

4

16½

34

Note:
Holdfast hole patterns and spacing for both the front apron and benchtop are depicted as built in the accompanying text. Actual hole patterns and spacing are at the builder's discretion.

Moveable Planing Stop

Benchtop

Optional metal support plate to protect front edge of planing stop opening

Bracket for ⅜ bolt for securing crochet to bench

Front Outside Apron

Glue Block

Brackets for securing top and front panel to leg assemblies

Leg Stretcher

Front Left Leg Assembly

Cutaway View

Front Inside Apron

Shelf

Glue Blocks (4 required)

Front Outside Apron

Front Inside Apron

Notch for Bracket

Mounting Bracket

Crochet

Exploded Front Apron

Top View
72

Front Inside Apron

1½ typ.

2½

7

45

4

⅜

11¼

3

5¼

3

10¾

5¼

1½ typ.

⁷⁄₁₆ dia. holes for holdfasts

⁷⁄₁₆ dia. through hole for ⅜ bolt with 1" dia. x ½ deep countersink to recess mounting hardware (typ. for sides and top)

64

⁷⁄₁₆ dia. holes for attaching crochet to apron

2 typ.

4

3⅝

¾

2¼

Front Outside Apron

Top View
72

1½ typ.

1½

2½

7

45

4

⅜

11¼

3

5¼

3

10¾

64

Glue Block

Back Inside Apron (shaded area)

4

Back Outside Apron

113

Exploded View

Long Leg Board
Top Mounting Plate
Long Leg Board
Short Leg Board
Long Leg Board
Short Leg Board
Leg Front Plate
Leg Stretcher
Shelf Support

Shelf Support

Top Mounting Plate

Leg Stretcher

Leg Support Assembly

Short Leg Board

Long Leg Board

Leg Front Plate

Top View

4

12⅜

10⅝

3

5⅜

2¼

Crochet Detail

¾

1½

4

2

3⅜

3

Crochet
1" sq. grid

Side View

¾

14½

1

Top View

53

16½

8¼

2

½

¾

3

20½

2
typ.

20½

Shelf Assembly

Planing Stop

12

2½

2½

Section Through Top

1½

22½

18

Benchtop, Inside

12¾

2¼

View of Benchtop with Top Boards Removed

6

6

45

Holdfast holes to match top board

A NOUVEAU ROUBO: A few nights ago my 6-year-old asked me what my favorite *thing* was in the whole wide world. What one thing would I want to keep if the rest of my things were taken away? My answer: This bench. Her answer: The family bank account.

Chapter Seven

The French Workbench

While the English workbench might be a fascinating evolutionary dead end, the so-called French bench is something that has survived in many forms. It has evolved. It has been corrupted. Gaze at the workbench drawings in Roubo's enormous *L'Art du menuisier* (*The Art of the Woodworker*, 1769-1775) and compare them to the workbench drawings in the 20th-century tool catalog by La Forge Royale. Some details have changed in the 150 years between the printings of those two books, but the same DNA courses through both illustrations.

This form of bench shows up in the famous reconstruction of the Dominy family workshop at Winterthur, which was in operation in the 18th and 19th centuries. And whenever I get to lay my own hands on an old workbench, either in a collection or in the shop of a craftsman, I can see many ways that Roubo's book echoed in the benches built in the Colonies.

You can see it in the massive and thick tops that are free of aprons or other supporting mechanisms. You can see it in the simple workholding devices. These benches will typically have a vise (perhaps two), a planing stop and some device for propping up the edges of a long piece of work so you can work on an edge.

Other than that, it is only a massive three-dimensional clamping surface. It is pure overbuilt function, and that is its charm. It will hold any board for building furniture, and it doesn't care if you use power tools, hand tools or some blend of the two.

In the more than ten years since I built this bench, I've made a few modifications to the original French form, but the bottom line is this: I have yet to find a workholding task that challenges this bench. I've built Windsor chairs, Shaker cabinets, Creole tables, boxes big and small, contemporary shelves, router jigs and who knows what else. Curved stuff, straight stuff, small pieces, large panels and even some 8'-long 2x4s all stayed put without putting me out. In other words, I wouldn't trade this bench for anyone else's.

There's a price to pay to build the French bench. You need to devote some more labor, wood and lifting to the task. Oh, and a gallon of glue, if you build the bench using construction materials.

There are other ways to build this bench which you could consider that involve less laminating. You could build it exactly like Roubo

specified and use a single massive slab for the top. Find someone who owns a band saw mill (the Wood-Mizer sawmill company keeps a data base of people who do custom cutting). Then you have to dry the slab, or find someone with a kiln. And you have to be able to process it – check the next chapter for details.

Another option I've tried uses laminated construction beams for the bench. You can get these construction beams in enormous thicknesses, widths and lengths. And they are already glued up and fairly square. Of course, they aren't something you will find at the home center, so you're going to have to find someone who supplies them to the trades and then find a way to have them be delivered to your shop. They are ugly as all get-out. But they work.

And if you look around, you might find other ways to build this bench. When I was in Germany in 2006 I visited the Residenz in Wurzburg, an enormous palace built for the bishop princes that ruled that area. While the building was impressive, I was most smitten by some of the materials being used by the artisans who were restoring one of the building's painted ceilings. The scaffolding was all supported by some impressive-looking laminations that were stacked up like children's building blocks. The laminated blocks looked like white pine 2x6s that had been glued up into slabs that were as wide as 16" and 6' long.

They were all perfectly dressed and finished with a film finish to boot. And I know they were a commercial product because many of them still had bar codes and labels (in German, dang it) stapled to the end grain. They looked like perfect bench-building materials for a French workbench – a fact that I didn't feel compelled to tell to my German tour guide.

"Simpler is better (except when complicated looks really cool)."

— Daiku-Dojo web site, daikudojo.org

Understanding the French Bench

I first encountered this style of bench while paging through a copy of volume one of Roubo's *l'Art du menuisier* during a business trip to New York City. Roubo was a professional 18th-century joiner and well-educated man, and his multi-volume work on the craft is one of the seminal works in the field.

I was actually looking at the book with its owner, Joel Moskowitz, to settle a fine (read: meaningless) point of disagreement about historical workbench heights. As we were yammering and flipping pages we hit plate 11, which shows this workbench for joiners. A light went on in my head. This bench had a lot of details that resembled my workbench back in our shop in Cincinnati. The front edge of Roubo's workbench was flush with the legs, a change I had made a few months earlier. The Roubo bench lacked any apron or other awkward supporting structure below the length of the top. I had just reworked the sliding deadman on my bench to remove clamping obstructions. But Roubo's bench was different than mine in other ways. Mostly, it was simpler and more massive than my bench, which was sturdy enough (I thought at the time) and had been cluttered by clamping gizmos.

When I returned to the office after my trip to New York City, my head was buzzing with ideas about this French bench. And so I sat down and started looking at every image of old workbenches I could find in my books at home and work. It quickly became evident that there are some important differences between the Roubo bench and some modern benches:

Size and mass: In his text, Roubo specified that a proper workbench's top should be thick and long – as much as 6" thick and between 6' and 12' long. The thickness adds weight, provides strength to the workbench's base (more on that point later) and makes the top stiff so you don't need an apron below for support. Why is this an important detail? Aprons obstruct your clamps when you secure anything to your bench. If you've ever used a bench without an apron, you know how liberating this feature is. As to the length, make your bench as long as your shop will permit with at least a couple feet of clearance at each end. A long bench allows you to assemble projects at one end and continue to cut, plane, rout and sand at the other. A large workbench actually saves space because you don't have to build an assembly bench. As to the bench's width, you want to be able to clamp across the width of your bench; and tops that are wider than 27" will start to interfere with using a common 30" clamp. Similarly, a bench narrower than 18" will be tippy unless braced against a wall.

Placement of the top: The workbench's top is placed on the base of the bench so that the legs and stretchers are flush to the front edge of the benchtop – there's no overhang at the front or at the back. This design feature allows you to use your bench's legs and stretchers as a clamping surface. When you are working on anything wide – such as mortising a door's edge – you can secure it easily to the legs or stretchers with a clamp.

Simple workholding: To work on the edge of a board, Roubo shows a hook (it's called a *crochet* – French for *hook*) at the location where most benches have a metal face vise. The shape of the crochet allows it to grab one end of the work and immobilize it when you work from right to left, such as with a plane. You can use a wide variety of methods to support your work from below: holdfasts in the legs, a sliding deadman (if you have one) or even a 2x4 clamped to the legs. For working on the faces of boards, you work against the single planing stop (metal teeth are optional) or you can use the holdfasts

EVERYTHING YOU NEED TO KNOW: When I built this French workbench, all I had in the way of instruction was this plate and a few rough dimensions passed to me by a French-Canadian woodworker. The lack of detail wasn't a big deal because there aren't too many details to attend to.

in the top in a variety of manners. The holdfasts can be used directly on the work (such as when you are drilling or mortising) or you can use the holdfasts to secure thin scraps of wood (battens or a doe's foot) to your benchtop to work against.

Unusual joinery: The legs of the Roubo workbench are joined to the top with a sliding dovetail and through-tenon. For any woodworker with a passing knowledge of the properties of wood, this looks like disaster. After all, the top will expand and contract while the stretchers below will not. Will this bench self-destruct? No. This bench is not a dining room table, where the strength of the structure comes from the joinery between the legs and aprons. The vast majority of the strength of this workbench comes from the top. There are no aprons (hurrah!) and the stretchers are quite small. So when the top shrinks and expands, the only thing that really happens is that the joints at the stretchers open up a little and the bench gets a little bit of an A-frame shape. After a year of work, I measured the distortion of the workbench's base. It was indeed an A-frame shape, but barely. At the front of the bench, the top of the bench was 1/8" narrower than it was at the floor. This distortion did not in any way interfere with clamping or securing my work.

A leg vise: Roubo suggests adding a leg vise to the front of the workbench, though it is not shown on the bench in his primary drawing. I was a bit torn as to what to do. I was interested in the cro-

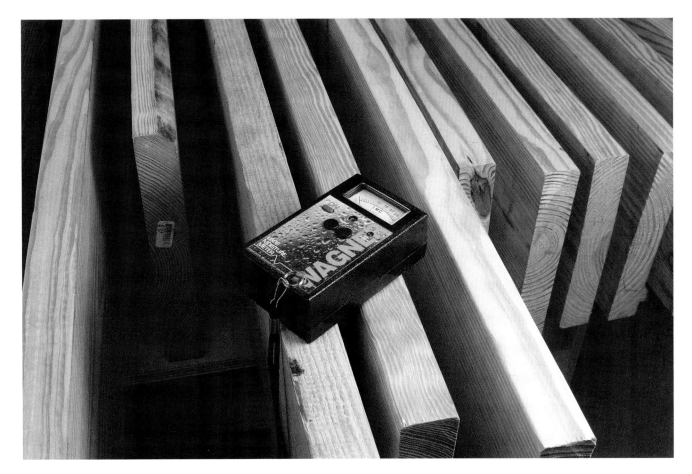

NAVIGATE THE WATER: Get a moisture meter if you want to avoid surprises. When working with softwoods, you can use the moisture meter to separate the wet boards from the dry ones. You'll know when the wood reaches equilibrium with your shop, and you'll be able to work with boards that aren't at equilibrium with confidence.

chet (because I'd never tried one), but the leg vise seemed a bit more familiar to me. I decided to build both. Getting the crochet and vise jaws positioned correctly took some care, but it was the right decision to add both because it expanded my thoughts on workholding.

Use the Wood's Moisture to Your Advantage

Like my English bench, I built the French one using Southern yellow pine, a construction material typically used as joists or (when treated with preservatives) for decks. I purchased all of the wood for this bench (with a bit of stock left over) for $250 at my local home center. You should be aware that softwoods such as Southern yellow pine, hemlock and fir will not be as dry as your typical kiln-dried hardwood. The moisture content of yellow pine – sometimes called longleaf pine – is at equilibrium in our shop at about 10 percent. The stuff straight from the store usually is wetter. With this batch of pine some of the boards were as wet as 17 percent. (I have worked with fir from a home center that was so wet that it sprayed a stream of water when I ripped it on the table saw.)

Don't be alarmed by the high moisture content. You can use it to your advantage when building this bench. You need a moisture meter to do this, however. Mark every board with its moisture content and then segregate the boards. Choose the wettest boards for the top and

legs, those parts will shrink on the stretchers of the bench, which should have a lower moisture content than the other parts. This approach will keep the joints tight and will slightly distort the base's shape, which is going to happen anyway.

At the lumberyard, take your time when picking your boards, and use your eyes and your moisture meter to guide your choices. Pull the boards from the rack that are as clear of knots, splits, shakes and bark as possible. Don't be afraid to ask the people at the home center to open a new bunk of material for you – it typically is stored in the racks above the open bunk. Use your moisture meter to find the driest ones and make a pile of possible boards. If you pull more boards than you need for the bench, examine them all closely for twist and wind.

If you don't have a moisture meter, a good way to judge wetness is by roughly gauging the weight of the board in question. Wetter boards weigh quite a bit more. Sometimes the extra weight is resin – yellow pine is sticky stuff. If the end grain doesn't feel cool to the touch, grab these heavier boards.

As noted in the chapter on the English bench: the wider the softwood stock, the clearer and straighter it will be. Don't buy 2x4s for this project. Please. They are the worst when it comes to knots, bow, twist and wind. You might think, "I am saving time because I won't have to rip anything." That is a fool's paradise. Stick to 2x12s and 2x10s and rip out the boards you need for each component.

ARROWS GUIDE THE GLUE-UP: Mark the direction the grain is running on each edge as you pick your boards for each top section. This also will make life easier when (or if) you true up the top with a handplane.

EXTEND-A-BED: Dealing with 8'-long stock on any power jointer is difficult. The beds are not really designed to handle this size stock. And because the boards weigh a lot, even keeping them under control is difficult. That's why I recommend you set up some sort of infeed and outfeed support system. It will help hold the board so you can focus on moving it steadily across the cutterhead.

A PAIN IN THE PINE:
In this assembly you can see how the board on the left is bowed. I positioned the concave side of the bow toward the inside of the assembly. Clamp pressure in the middle of this assembly will flatten the entire board against its neighbor.

DON'T SKIMP ON GLUE:
You want a thin, consistent film of glue on the board. I pour a line of glue down the board and spread it (quickly now!) with cardboard and then stack it on its neighbor. This trick gives you a little more time to get the clamps on.

Basic Joinery Made Easier

This bench can be built by a beginner. I know several people who built this bench as their first-ever woodworking project. (Before even building the obligatory set of bookshelves.) All told, there are 12 housed joints in this bench and nothing is complex or angled. And here's a bonus: You don't have to cut any tenons when building this bench – though it is entirely mortise-and-tenon construction. All of the tenons on the legs and stretchers are created when laminating the boards together. The longer boards in the lamination become the tenons. The shorter boards act as the tenons' shoulders.

All of the joints in this bench are drawbored. This early and nearly forgotten technique will make all of your joints stouter. But most of the work in this bench is in gluing up the boards to create the top,

legs and stretchers. I'd start by buying a gallon of a slow-setting glue, such as Titebond Extend, and making sure your powered planer and powered jointer are tuned up.

Good Stock Preparation

This project can be built with a 6" power jointer and 13" portable planer – you don't need industrial equipment. Begin by ripping all your boards down to the sizes you'll need for your laminations. I ripped them 1/4" oversize to allow for trimming after everything was glued up. Remember that dimensional lumberyard stock is sold undersized. A 2x12 is actually about 11" wide; a 2x10 is typically 9" wide in the real world.

ON THE COLLECTING OF CLAMPS: How many clamps does it take to make a workbench top? Answer: As many as you have. No matter how many clamps we own, I always dig deep into our collection for big glue-ups.

EDGE PATROL: When you start assembling your four top sections you want the joints to be tight. Because these assemblies are so big, you won't be able to use clamp pressure to remove any gaps. Take your time and do it right.

Then plane and joint all your boards to a finished thickness of 1¼". If your stock can finish out a little thicker, then let it. Embrace the extra weight and thickness. I recommend beginning gluing up the top in sections, four boards to a section. This allows you to then run the completed section over a 6" jointer and through your planer to true it.

Because you're going to machine or handplane these sections after assembly, you want to make sure all the grain is running in the same direction in the boards.

The other thing to watch for is which way the boards bow. No matter how carefully you prepare your stock, some of the boards are likely to have a small bow. Plan your sections so the bow faces the inside of the assembly.

Here's another tip about surfacing your lumber. Ignore this paragraph if you are using a well-seasoned hardwood. It doesn't apply. When you work with softwoods, especially yellow pine, you are better off surfacing whatever wood you are going to be working with for the next day only. Do your business with that batch, then surface the next batch for the next day's work.

I know that this seems like it's a pain. It is. But it's good advice. Softwoods tend to shift around after you surface them. And if you leave them overnight they will do circus tricks for you. ("Roll over!") This will happen even if the boards appear to be at equilibrium with your shop. Once you get them glued up into a top section, they might still move around a bit, but they will settle down soon enough. And then they become quite stable. I'm sure there is a tree scientist somewhere who could confirm, explain or mock this assertion. But I've found it to be true after surfacing thousands of board feet of the stuff for furniture-grade work.

So work in stages. It will save you some trouble and prevent you from reworking your boards to get them flat again.

HERE'S A CHEAT: If you're having problems getting your assemblies to mate perfectly, take a couple swipes down the middle with a block plane. This can remove material in the middle that is interfering with clamping.

Tricks for Gluing the Top

Gluing up Southern yellow pine can try your patience. The wood is dense and resinous, so it resists glue penetration more than some other pines. The way to get around the resin problem is to remove it at the surface by wiping the resinous areas with acetone right before applying glue. The way to get around the density issue is to allow each assembly to stay in the clamps for four hours. This is not arbitrary or overcautious – it's the recommendation from a technical specialist at Franklin International, the company that makes Titebond.

A common complaint that I hear from people trying to treat this construction lumber like a cabinet wood is that it will sometimes come apart at the seams, especially near the ends. I had this happen in an early bench of mine, and it was because I was in a hurry. In our shop we'll clamp up panels for 30 minutes and then take them out of the clamps. That's not always a good idea with yellow pine.

You can fill the splits with epoxy if you like. Or you can rip apart the joint at the glue line and try again. In my instance, I filled the crack. It served as a reminder to slow down a bit.

DON'T BURN A COMMUTATOR: No matter how butch your circular saw is, don't make this cut by starting with a full-depth pass. Make the finished cut in two or three passes; you'll get less burning and it will be easier to clean up the ends.

LOOK MA, NO TENON SAW: The tenons on the legs and stretchers are formed during the lamination process. This saves you from having to cut tenons on the end of a 5'-long stretcher – a real trick to do well.

YOUR 18-GAUGE BUDDIES: The plywood spacers ensure your leg tenons will be exactly 2" long and square. A couple short brads are all the holding power you need for this temporary joint.

KNOCK ON WOOD: A rap with a hammer will loosen the plywood spacers. There might be glue squeeze-out in the corner between the shoulder and cheek. Chisel it out and the tenon is complete.

Apply clamps every 12" or so on your top assembly. Start at the middle and work out to the ends, pushing and pulling your boards into alignment as you go. After all four assemblies are complete, joint and plane them to clean up the faces and edges. Keep them as thick and as wide as you can. Then arrange them as they'll appear in the finished assembly and joint all the edges to get airtight joints.

If you are skilled with a handplane, I think you'll find this an excellent task for a jointer plane. Two of my three joints for the top needed to be tuned with a handplane to be at their best. It might seem a daunting task because the edge is so big, but that actually is an advantage because your plane won't tip off the edge. I also did some further tweaking with a block plane.

If you are confident that your joints are sound, you can clamp up the entire top during one big gut-wrenching moment. I did it. I didn't enjoy it. But it worked. If you're not feeling frosty, glue two small sections into one. Then either add a single section at a time to that chunk or glue up a separate hunk of two sections and then join the two hunks.

Be advised that whenever you release an assembly from clamps you should check the edge again before gluing on another chunk. Clamps, glue and – I don't know, the alignment of the stars – can bend a jointed straight edge.

When your top is complete, trim the ends square using a circular saw and a straightedge guide. Or you can use a big handsaw. If you go the circular saw route, you'll need to cut from both the top and the bottom of the benchtop, so be sure to carry your layout lines around the sides and bottom of the piece. After squaring the ends, clean up your sawblade marks with a block plane. First moisten the end grain with some alcohol and then tidy things up.

Making Tenons Out of Nothing

The next task is to glue up the legs and stretchers. These laminations are easier than the top pieces because they are shorter. But there is another challenge. You're going to leave some of these individual boards a bit longer so that they will become the tenons you need.

TWO RIPS MAKE ONE TRACK: Make the ½" x ½" chamfer on the long stretchers by simply ripping it on the table saw. Using a chamfer bit in a router is much slower because you will have to make several passes.

TENACIOUS TENONS: With all the legs and stretchers complete, I then dressed the glued-up edges on the powered jointer and then with a hand-plane. This is what the completed and huge tenons look like.

MEASURING WITHOUT MATH: The less you measure, the more accurate you will become. Using the tenon to mark out your mortises reduces the chance of a measuring error. And it is faster, too.

You might be asking yourself how you'll get a perfect tenon with these laminations sliding around as you're clamping them. After some head-scratching I found an easy way to get perfect tenons. First, make sure all your pieces are crosscut square across both the width and the thickness.

Now get some scrap plywood, anything thicker than ¼" will do fine. Cut it so it is as long as your tenons (2" long for the leg tenons; 2½" long for the stretchers). And cut it so it's wider than the assembled lamination (7" wide for the legs; 6" wide for the stretchers).

Before you glue up your legs and stretchers, nail one of these boards to the pieces that will form the tenon's face cheek. Now glue up the layers and butt the two outside laminations against these plywood spacers.

To keep all the leg parts in alignment during glue-up, don't be afraid to put a couple clamps along the length of the leg to align the pieces lengthwise. This extra clamping also guarantees a well-formed

tenon. As soon as your clamps are set, knock the spacer off the assembly with a hammer. You don't want the spacer to accidentally get glued to your leg.

If you are particularly worried about the spacer becoming part of the permanent exhibit, then rub some wax or paraffin on the spacer before nailing it down. Wax is an oil; glue is water. That should help.

Before you move to gluing up the stretchers, you need to decide if you want a sliding deadman on your bench. If the answer is yes (and I hope it is), then cut two ½" x ½" chamfers on the long edges of the board that will face the outside of the bench. The deadman will slide on this track. Resist using a groove to guide the sliding deadman, as is done with sliding doors in casework. It can fill up with chips.

Assembling the stretchers uses the same routine as the legs. Use plywood spacers on the ends of the long board in the lamination to properly position the shorter board and create the tenons.

Making Massive Leg Mortises

The mortises in the legs are quite large. As a result, you won't be able to use a mortising machine (at least, not without tremendous difficulty). And making these mortises by chisel alone would also be more work than necessary.

The best solution is, quite honestly, to drill out the mortises and then clean up the corners with a chisel. If you have a drill press and a 1¼" Forstner bit, you're golden. If you are using a brace and bit with an expansive bit, that also will work – just be sure to use a brace with a large swing. 14" is about right.

The first step is to mark out the locations of all the mortises on the legs. Measure up 5" from the bottom of the legs and then use the tenon itself – like a ruler – to lay out the mortise location. This trick reduces measuring errors.

If you're going to drill out these mortises with a Forstner bit, set your drill press for 1,200 rpm (or in that neighborhood). That's a good speed for both clearing chips, reducing burning and getting the job done. When I make mortises with a Forstner, I make many overlapping holes, to the point where I only have the corners to clean up. I do everything I can to avoid chiseling the long-grain walls of the mortise. This is where the joint's strength comes from, and chiseling it almost always introduces a sloppy or irregular fit.

BEGIN THE BOREDOM: Begin the mortise by defining the beginning and ending of the joint with your Forstner bit.

THE BORING MIDDLE PART: Then clean up the waste between as shown above.

HUNT THE HUMPS: Now clean up the little triangles of waste along the long-grain walls of the mortise. The more you bore, the smaller the triangles get.

BORED BOARD: You're done when you can put the bit in the joint and it will slide freely left to right in the mortise.

Make each leg mortise a little deeper (I like ¹/₈") than needed. This means that the two mortises in each leg will meet one another in the middle. This is an asset because this gap gives a place for the excess glue to go during assembly.

To complete the joint you can square up the corners with a chisel (as I did) or you can clip the corners of your tenon with a chisel or a coarse rasp. I have found that squaring the corners of the mortise is almost always the faster technique. Your corner work will be more accurate if you begin your cut in the right place. Don't place the chisel where you want the corner to be and wail away. That makes the tool hard to steer. Take a couple smaller bites first and you will be driving the chisel – not the other way around.

Details on the Legs

Before you dive into assembling the base, take care of a few details now to save hassles later. First, plane a ¹/₄" x ¹/₄" chamfer on the bottom edge of the legs. This chamfer prevents your legs from snagging on something on your floor and ripping out some grain when you drag or push your bench to a new location. Yes, even at 350 pounds, you can move this bench around – and you will.

Next up is an important decision. If you're going to install a leg vise in your bench, cut a big notch in the front left leg for the guide that keeps the jaw parallel. If you want my advice, I'd go ahead and cut this notch, even if you're not sold on the utility of the leg vise. I really like its ability to secure small parts and I find it as tough as many metal-jawed vises I've used. You also should go ahead and drill the 1³/₈"-diameter hole in the leg for the vise's screw. Its location is shown in the construction drawing.

The other detail is to drill holes in the legs for your hold-downs. Before you do this, you need to decide on their diameter, and that really depends on which hold-down you purchase.

Assembling the Base

The base is assembled by drawboring the joints together. This technique allows you to assemble the base without any clamps (so you don't have to buy any 6'-long clamps for this job). You can also assemble this base one joint at a time – that's the beauty of this technique. Here's drawboring in a nutshell: Drill a hole through the disassembled mortise. Assemble the joint dry and transfer the hole's location onto the mating tenon cheek. Disassemble the joint and drill the hole through the tenon – but offset it a bit toward the shoulder. When you

CORNERED ANIMAL: A corner chisel is expensive, and it is a trick to sharpen. But when you need one, it's worth the hassle. This operation can be carried out with a standard bench chisel, but it takes longer.

SHAVE YOUR LEGS: Before assembly, dress your legs for the final time. They should be straight and true; a smoothing plane removes so little material that it's unlikely to take your legs out of square.

CHOP THE NOTCH: The notch for the vise is ½" wide, 4" long and runs through the entire leg. The best way to cut it is to saw out the cheeks (I used a band saw) and then use a mortise chisel and mallet to pop out the waste. This is both easy and fun.

drive a peg through the completed joint, the peg will draw the bores together, locking them mechanically. It's a bit of 17th-century magic.

Here are the details for this bench: With the joint disassembled, drill the ³/₈" holes through the mortise using an auger bit. Assemble the joint and mark the hole's centerpoint location with a prick of a ³/₈" brad-point bit. Remove the tenon and drill the hole for the peg a bit closer to the shoulder of the tenon – ³/₃₂" to ¹/₈" will do the job. Pick the larger offset if your legs are particularly wet (which means you have more shrinkage ahead of you).

Assemble the joint without glue and twist a drawbore pin into the joint to begin aligning the holes and check the fit of the shoulder. A drawbore pin is a tapered metal drift pin (you can buy them at Sears). The metal pin allows you to check the fit of your components and to deform the wood a bit to prepare a path for a more fragile wooden peg. If, after inserting the drawbore pin, you see any gaps, find the extra material or dried glue that is interfering with a good fit and chisel it out now.

When the joint fits tightly, reassemble it with glue and whittle the ends of two ³/₈" x 4" pegs so they look like elongated pencils. For most furniture jobs, I use a ¹/₄"-diameter peg when drawboring. But because of the scale of this project, ³/₈"-diameter oak stock is far better. (And even better than that is white oak stock that has been rived and is bone dry.)

POINT TO THE MIDDLE: Assemble the joint without glue and use a brad-point bit to mark the center of the hole on the tenon's cheek.

FOREARM TORQUE: Because of the depth of these holes in your legs, you're going to want to make them with an auger that's powered by a brace and bit. These are powerful tools – and this will get you warmed up for boring out the mortises in the underside of the top.

OK, THIS IS FUSSY: A piece of scrap in the mortise reduces tear-out when you drill into the mortise cheek. It's probably unnecessary to the strength of this bench, but I relish overbuilding joints for workbenches.

THE OFFSET: Remove the tenon and mark the location of the peg hole in the tenon. It should be closer to the tenon's shoulder than the original mark. All these fussy lines and measuring of offsets is for the beginner. After a dozen joints, you will drawbore through instinct.

Twist one of the drawbore pins into one of the two holes and then drive a wooden peg into the adjacent hole. Remove the steel drawbore pin and drive the second peg in. Trim the pegs flush with a saw and chisel. Look ma, no clamps.

And You Thought the Leg Mortises Were Big?

If you've ever built a table before you're probably a bit concerned about how the top connects to the base. Your first reaction might be that this design detail is simply the product of an 18th-century woodworker who didn't understand seasonal wood movement. After all, the top will expand and contract but the base will not. It seems like a disaster waiting to happen.

But it's not.

By tenoning the legs into a top that is a little on the wet side (as yours undoubtedly is), the bench's design is counting on the top shrinking and wracking the base a bit, making it slightly wider at the bottom than at the top and more stable.

If you're skittish about this design detail, here's an option: Make the two mortises for the rear legs an $^{1}/_{8}$" wider than necessary to allow the top to move without wracking the base. By widening the mortises for the rear legs only you'll keep the front edge of the top flush to the front legs – a critical detail. If you take this route, you'll still drawbore all four leg joints – the pins won't interfere with wood movement.

The original bench in the Roubo volumes showed the tenons passing all the way through the top. If you are confident enough to attempt this, go forward with my blessing. I made the tenons go only halfway through the top and then drawbored them to the base without glue. This accomplished the same mechanical integration of-

fered by the original design. And yes, this is an authentic Roubo detail. Volume 3 of his book shows a bench with blind tenons (it's plate 279).

Lay out your mortises on the underside of the benchtop by using the base itself. How's that? Turn your top upside down on sawhorses and place the base in position, also upside down. Mark for the mortises. Move or remove the base and bore out the waste using a $^{3}/_{4}$" auger bit. If you're going to use an electric drill for this operation, use a corded one. You can cook a cordless drill in short order with this operation.

Clean out the waste with a mortise chisel and use a combination square to confirm that the mortise walls are both square and deep enough to accept the leg tenons. You don't want to fit these joints any more than you have to – the base is about 100 pounds.

If you've opted for the sliding deadman, you'll need to mill a $^{5}/_{8}$"-wide x 1"-deep groove in the underside of the top for the deadman before attaching the top and base. After I milled this groove, disaster struck. The top slid off the sawhorses and landed on the corner with the groove. There was a snap, followed by a brief cloudburst of cursing. I vowed to fix the joint with glue (which I did, and seamlessly) and then to reinforce this area with a steel strip (which I didn't). After a

PINNED AND PONDERED: Reassemble the joint and twist the draw-bore pin into the joint. Check the fit of your components. Don't worry too much about a gap on the inside of the base. Focus on the outside, the show side. After this dress rehearsal, add glue and drive the pegs home.

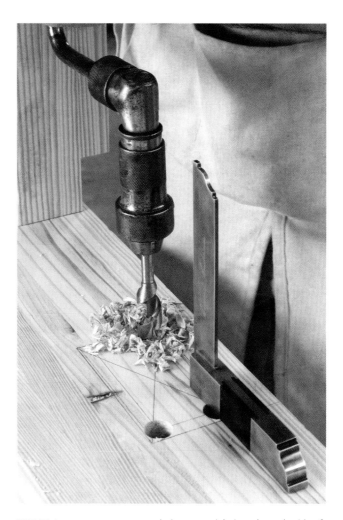

TRY IT: A try square ensures your holes are straight into the underside of the top. After drilling three of these mortises, you'll have the confidence to do the fourth without the square.

PLACE AND TRACE: Center the top on the underside of the bench and make sure the front legs will be flush to the front edge of the bench. If the top has an overhang at the back you can take care of that after the top reaches equilibrium. Knife around the four tenons. Push the base aside or remove it. Then bore out the waste.

couple years of hard use, the edge is solid, and my thoughts about a steel strip diminished.

I drawbored the top to the base, but I didn't use glue in these joints. If I ever need to remove the top, I can drill out the ³/₈" pegs to dismantle the assembly. Follow the same drilling and pegging procedure you used to drawbore the joints in the base. The only difference is the length of the pegs; these are 6" long.

Turn the bench onto its feet. Stand on it. Park a car's engine on it if you like. I've found that this bench is up to any task. Before you start adding the gizmos that hold your work, take an hour or so to flatten the top. A jack plane and a jointer plane are the most effective tools for this operation. See the chapter on maintenance and appliances for more information on flattening a top.

Workholding Details

If you're going to add the crochet to the bench, take care to make sure the grain direction runs straight from the tip to the far corner – this is stronger than making it parallel to the top's edge. I made the crochet by face-gluing three pieces of 1"-thick ash. I cut the shape out on the band saw and then cleaned up the sawblade marks with a spokeshave

In Woodworking, the Question is often the Answer

There is an old expression that has nothing to do with woodworking, but it has turned out to be one of the guiding principles in my work.

The expression goes something like this: "If you have to ask the question, then you already know the answer."

I know that it sounds like some nonsense that a smooth-talking corporate trainer might spin to baffle you, but allow me to give you a real-world example of how useful it is in the shop.

As I was building the French workbench it came time to attach the massive 230-pound top to the 100-pound base, and I was facing the task of drawboring the four massive joints.

This extra step was going to require a couple hours of work and serious heavy lifting. I was going to have to fit the base into the top, remove the base to bore the holes for the pegs and then fit it again and remove it again to mark and bore the offset holes in the tenons.

It was about 5 P.M., and it would be so much easier to just drop the top onto the base, let gravity hold everything together and call it a day. The question then flashed in my head: "Do I really need to drawbore the top?"

I've found that these questions of expediency are like the old cartoons where the character is getting competing advice from an angel on one shoulder and a devil on the other. Questions such as these always come from the devil on the right shoulder of the cartoon cat (or woodworker).

When You Come to the Fork in the Road, Take it

For years I listened to and agonized over questions such as these. I debated them and tried to see both sides of the argument. However, eventually I realized that all these different questions were really just one question in disguise: Are you going to take a seemingly reasonable shortcut that will save you time now but cause regret later?

· Question: Should I strip the finish off my Morris chair project after the staining highlighted a couple small but disappointing toolmarks near the through-tenons?

· Question: Should I dovetail the rear joints in these drawers for my tool cabinet? No one will ever see them, and a lock-rabbet will be quite a bit faster.

· Question: Do I really need to test-fit this familiar joint before I glue it up?

· Question: Do I really need to check the jointer's fence to make sure it's still 90° to the bed?

In the case of the workbench, I actually asked the question out loud, and all of my fellow editors heard me and chimed in with advice. One editor said that gravity was more than enough to hold everything in place and that drawboring the top was likely an act of ridiculous excess.

The other editors were on the fence and so we assembled the bench and put it on its feet. The bench looked good all put together like that. It seemed rock solid, like I could park my old Volkswagen on it. I was ready to go home and have a beer.

ASK YOURSELF: I seem to mutter to myself a lot while making chairs, and I also find myself remaking the complex curved parts quite a bit. The two things are related.

Then one of the editors went up to the end of the bench and gave it several king-size hip checks. Something caught my eye. I looked closely at where the legs met the top as the editor gave it a few more hip checks.

Though it was slight, the bench base was wracking with every shove. After years of planing on this bench, this wracking would become a problem. So I fetched my drawbore pins from my tool chest and got ready for a long evening. I had already wasted an hour testing out a question to which I already knew the answer.

As I drove home later that evening (ready for two beers), I wondered if this philosophy could become immobilizing for some. That is, every question could lead to a fussy downward spiral of extra work that resulted in nothing ever getting done.

But I don't think so. Every project is a series of operations, many of which are familiar and don't generate these questions. But when we stumble into new territory, these questions are the angel on our left shoulder telling us to first slow down and figure things out.

And if we listen, then the next time we encounter the same problem there won't be any questions – just action.

A TRENCHER: Mill the groove for the deadman using an upcut spiral bit in your plunge router. An edge guide makes this operation a snap. This groove is deep to allow the deadman to be removed or modified.

HOOKED ON THE HOOK: Here you can see the proper grain direction for a crochet. This feature and the shape of the crochet allows it to grab your work and wedge it against the benchtop. It is surprisingly effective.

DEAD ON: To cut the trench on the bottom edge, mark out the shape on the front edge of the deadman, then set your table saw's blade to 45° and line things up with your marks. Make one pass, turn the deadman around and make a second pass to finish the cut. Clean up the work with a chisel.

and a card scraper. Drill clearance holes in the crochet for $1/2$" x 6" lag bolts and $1/2$" washers. Drill pilot holes in the benchtop, using the holes in the crochet as a template. Attach the crochet to the benchtop with the end of the crochet flush to the end of the benchtop. I centered the crochet on the top's thickness. If you use a plow plane in your work, you'll want to lower the crochet a bit so your plow's fence will clear the crochet.

The planing stop is one of the most important parts of the bench. It is simply a piece of 2" x 2" x 12" ash that is friction-fit into a 2" x 2" mortise in the benchtop. You knock the planing stop up and down with your mallet. This planing stop can be a simple stick of wood, or it can have a toothed metal stop embedded in it. It's your choice.

The leg vise is a simple affair to make if you purchase an inexpensive metal vise screw. The vise comes with a threaded metal collar that you screw to the inside of the leg, centered on the $1^{1}/4$" hole you drilled before assembly.

The jaw has a slight coffin shape as shown in the drawings. And I planed a chamfer on three edges to soften the look. The chamfer on the top edge is the only critical one. It allows better access to your work when working at an angle with a plane, chisel or rasp.

The parallel guide is tenoned and pegged into the jaw. It is probably the part of the vise that is most unfamiliar to our 21st century eyes. The parallel guide is drilled with two offset rows of $3/8$" holes on 1" centers. By placing a $3/8$" steel pin in one of the holes in front of the leg and advancing the bench screw, the peg will then jam against the leg and pivot the top of your jaw against your work. This provides tremendous workholding power, equal to a metal vise as near as I can tell. The only downside is that you have to move the pin around for different thicknesses of work. It's a small price to pay for the small price (and great benefits) of the bench screw.

I made my own vise handle with a piece of 1" x 1" x 15" ash left over from the crochet. I planed it to an octagonal shape and then secured it in the bench screw by driving $3/8$" pegs (left over from drawboring) through each end. You could buy a vise handle, but this one is much more tactile and appropriate.

The sliding deadman is a gizmo that you can add now or wait on. You might not find your work needs it, however it's so quick to make you should give it a try. First plow out the triangular trench on the bottom edge of the deadman using your table saw. Then cut the $5/8$" x 1"-long tenon on the top. Tweak the tenon's thickness and shape until the deadman fits up into the groove and then onto the track below.

Once the deadman fits, cut the curved shape on the long edges. The curve allows you to get your hand between the deadman and leg when the deadman is pushed up against the leg. Then drill the two rows of offset holes on 2" centers. You can make a dedicated peg to place in these holes or you can make the holes the same size as the shaft on your holdfast and use one of those to support your work.

Finally, you want to drill holes in the top for holdfasts. Their location isn't arbitrary. The hole near the planing stop allows me to put a batten in front of the planing stop and secure it with the holdfast, which allows me to plane wide panels against the batten.

The holes along the back edge allow me to secure thin battens up against the long edges of long boards. These are ideal for controlling your stock from the side, which is helpful when planing at an angle to the grain or across the grain. My advice is to drill these few holes

NOW WITH A SHELF: I didn't have time to make the shelf below the bench when I first built it. One afternoon I fixed that situation. I haven't actually seen the shelf for a couple years – it's covered in parts, tools and appliances.

TONGUES & GROOVES: You could simply butt the edges of the shelves together, but a tongue-in-groove shelf is stronger, traditional and nicer.

FIT THE END: Shown is one of the shelf pieces for the end with its notches cut. You also can see the ledgers beneath the shelf pieces.

and add more when needed. With the holes drilled, you can finish the bench if you please. I applied a couple coats of an oil/varnish blend.

When I completed the bench I soon realized something unexpected. Though building the bench itself was an adventure, the real journey began when I started using the bench. With the holdfasts, crochet and battens in my arsenal I found new ways to work just about every time I stepped up to the bench.

A Flexible Bench

You do not have to add all the bench accessories shown to create a working bench. In fact, you might want to try this bench in its purest form first: a crochet, planing stop and holdfast holes. You can accomplish every major workholding task with this setup (plus some holdfasts).

The leg vise and sliding deadman are nice additions. The leg vise helps hold small work. And the deadman offers quick and flexible support when holding wide boards or doors on edge.

Another ugrade I recommend is the shelf shown in Roubo's volume. When I built the bench, I had a deadline based on when the photographer had to take a picture of it. An hour before show time I was still building the bench – putting the finishing touches on the leg vise to be exact. I had always meant to put a tongue-and-groove shelf below the workbench like the original, but I simply ran out of time. One day during lunch I resolved to correct that omission.

I stopped by the home center and picked up enough Southern yellow pine for the job – two 8'-long 2x12s for the shelves and one 8'-long 2x6 for the ledgers beneath the shelves. This was 30 percent more wood than I needed, but it gave me clear, straight stock.

First joint and plane all the stock down to 1¼" thick. Rip the ledgers from the 2x6 and the shelf planks from the 2x12s. Crosscut the ledgers to length after double-checking your measurements against your bench. Clamp them in place on the stretchers so that the bottom edge of each ledger is flush with the bottom edge of its mating stretcher. Screw the ledgers to the stretchers with #10 x 2" screws. I used four screws in each long stretcher and two in each end stretcher.

Now you can crosscut your shelves easily and fit them on top of the ledgers and between the stretchers. Now plow a ½" x ½" groove along one long edge of each shelf plank. I used a dado stack in my table saw. Now reduce the height of the dado stack to ⅜" and cut the

Shelf for the French Workbench

NO.	PART	SIZES (INCHES)			MATERIAL
		T	W	L	
☐ 2	Long ledgers	1¼	1¼	56	Yellow pine
☐ 2	Short ledgers	1¼	1¼	14	Yellow pine
☐ 6	Shelf planks	1¼	11	19	Yellow pine

Fig. 15.

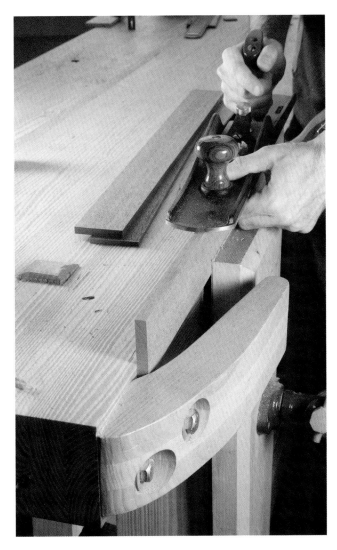

CROCHET AND VISE: This isn't a traditional setup but it is an effective one. I like using the crochet and leg vise in tandem. Nothing ever slips.

CLAMPING PLATFORM: One of the best features of the French workbench is also the least obvious: the top. The thick, stiff top is a superb clamping surface, especially with the lack of aprons below it.

WORKING ON EDGES: Holdfasts in the legs and a scrapwood ledger support the work from below. The crochet wedges the work against the benchtop and legs.

rabbets on the opposite long edge that will create the tongue. The fit between the tongue and its groove shouldn't be too tight. You want the pieces to slide together easily.

Plane your shelves flat. Chamfer the long edges of each shelf. A small $^1/_8$" x $^1/_8$" chamfer will make the long edges more robust. Place five of the shelves on the ledgers and center them between the legs. You should have about a $4^1/_4$" gap between the shelves and the end stretchers. Measure this gap and then rip your sixth shelf. One piece will go on one end; the other will go on the other end.

My wood was pretty wet (15 percent moisture content). So these boards will shrink up a bit as they come in equilibrium with the shop. So I didn't leave much of a gap between the shelves, just $^1/_{32}$" or so. Now place the shelf pieces for the ends up against the legs and lay out the notches that will allow each end piece to fit around the legs. Cut the notches and clean up your work with a chisel.

With everything fit in place, you can then secure the shelves to their ledgers. I used Miller Dowels without glue. These stepped and tapered dowels are great if you ever need to knock something apart to move it. A couple coats of oil/varnish blend and you're done.

Shop Testing the French Workbench

I'm often asked how I like my French workbench, or if I'll ever come to my senses and simply buy a continental workbench like the rest of the world. This French bench has been the center of my work for more than two years now, and I cannot imagine ever getting rid of it.

I've made changes. I added a wagon vise in the end-vise position plus a matching row of dog holes. I made this modification to help me work across the grain of boards with my handplanes (mostly my jointer and fore planes). A wagon vise is faster than using the battens-plus-holdfasts method – but it's not better.

The wagon vise is worth a few sentences of explanation. I found a drawing of it in an early 20th-century French woodworking catalog. And it pops its head up every once in a while (most recently I saw it in an issue of *Woodsmith* magazine). But the wagon vise has never been nearly as popular as the classic tail vise.

Because my wagon vise was a retrofit, it also was a compromise. I first hacked out a large through-mortise in the benchtop and installed a small metal vise screw in the mortise. (This screw is usually used in making homemade veneer presses, but it is more than stout enough

PIERRE, MEET JACK: Though a sliding deadman isn't original to the French bench (that I can find), it is a highly recommended addition to the bench. When your French friends come for a visit you can remove it.

SAWING TENONS: A leg vise offers a wide expanse of gripping surface. You can clamp your work, assume it will stay put and focus on cutting to your knife lines.

WORKING ON FACES: Holdfasts and battens keep the work from skittering around on your benchtop.

for this application). I attached the end of the vise's screw to a wooden block that had a couple holes bored through it for round bench dogs.

Once I added a little track below the bench to keep the vise block steady, I thought I was in business. I was mistaken. The vise screw was applying a lot of pressure to the 2" block of end grain at the end of the bench. I got a little worried that the whole thing would self-destruct if someone applied a lot of pressure to the vise screw. And so I added a thick end cap to the bench using 6"-long carriage bolts and washers. That seemed to make everything really tight and sturdy. But was it worth all the trouble? I think the jury is still out. The biggest advantage the wagon vise offers over a Wonder Dog system is the ability to plane thin stock with ease. Plus the wagon vise is a bit faster to use. So think carefully before you make this modification to your bench. It helps, but it is not a cure-all.

One more note: If you simply screw the wagon vise's threaded casting to your bench (instead of bolting it through the benchtop) it will be great for applying pressure to pinch stuff between the dogs, but it will be ineffective for disassembling things. Using the dogs of the

wagon vise to pull apart a frame assembly is more likely to pull the vise's threaded casting right out of the bench, screws and all. I know that it sounds like I don't like my wagon vise – but that's not true. I use it all the time. I like it. I just don't want to sell it to you as the most perfect solution of all time. If it were, then what you are holding in your hands would be a pamphlet instead of a book.

I think that I learned a lot about building vises after making several of them. The rules I outlined earlier in this book for workbenches should have one special caveat for woodworkers making vises. Remember the rule about overbuilding your workbench? When it comes to making your own vises, there is no such thing as overbuilt. Make all the components of a homemade vise as stout as possible with thick, tough woods.

Other modifications to the stock French bench: I've messed with the sliding deadman during the last couple years so that it uses the Stanley No. 203 bench bracket instead of a wooden peg. That change was in the name of science, not necessity. I wanted to know how the bench bracket compared to the wooden peg. The No. 203 is cool and

The French Workbench

NO.	PART	SIZES (INCHES)			MATERIAL	NOTES
		T	W	L		
❑ 1	Top	4	24	96	Yellow pine	
❑ 4	Legs	5	5	32	Yellow pine	2" TOE
❑ 2	Long stretchers	2½	3¾	61	Yellow pine	2½" TBE
❑ 2	End stretchers	2½	3	19	Yellow pine	2½" TBE
❑ 1	Deadman	1¼	8	22½	Yellow pine	⅝" x 1½" TOE
❑ 1	Leg vise	1¾	8	33¾	Ash	¾" x ¾" chamfer on three edges
❑ 1	Vise handle	1	1	15	Ash	Octagonal
❑ 1	Vise's parallel guide	½	3	17	Ash	Drilled with ⅜" holes
❑ 1	Planing stop	2	2	12	Ash	Friction-fit into 2" x 2" mortise
❑ 1	Crochet	3	4	13	Ash	

KEY: TOE = tenon on one end; TBE = tenon, both ends

helps out in some situations by stabilizing your work. But is it a do-or-die modification that you should make? Not really.

In fact, there's only one modification I've made in the last two years that I think is essential: Add some leather to the jaws of the leg vise. This makes the vise grip even better with less pressure.

Apart from that $15, 15-minute fix, I think you can build this bench as is. After working on it you might come up with modifications that suit your work. And this is the true beauty of this bench. Its open architecture allows you to add vises or other workholding devices with little fuss. Want a quick-release vise? No problem – there are no aprons to restrict the bars of the vise. How about adding a twin-screw vise in the end-vise position? Again – not a problem.

This bench is like an empty canvas or a lump of clay. It is designed to be altered. And because you won't be the same kind of woodworker in 10 years time (this I guarantee) you're going to want a bench that will change with you. This bench just might save you from building another bench (or even two) as your skills deepen and your workholding needs become more complicated.

PLANING PANELS: Secure a batten (of any thickness) against your planing stop with a holdfast and you can work wide stock with ease.

SAW PANELS OF ANY WIDTH: The deadman, leg vise and a bar clamp (or two) will allow you to hold any panel for sawing.

"I have a friend who was involved a few years ago in the construction of a nightclub in Mexico. Much of it was cast concrete. The forms were made of timbers sawn to order on the spot by a couple of guys with handsaws and big arms. You wanted a 2x8? They would cut it from a larger timber right then and there. No pit saw, no power saws. "Got to tell you, boys and girls, I like hand tools and am very interested in saws and saw skills, but there comes a limit. For something like that I'd rather have a Skil Saw than saw skill."

— Joe Sullivan, quoted on the Knots forum, March 11, 2007

LE ROUBO

Top View

Front View

Left Side

135

Leg Vise Jaw

Leg Vise Arrangement

Crochet

1" sq. grid

Planing Stop

Parallel Guide
(½ in. thick)

Holes for pegging tenon

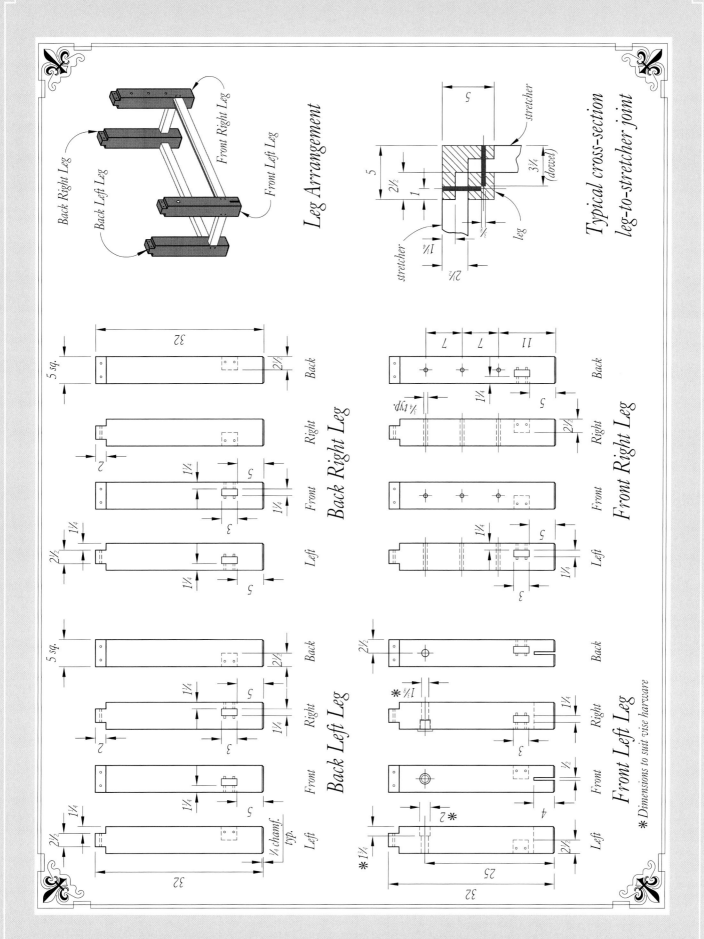

Leg Arrangement

Back Right Leg
Back Left Leg
Front Right Leg
Front Left Leg

Typical cross-section
leg-to-stretcher joint

stretcher
stretcher
leg
(dowel)

Back Right Leg
Back
Right
Front
Left

Front Right Leg
Back
Right
Front
Left

Back Left Leg
Back
Right
Front
Left

Front Left Leg
Back
Right
Front
Left

* Dimensions to suit vise hardware

137

Stretcher Arrangement

Front and Rear Stretchers

Deadman

End Stretcher
(2 req'd)

Underside of Bench

Typ. Cross-Section
Leg-to-Top Joint

Vise Handle

MASSIVE: Once I finally made the leap to making a French bench in its 100-percent massiveness, I knew I could never go back. The only thing more stout would be a bench carved from solid rock.

Chapter Eight

The Ancient Roubo

There is something almost spooky about the allure of the ancient French workbench, with its sliding dovetail through-joints and massive proportions.

Even though these joints greatly complicate construction and add to your maintenance chores after it's built, I know hundreds of wood-workers have built a workbench this way – despite the downsides.

I know this because I helped many of them. I also know this because I am one of them – I'm in love with this particular form.

During the last 10 years of teaching people to build this bench I have figured out how to make this workbench by employing a wide variety of tools, from using hand tools alone all the way up to using chain mortisers and industrial milling equipment.

So this chapter is a little different than other descriptions of building a workbench. Instead of focusing on one specific set of operations, I am going to discuss the different approaches available and how they compare. I think you'll see that combining hand tools, electric hand tools and some machinery is the best way to make this bench.

About the Bench
This bench has only 12 joints, all of them variations on the mortise and tenon. So at its heart, this bench is about sawing and chiseling to a line, and little more. What's difficult about the bench is the scale of the components. Cutting a sliding dovetail in ³/₄" material is one thing. Cutting it on a leg that is 3¹/₂" thick x 6" wide is quite another.

If you're reading this chapter, you are probably deeply interested in the old French forms and don't want to compromise on the joints or the size of the components. So let's revisit Roubo's description of the workbench from the 18th century. Here I have excerpted only the sections on the joints and sizes of the parts.

The top is made of a plank or table of 5-6 thumbs (inches) thickness by 20-22 thumbs in width. For its length, that varies from 6 to 12 feet, but the normal length is 9 feet. This bench is of elm or beech wood but more commonly the latter, which is very solid and of a tighter/denser grain than the other...

The legs of the bench are of hard oak, very firm, 6 thumbs in width by 3-4 in thickness. They are assembled on [to the] top by tenon and a dovetailed tenon in the style of a slip joint/bridle joint...

PLATE 11: I have built several benches using only this drawing as my guide.

"The workbench is the first and most necessary of the woodworking tools."

— A.-J. Roubo, *l'Art du menuisier*

THE DREAM: These thick oak slabs from 18th-century trees have been drying for 13 years, but they are still too wet for furniture (20 percent to 60 percent moisture content). But you can use them for building a bench.

HOME LEFTOVERS: These yellow pine 6x6x8s were $10 each and were left over from the log cabin industry. They were a little knotty in places, but they made some excellent workbenches.

The joinery/construction of these legs should be extremely straight, especially along the width. To make them still stronger, you enlarge the mortises at the top in order to place in the corners pieces of wood that you drive into the tenon, which makes them split, such that they spread the tail end of the tenons in the mortises and consequently they cannot come loose...

All around the edge of the bench and at 4-5 thumbs from the base of the legs are assembled four crosspieces [stretchers] of 4 thumbs wide at least by 2 thumbs thickness. The base of the bench is filled by planks supported by cleats which are secured to the crosspieces of the workbench, figure f, figure 4. You should note to put the length of these planks on the width of the bench [place them side-by-side with the grain running front to back] so as to provide more strength as one can see in figure 1.

WOOD-MIZER: Even a small band-saw mill can deal with the parts for a workbench. Look for a custom cutter who is just a little on the crazy side (you will not find this a difficult task).

So now we know the range of part sizes we should look for. And this is the first obstacle – finding large slabs of wood that are suitable for this bench.

You are not going to find these at your neighborhood lumberyard. Perhaps the closest thing you will find is 16/4-thick poplar, which is stocked by many professional yards for contractors. My advice, however, is to skip the lumberyard.

The best place to find thick stock is, in my experience, the Internet, particularly the digital want ads, such as those on Craigslist. Make it a habit to look for reclaimed beams from old buildings that have been torn down, or scrap that is left over from building log homes. You probably will even find a custom sawyer who owns a portable band-saw mill.

The good news about reclaimed lumber is that it's almost always fully acclimated. The bad news is it is usually full of metal, holes or joints from its previous life.

The good news about a custom sawyer is that you can get your parts cut exactly as you like from species that you want. The downside is the lumber is usually sopping wet and needs to dry out before becoming a bench – perhaps for a couple years or more.

Thick slabs are difficult to dry – commercial kilns in my area won't touch them. So your best bet is to cut them to nearly finished length and let them air-dry. How long? As long as you can. All the rules for air-drying wood go out the window when you deal with thick slabs. Slabs can take many years to reach equilibrium. But when they finally do, they don't move much after that.

OUT OF LINE: Here you can see how the end grain of the dovetail and tenon is proud of the benchtop. A few swipes with a jointer plane will get it back in line.

Optimally, you will not start building your bench until all the "free water" has left the wood and all that was left is "bound water" – water molecules that are literally bound to the cell walls. This is usually when the wood is about 20 percent moisture; it's also when the board will start to distort as it dries.

If you are using wet wood, your best bet is to build the bench as quickly as possible. The stout joints seem to keep the pieces from distorting as much as if they were drying out in the yard.

If this discussion makes you think about building your bench from laminated kiln-dried hardwoods, then you are still a bit sane. You do have to be a little nuts (or a timber-framer) to build this bench.

Downsides of the Bench

So the chances are that your wood is going to be a little wet. What does that really mean? For the most part, it means you are going to have to flatten your benchtop every six months or so for a few years, depending on the tolerances you require for your work.

In addition to that, you will have to plane down the end grain of the through-tenons/sliding dovetails that protrude through the bench-top. You might have to do this three or four times a year at first as the top shrinks around the leg joints.

The upside to this is that you will learn exactly how wonky a benchtop needs to be to be unworkable. That's a good thing to know.

The other thing you'll find is that the overall bench can become vaguely A-shaped when viewed from its ends. This is the result of the benchtop shrinking and the lower stretchers keeping the legs the same distance apart at the floor. The shoulders of your tenons down there might open up a bit. And the top of your benchtop will no longer be 90° to the front surface of your workbench.

While I am sure that is a problem for some sorts of work, I have not found it to be troublesome, and I am fairly fussy. You can still clamp stuff to your legs and stretchers to work on parts; you just cannot use the top and leg as a reliable gauge of 90°.

Oh, and the ends of your benchtop might check. Mine have. Usually the checks go nowhere. But if that will make you lie awake at night, call the Sjöberg of Sweden bench-making company.

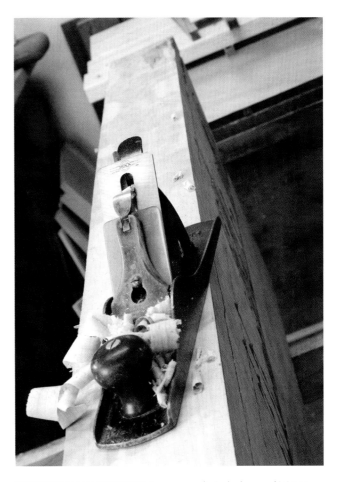

BETTER THAN MACHINERY: I recommend a jack plane and jointer plane for truing up the edges of your benchtop pieces. It's fast, and it's something one person can easily accomplish.

Perfectly aligned joints will become misaligned. This has no bearing on the function of the bench, but it is ugly to some.

For me, all these "disadvantages" are merely part of building a bench like this. And its advantages far outweigh its negatives. To wit: Once the bench reaches equilibrium it will basically stop moving. Also, the sizes of the components ensure the bench will be a mono-lithic and perfect woodworking surface. And all the little "unsightly" things will make it look like a bona-fide ancient French workbench. This is what these benches are supposed to look like.

Have you run away screaming yet? No? Let's get started.

The Benchtop

I always start by making the benchtop because its final size determines the lengths of the stretchers. If the benchtop ends up ⅛" too wide, you aren't going to run it through a table saw, are you? No. You just change the size of the stretchers below to compensate.

If you are fortunate enough to find a single slab that will be your top, count yourself as lucky. And if you also can orient the heart side of the slab out as the benchtop's working surface, you should buy a lottery ticket that day. If you can orient the heart side of the tree up, then the top will distort in a way that will help keep the sliding dovetail joints closed.

If you don't have a single slab, you'll need to glue up the top from two or more boards. I have found that machines are not much help in making these edge joints. Even when using industrial equipment and

CHECK THE JOINT: Not only does the seam have to close under its own weight, but the slab should be flat as well.

SLAB COMPLETE: Even a one-seam benchtop is a challenge in 6"-thick material. Take your time and do it right. When the clamps come off, dress the underside of the benchtop flat.

a team of experienced woodworkers, it is difficult to get a glue-ready joint on the edge of a 6"-thick slab.

That's why I prefer to use handplanes for this joint. I use a jack plane to get the edge as straight and square as possible. Then I follow up with a jointer plane to get it smooth and perfectly true.

It might be tempting to use a spring joint here, but I don't recommend it. Most of the spring joints I've seen in huge benchtops have opened up a bit after a couple years. The benchtops don't fail, but no one likes to see an open seam.

So go for perfect. Don't settle for less.

Gluing up a huge benchtop is no different than any other panel glue-up. The primary job of the clamps is to squeeze out any excess glue and hold the edges in close proximity so the glue can do its job. If you have done a good job with the plane, you should only need a bar clamp every 12" or so along the assembly.

What glue should you use? Good question. I love hide glue, and I'm not a big fan of modern yellow glues. But for this joint I almost always use epoxy. It's expensive, but it has two enormous advantages: It will bond wet wood and it fills gaps. No other woodworking glue does that.

Once the glue has cured, scrape off the squeeze-out and flatten the underside of the benchtop – don't fuss with the working surface. Get the underside as flat as possible, but don't worry about its smoothness. Check this surface with your winding sticks and make sure it's not twisted.

Now true-up the front edge of the benchtop with your handplanes. Get it straight and square to the underside of your top. With any luck, the back edge of your benchtop will be close to parallel with the front

HARD WORK: But it's worth it. Hold the saw tote with both hands and the tool's teeth facing away from you. This stance is easier on your back than bending over the benchtop.

MAGIC TRIANGLE: If you use this simple and ancient marking system, you are much less likely to make a fatal error in mortising. I know this from dealing with the mistakes of students who eschewed the triangle.

edge. If it's more than ¼" out, you might consider working the back edge with a jack plane to get the edges parallel. But don't go crazy.

The last step on the benchtop is to cut its ends square and to final size. I have tried every known power-tool solution out there. Most table saws can't deal with 6" material. Nor can a typical circular saw.

If you are timber framer, you probably have access to enormous circular saws that can make the cut in one easy pass. But for the rest of us, the handsaw is the best weapon.

My favorite technique is to first make a deep kerf (2") on the benchtop with a circular saw, indicating where I should saw. Then I saw off the end with a 7-point crosscut handsaw. The kerf guides my saw and also helps me plane the ends to square.

Base Joinery

Here's how I typically make the base pieces: I first cut the sliding dovetail and tenon on the tops of the legs. Then I cut the mortises in the legs for the stretcher pieces.

I turn the benchtop upside down on my sawbenches and position the legs where they ultimately will enter the benchtop. Then I can determine the lengths of my four stretchers.

I cut the stretchers to length and loosely tenon them (they will be drawbored). Finally I clamp up the dry base on the underside of the top and make sure it's the right size and shape. Easy.

Before we start into the base's joinery, here's the dirty little secret about it: The stretcher-to-leg joint isn't all that important. It can and should be loose because it plays little role in the strength of the bench. In fact, tight joints there can actually make assembly impossible or difficult.

The real strength of this workbench is the joint between the tops of the legs and the benchtop. Heck, many early workbenches (Roman times up until the 1600s) didn't even have stretchers or a shelf. My theory is that stretchers were originally added to make it easy to add a handy shelf for holding bench planes and other tools.

So focus all your attention on getting the sliding dovetails and through-tenons perfect.

Begin by marking up your four legs with a cabinetmaker's triangle so you can keep all the parts straight during construction.

DOVETAIL JIG: If I were making these benches in a production environment I might use a jig such as this. But if you are building one bench only, get your handsaw.

The Dovetail and the Tenon

This joint looks difficult, but it's really not. To lay it out, first mark a ³⁄₈" shoulder on the inside of the leg. This small shoulder helps prevent the top from sagging (so says M. Roubo). Then divide the remainder of the leg's thickness into the remainder of the joint. The dovetail and the tenon are each 1¼" thick – what's left is the space between them (this is an ideal layout for a 3½"-thick leg).

Roubo doesn't tell us what the slope of the dovetail is, and the drawing of it is a bit confusing. I have found that a 30° slope looks right and is plenty strong. But feel free to do your own thing – I don't think it matters much.

Cutting the dovetail is best done with handsaws. During some classes we have made jigs that hold the leg at a 30° and use a band saw. But usually by the time you get everything set up on the machine you could have been long done with the joint if you'd worked by hand.

I usually cut the dovetail with a tenon saw until the saw bottoms out and the spine won't allow me to cut any deeper. Then I finish the cut with a rip panel saw or rip handsaw. Then I use a fine carcase saw (filed crosscut) to cut the shoulder.

Cutting the straight tenon cheeks is honestly easiest on a band saw – any band saw can handle this cut. Cut the back cheek of the dovetail, the front cheek of the tenon and then the back cheek of the tenon. Then saw out the waste between the tenon and dovetail.

TAKE IT EASY: Lay out the dovetail on the front of the leg and its edges. Then you can follow both lines as you saw. Drop the handle as you saw to follow only the line you can see. Then remove the saw, walk around to the other side and focus similarly on the other line.

JOB FOR A BAND SAW: Because this cut is straight and deep, the band saw is the best machine for the job. Take your time and don't let the blade wander.

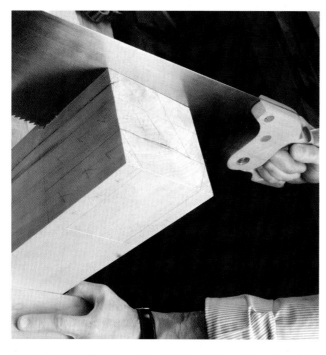

DEEP CUTS: Just like when cutting the dovetail, drop the handle and follow the line as you saw. Then walk around to the other side of the leg and do the same operation on the other face. Then you can remove the waste between the two kerfs.

BASHING OUT: A mortise chisel can remove this waste. Make deep cuts by the baseline. Then place the tip of your chisel in the end grain of the waste and rive out the waste between.

If you don't have a band saw, you definitely can cut this by hand. It's not difficult, just slow. After making all the cheek cuts, you need to remove the waste between the tenon and dovetail. I usually do this with a mortising chisel and work down by the baseline of the joint. Another solution is to bore a large-diameter hole near the baseline and pop the waste out with a chisel.

No matter how you cut these joints they need to be inspected afterward. Set a sliding bevel to 30° and inspect the dovetail slopes. Look for bumps and true up each surface so it is straight and 30°.

With a long combination square, check the face cheeks of the dovetail and the tenon. Pare away any humps.

Stretcher Mortises

You want your stretchers about 4" from the floor – no more. This 4" space allows you to get a boot or shoe under the stretcher while planing. You will find traversing with a plane and sawing is much easier if you can get your feet involved in pulling your body forward.

Lay out the locations of the mortises. The mortises should be one-third as wide as the stretchers are thick. If your stretchers are 3" thick, then your mortises should be 1" wide. Typically mortises like this should be about 5" deep. Because the stretchers don't add much strength to the bench, you will be fine with 3"- or 4"-deep mortises.

With deep mortises, I bore out as much waste as I can with an auger or at the drill press. Then I clean up the walls with a paring chisel and I clean up the corners with a ½" mortising chisel.

READY FOR MORTISING: With the joints on the tops of the legs cut, regroup the four legs to begin laying out the mortises for the stretchers.

FINAL CHOPS: No matter how you cut your mortises, you'll need to clean up each cavity with a bench chisel and some well-placed chops.

TRANSFER TIME: Clamp up your base pieces and move them into position on the underside of your benchtop.

KNIFE, THEN LEAD: After knifing in the shape of the joint, follow that with a mechanical pencil to make sure the knife lines are visible.

An industrial mortising machine isn't an option for most woodworkers. However, if you have one, this is a great place to use it.

Cutting the matching tenons on the stretchers is simple work. Use whatever tools you prefer. A handsaw, band saw or table saw are all good choices, and I have had good luck with all three. Just remember not to make these joints tight. You should be able to seat all the tenons in their mortises with light hand pressure. If you have to use a mallet, they are too tight.

Dry-fit and Mark

Now comes one of the most critical steps: Transferring the shape of the tops of the legs onto the underside of the benchtop. Dry-fit your workbench's base together and place it on the underside of the benchtop, which still should be upside down on sawbenches. Clamp all eight joints, applying the clamps across the stretchers.

Shift the base assembly around until the front legs are flush to the front edge of the benchtop and the base itself is centered on the top. Carefully trace the shape of each sliding dovetail and tenon onto the

EXPERIMENT: Even a high-quality track saw had difficulty cutting this joint perfectly. Every joint needed a bit of fussing afterward to fit its leg.

CLEAN: The nice thing about using the circular saw was the cut was quite crisp, all things considered. It just wasn't accurate.

ACCURATE AND SAFE: Even first-time bench builders are able to make this cut with ease. Stand the benchtop on its edge. Saw from one side down to the baseline. Then go around to the other side of the top and repeat.

HUNGRY CHISEL: The waste is surprisingly easy to knock out with a chisel and mallet. Take care not to go too deep (it's easy to do) because that will weaken the joint.

FLOORING TOOL: A router plane makes flattening the floor of the socket an easy task. Take small bites to get a smooth joinery surface.

underside of the benchtop. Use a knife at first, then follow the knife with a fine-point mechanical pencil to make the knife lines more visible.

After I mark around all four legs, I go back and inspect the marks for all four legs again. If the base shifted, I'll need to start again. After I'm happy that the marks are in the right place, I remove the base and transfer the joinery marks from the underside of the top to the working surface of the top.

Cut the Dovetail Socket

I haven't found a satisfying way to cut the dovetail socket with machines or powered hand tools, but perhaps the solution has eluded me.

For a few years, I tried to cut the dovetail slope with a high-quality circular saw with a track system. This worked OK, except when the sawblade deflected a bit, which is a common problem in deep cuts.

So every joint needed a bunch of tuning after cutting. The circular saw wasn't a total bust, however. If you have one, it's a great tool for kerfing the waste in the dovetail socket, which makes the waste easier to remove with a chisel.

So in the end, my favorite way to cut the dovetail slope is with a carcase saw or handsaw. It's not difficult to follow your lines if you take your time.

After I saw out the dovetail slope, I kerf the waste between the dovetail cuts with a handsaw or circular saw. I pop out the waste with a chisel driven by a mallet. Then I clean up the floor of the socket with a router plane and the widest chisel available.

Compare each socket to its mate using a sliding bevel to get a preview of how they will fit.

CLEAN THE CORNERS: Use the flat floor left by the router plane to pare into the corners of the socket.

THE LONE CHISEL: Cutting the mortise with just a chisel is slow, heavy work. And it's not the satisfying kind.

HOLES FIRST: Deep cuts with an auger bit make it much easier to remove the waste in the mortise. Bore in from both faces of the benchtop – meeting in the middle. Do the same with the chisels.

Mortise the Top

Without a doubt the biggest challenge of this workbench is making the through-mortises in the top. There is a lot of meat that needs to be removed and you need to be accurate. I have tried a lot of different methods and have settled on a technique that uses a corded drill, a jigsaw and a chisel.

The first time I made this bench, I tried mortising it like a cabinet door. I used only a mortise chisel – no other cutting tools. It was a slog, and I don't recommend it.

Next I took a timber-framer's approach and bored out most of the waste with an auger bit driven by a brace and bit. Then I cleaned out the mortise with a mortise chisel and bench chisels. This is totally doable, though it is a little slow.

After a tip from Jameel Abraham I switched to boring out the waste with a corded drill and a special Japanese-made bit that is designed for deep, accurate cuts. Called a "Nailchipper" bit and made by WoodOwl, these bits dive into tough woods without cooking your drill.

WHO? WOODOWL: These amazing bits plunge into the wood without jamming – the first time you use one it's shocking. Here the maker is working against a guide to keep the bit as straight as possible during the plunge.

With the help of these bits, a two-day job turned into something that took only a few hours.

The next improvement to the process was a trick of my own. While building one of these benches at home I tried kerfing all the waste left behind with a jigsaw. I worked on both faces of the joint and sawed right up to the line. I made a lot of kerfs, even more than are shown in the photo.

Then I took a wide chisel and removed the waste. As soon as the kerfs inside the mortise disappeared, I was done and had a perfectly straight, perfectly sized mortise. It was like magic.

The Planing Stop

While you're in the mortising mood, lay out and mortise the benchtop for a wooden planing stop. They are typically 3" x 3" x 12" and are friction-fit in a mortise in the benchtop.

The old benches also had a toothed piece of ironwork embedded in the movable stick.

Make the mortise now – before assembly. You can fit the wooden stop in its mortise later on.

KERF THAT MORTISE: Using a long jigsaw blade, kerf the waste all around the mortise, paying particular attention not to cross your layout lines (top). Then come back with a chisel and remove all the nubbins of waste (above). When the kerfs in the joint disappear, your joint is complete.

WEDGE THE GAP: Glue and wedges can close up (almost) any open seam around the tenons or dovetails. Hit the wedge until it stops moving. Then stop hitting it.

Assembly

The workbench comes together all at once. The base parts are bored for ⅝" drawbore pegs and the mortises are painted with glue (it doesn't hurt). Then you assemble the base on the floor of your shop and paint the tops of the legs with hide glue (hide glue is a lubricant).

Drop the benchtop onto the base. Drive the drawbore pegs. Wedge the joints that protrude through the top. Drink a beer.

Here are some important details about the operation. I now use ⅝" drawbore pegs (usually oak or locust) to assemble the bench base – one per joint. These large pegs almost never split during the sometimes-violent assembly process.

Each drawbore peg is shaved to size, pointed like a pencil and then rubbed with paraffin to ease assembly.

The ⅝" through-holes for the pegs in the legs and tenons are offset from one another by ⅛", perhaps ⅟₃₂" less if your base is indeed made of hard, dry wood like Roubo recommends. When you drive the pegs in, they will draw the two offset bores together – drawboring.

So clean off all the toolmarks on the base pieces and drill your ⅝"-diameter holes for drawboring. It's also a good idea to chamfer the leading rim of the joints on the top of each leg. You don't need much chamfer – only ⅟₁₆".

Compare all your male and female joints to make sure they will go together. If you need to do a test fit, feel free. Just realize that getting the legs out of the joints in the tops can be a bear.

Before assembly, it's also a good idea to make some 1¼"-wide wooden wedges to drive into the joints through the benchtop. These wedges should have a shallow slope – 6° or 8° is about right. I make my wedges out of white oak whenever possible.

Before you begin assembly, decide what glue to use (though glue isn't a big part of the bench's strength). If the wood is still wet, use epoxy. If it's fairly dry, use liquid hide glue, which acts as a lubricant and is reversible if something goes horribly wrong during assembly.

TIME FOR A BEVERAGE: With the wedges in and the drawbores pounded home, put the sledge down and let the bench sit overnight before you continue.

COARSE IS BETTER: A crosscut handsaw will make short work of the protruding tenons. Who cares if the teeth scratch the benchtop? You haven't flattened it yet.

Paint the insides of the leg mortises with glue and put the stretchers in place. The bench base should be on a stout floor. Paint the joints on the tops of the legs with glue. With a helper, drop the benchtop onto the leg joints. It should get stuck or wedged onto the joints.

Lift up one end of the benchtop about 6" and drop it to the floor. Have your helper do the same at the other end. Each hit should drive the bench parts together. It's OK if the bottoms of the legs get a little roughed up by the process.

I have yet to find a bench that could not be assembled this way – the weight of the bench and gravity does the work. I have tried many other methods that work, including a sledgehammer, but this is the best way in my experience.

Once the top is seated fully, wedge any gaps in the benchtop. Be cautious if you drive wedges into the dovetail slope because you can rive off the front of the benchtop.

Now drive in the drawbore pegs. I like to use a heavy sledge and tap them gently in.

Let the bench stand overnight before flushing things up or flattening the top.

SHINY FOR NOW: What I like about an oil finish is it doesn't make the surface slippery (once the oil has cured). A straight oil finish offers little protection against water or spills, but it looks a bit more finished than leaving the bench bare.

NO FRILLS: I made this leg vise to match the simple one in Roubo. No parallel guide. No garter.

Flushing, Flattening and Finishing

After the glue has dried, you can trim all the joints flush using a hand saw or (if you are a masochist) a slow-cutting flush-cut saw. Then clean up the joints with a plane.

I also bore all my holdfast holes at this point. I like two rows of holdfasts: One near the back edge of the workbench and a second row – staggered to fall between the position of the back row holes – about 6" to 8" closer to the front edge.

At this stage I flatten my benchtop with a jack plane, jointer plane and winding sticks. As mentioned before, there are lots of ways to finish a bench – from no finish all the way up to a homemade blend of equal parts boiled linseed oil, varnish and paint thinner.

For this bench, I used a toothing plane to lightly scratch the benchtop all over and roughen its surface a bit – slippery benchtops are the worst. Then I applied two coats of boiled linseed oil. And I got to work on the vise.

A Simple Leg Vise

I love leg vises, but most of the ones I've made were complex affairs with gizmos that make the vise easier to use, such as a parallel guide and garter.

For this vise, I decided to go primitive and copy the vise shown in Roubo. So the hub of the vise is much lower than usual. And there is no parallel guide or garter.

How does the vise work? To make the jaw clamp parallel to the benchtop, I place a tapered stick between the leg and jaw at the floor. This one stick – an offcut from tapering a table leg – handles about 90 percent of my clamping needs. And I don't need to bend over to move it, like you do with a parallel guide. I just move it with my foot.

The lack of a garter isn't as annoying as I thought it would be. I simply have to pull the chop back when I release the jaws.

While this vise isn't as convenient as more complex leg vises, it does have one undeniable virtue: It's dead simple. There is almost nothing that can break, jam, bend or get clogged by detritus. It's definitely a low-maintenance vise.

And even after two years of using it, I haven't been tempted to upgrade it.

RELIEF: The inside of the jaw is relieved about ⅛", which gives the vice more clamping power at the top of its jaw.

SLEEVED: One of the sweet features of a French bench is the ability to sleeve assemblies over the cantilevers.

FIN: I always try to leave some sort of trace behind about who made the workbench I just finished.

Shelf Details

While I'm not a fan of transforming the base of a workbench into a tool cabinet, I think every bench can benefit from a simple shelf.

I always add the shelf onto the bench after it is assembled, and I make it easily removable in case it ever needs to be repaired. The shelf is simple: The bottom boards sit on cleats that are nailed to the inside faces of the stretchers.

The first step is to make cleats from some scraps leftover from building the bench. I usually use 1½" x 1½" material for cleats, which makes for a stout shelf.

I nail these to the bottom inside edge of all four stretchers.

The boards for the shelf ideally should run from front to back. This makes for a stronger shelf and allows you to use shorter offcuts to make the shelf. But it also requires more joinery work.

Each board should be joined to its neighbor with a tongue-and-groove joint or a shiplap joint – but no glue. This will allow the bottom boards to expand and contract and prevent ugly gaps opening up in the shelf.

I cut the joints on the edges and then fit the boards onto the cleats. I usually nail the bottom boards to the cleats, though you can simply let gravity hold them in place.

BOTTOM CLEAT: This cleat is smaller than I usually use, but it will do. I fasten the cleat to the stretchers with cut nails.

Ancient Roubo

6' Version

NO.	PART	SIZES (INCHES)			MATERIAL	NOTES
		T	W	L		
❑ 1	Top	$4^{7}/_{8}$	20	72	Cherry	
❑ 4	Legs	4	$5^{1}/_{2}$	34	Cottonwood	
❑ 2	Long stretchers	$2^{1}/_{2}$	5	$42^{3}/_{4}$	Pine	3" TBE
❑ 2	Short stretchers	$2^{1}/_{2}$	5	$17^{1}/_{2}$	Pine	$2^{3}/_{4}$" TBE

8' Version

NO.	PART	SIZES (INCHES)			MATERIAL	NOTES
		T	W	L		
❑ 1	Top	6	22	96	Oak	
❑ 4	Legs	$3^{1}/_{2}$	$6^{1}/_{4}$	33	Oak	
❑ 2	Long stretchers	$1^{1}/_{2}$	4	57	Oak	3" TBE
❑ 2	Short stretchers	$1^{1}/_{2}$	4	19	Oak	2" TBE

Leg Vise

NO.	PART	SIZES (INCHES)			MATERIAL	NOTES
		T	W	L		
❑ 1	Leg vise jaw	$1^{7}/_{8}$	8	33	Hardwood	

KEY: TBE = tenon, both ends

LE OLDE SCHOOL ROUBO

Top View

20

14

3

Optional Tail
Vise Chop

72

Front View

4⅛

8

8

10

5½

3

37

10

Left Side

1

12

3

34

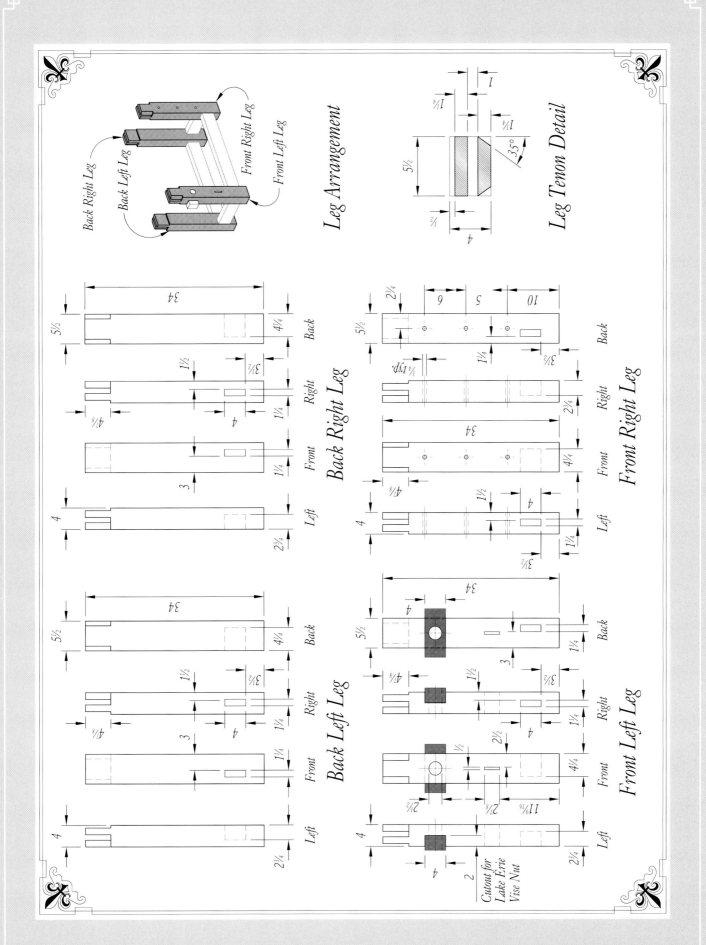

Leg Arrangement

Back Right Leg

Back Left Leg

Front Right Leg

Front Left Leg

Leg Tenon Detail

Back Right Leg

Back

Right

Front

Left

Back Left Leg

Back

Right

Front

Left

Front Right Leg

Back

Right

Front

Left

Front Left Leg

Back

Right

Front

Left

Cutout for
Lake Erie
Vise Nut

Leg Vise Arrangement

Leg Vise Chop

Parallel Guide
(1/2 in. thick)

Leg Vise Chop

Exploded View

Side Stretcher

Short Shelf Support

Front Stretcher

Long Shelf Support

Long Shelf Support

Long Shelf Support

Rear Stretcher

Side Stretcher

Short Shelf Support

Cutaway View

Shelf Cross Section

Long Shelf Support

Short Shelf Support

Shelf Assembly

Side Stretchers

Front and Rear Stretchers

HAPPILY EVER AFTER: Building a good bench is key, but what you do with it after it's complete is just as important. A flat benchtop will make your work predictable. And a handful of appliances (but not too many), will make your tools more accurate.

Chapter Nine

Maintenance & Appliances

Like any tool or machine, a workbench requires accessories (jigs, fixtures, appliances) and occasional maintenance to actually do anything of great value. A bench without a bench hook is a dining table. A bench with a cupped work surface is an exercise in bewilderment and wasted effort.

There are many appliances you can build for specialty work. Instead of my filching them from Robert Wearing's masterpiece, *Making Woodwork Aids & Devices* (Guild of Master Craftsman), I implore you to seek out his book, purchase it and read it. Later in this chapter, I will show you the basic woodworking appliances that every bench needs. But before you can build any appliance, you need to tend to one important chore: truing your benchtop.

There are a variety of ways to go about this, including some that are patently nuts. But before I march down that list of your options, I ask: Does the top need to be flat?

Whenever I'm in an old barn, workshop or even an antique mall, I can't resist poking around the guts of any old workbenches I find. When we take the kids on a hayride, I end up in the chicken house checking out the 18th-century wooden screws on a face vise. When we visit living history museums, the kids are chasing the animals, and I'm asking the guy dressed like a cooper if I can poke around the undercarriage of his bench.

I've found little evidence that these benches were flattened regularly. Many of them bear toolmarks that are deep and of varying ages. I've seen benches that are so worn from use that the edges look as round as a pillow. One bench was so worn away in one spot that the bench's 3"-thick top was less than an inch thick.

And when I check the 19th- and early 20th-century books, there's little attention given to the workbench top. While there is detailed instruction on sharpening, tool maintenance and the act of building a bench, flattening its top isn't often listed as routine shop maintenance. At most, they'll say the top should be flat.

There are several explanations:
1. Workbench flatness is overrated and a product of our modern obsession with granite plates and dial calipers.
2. Early woodworkers would use *planing trays* – a disposable workshop appliance that attached to the bench and allowed woodworkers to plane cabinet-scale parts at a variety of angles. (If you've never seen one of these, you will in this chapter.)

3. Or a flat workbench was so important to those who handplaned panels and furniture components that its flatness was a given.

I don't have the answer, but I suspect that all three are true to some degree. If you've ever done any handwork on a bench that was cupped, bowed or twisted, then you know that it's not a good way to work. The downward pressure from a plane can bend your work into a low spot in the bench. When using long planes in particular, a low spot will prevent you from ever planing the board flat.

You can use small wooden wedges under your stock to support it and prevent it from bending into a low spot on your bench, but the problem is that you will have difficulty knowing when your board is flat. A workbench top that is fairly flat is also a fair gauge of the flatness of other boards.

Two Solutions for Tops
So my recommendation is that if you can wield a handplane (even just enough to be trouble), then you should either use a planing tray or strive to keep your top fairly flat. You can overdo this. It's not necessary to flatten the top using methods that involve a machinist's straightedge and feeler gauges. And I would ward you away from methods that use a router that runs on a carriage suspended over your bench. I've watched people do this, and it is a lot of trouble to build these devices.

I think there are two smart paths: Learn to use a jointer plane (flattening a workbench top is the best practice for this) or remove your benchtop and take it to a cabinetshop that has a wide-belt sander.

"While we don't necessarily need more objects, we just might benefit from more making."

— John Dunnigan, from the essay "Understanding Furniture" in *Furniture Studio: The Heart of the Functional Arts* (The Furniture Society)

IN THE RIGHT LIGHT: Move your bench so that one end points to a window. This makes it easier to read your winding sticks as you look for gaps underneath them and alignment across their lengths.

LOOK FOR WARP: My winding sticks here are 36"-long aluminum angle. Place one winding stick at the far end of your bench and the other one about 24" away. Sight across them both, looking for high and low spots. Move the second winding stick another 24" and repeat.

CUP OR BOW? Now that I know the geography of the top, I'll drag one stick all along the top and watch the gap under the stick. This quick check confirms my suspicions about where the high spots are (and they are usually along the long edges of the top).

STOP SPELCHING: Before I get down to business, I'll cut a small chamfer (¹⁄₁₆" to ⅛") on the long edges of the top. This will prevent the grain from blowing out (the British call it spelching) when I plane cross-grain.

(Side note: Some workbench designs can be flattened using home woodworking machines. One such design has a benchtop that is made of two thick 10"-wide slabs with a 4"-wide tool tray screwed between them. Simply remove the screws and run each 10"-wide slab through your portable planer. Reassemble! Side, side note: I dislike tool trays, aka hamster beds.)

I can hear the workbench purists squirming from where I perch. Won't sending a workbench top through a wide-belt sander embed it with grit that will mar the work pieces of future projects? Not in my experience. Once you dust off the top and put a finish on it, such as an oil/varnish blend, the grit becomes part of the finish.

Plus, even if there is a little #220-grit in my benchtop, that's a lot kinder to my workpieces than what else gets embedded in my bench during my normal work: bits of dried glue, dyes, pigments, occasional stray metal filings.

Flatten it With a Handplane

Because I don't have a wide-belt sander, I prefer to use a handplane to do the job. It's a 30-minute job – and cheaper and easier than carting my top across town. The first time I ever tried to flatten a benchtop with a handplane (years ago) it was 100 percent successful, and I just barely knew what I was doing.

Flattening a benchtop is like flattening a board on one face. First you remove the high spots. These high spots could be at the corners or there could be a hump all along the middle (though I have never had one of these in my benchtop). Find the high spots using two winding sticks – parallel lengths of hardwood or aluminum angle that are longer than your bench is wide.

Mark the high spots (if you have any) in chalk and work them with a bit of spirited planing using a jack plane or fore plane set to take an aggressive cut using its cambered iron. Get things close. Check your results with your winding sticks.

Fetch your jointer plane and work the entire top using diagonal strokes that overlap. Repeat that process by going diagonally back the other way across the top. After each pass, your shavings will become more and more regular. When your shavings are full length, your top is flat (enough). Now plane the entire top with the grain and use slightly overlapping strokes. It should take two or three passes to produce regular full-length shavings. You are finished. So finish it with something simple and get back to work.

Need details? Visuals? I've prepared a pictorial essay of the process that should help you get started. My digital camera codes each photo with the time it was taken. The first photo was snapped at 10:46 A.M. By 11:44 A.M. I was done. And remember: I'd stopped to take 26 photos about the process, and each photo had to be illuminated with our photographic lights. I think the photography took longer than the actual work.

Appliances for the Bench

There are a galaxy of gizmos out there for you to make or buy for your bench. The ones I discuss are the essential appliances for building casework. I have a whole pile of them for making chairs and finishing that I won't deal with, plus more piles of one-off jigs that get recycled into smaller and smaller one-off jigs with every project.

The first one doesn't guide your tools. It holds them. If you position your workbench against a wall, a tool rack can hold a high density of tools right in front of you. I have worked out of tool chests, hanging cabinets, tool walls and roll-around bathroom cabinets (seriously!) and a simple tool rack above the bench is handy, though your tools will get dusty (so keep them oiled).

Here are the particulars: My rack is made using two sections of ³⁄₄" x 4" base moulding that we used to use in photo shoots at the magazine to hide ugly industrial vinyl base moulding. The two pieces of moulding are glued together with four ¹⁄₂"-thick spacers separating

IN MY CUPS: In general, my tops become cupped in use. So I remove the two high edges by working directly across the grain. In this instance the cup is slight, so I started with a jointer plane. If the cup is acute, start with a jack plane so you can take a thicker shaving.

ACROSS AND DOWN: Every stroke across the top should overlap. The shavings will give up easily (though I am told that the iron will dull more quickly). Work from one end of the top to the other. Then back down. Repeat until the plane's cutter can touch the hollow in the middle.

DIAGONAL MAKES A DIFFERENCE: Work across the top diagonally now, overlapping your strokes as before. Take care at the starting corner and stopping corner – your plane's sole won't have much support. You can proceed with speed during the middle strokes.

AND THE OTHER WAY: Switch directions and work diagonally the other way across the top. Repeat these two types of passes until you can make shavings at every point in a pass.

FINISH PLANING: Now reduce your depth of cut and use your jointer plane along the grain of the top (cutting cross-grain allows you to take a heavy cut). Overlap your stokes and repeat your passes until you are getting full-length shavings.

FOR THE OBSESSED: You don't have to smooth-plane your benchtop, but it's good practice with a large laminated surface. You can begin smooth-planing with the grain, there is no need for cross-grain or diagonal strokes.

CROSS-GRAIN SHAVINGS: When setting up your planes, here's what to shoot for. When working across the grain, this is what your shavings should look like. Take the heaviest cut you can manage and keep your work under control.

DIAGONAL SHAVINGS: Full-length shavings taken at 45° will look like thick ribbon. Shoot for a thickness of .006", perhaps a bit more.

FOR THE OBSESSED II: If you smooth-plane your benchtop, set your tool to take a shaving that is .002" or less. You can take even more if your top is behaving and you used a mild wood.

WIPE ON, WIPE OFF: Rag on two coats of an oil/varnish blend. When everything is dry, a coat of wax will help your top resist glue, but it will make it slippery (a bad thing – hand tool users don't want their stock sliding everywhere).

RIGHT AT HAND: An over-the-bench tool rack is an ideal and easy way to work at the bench. Racks do have downsides – tools can fall at inopportune times, damaging the work and (on occasion) the tool.

CRASH AT MY PAD: This pad never has to be fished from the garbage and is always the right size. I have been surprised by how much I use it.

the two. The ½"-thick space between the mouldings holds a remarkable array of hand tools. The ½" allows most tools to slip between the mouldings and stop at the ferrule of the handle.

Across the front of the moulding I added large Shaker pegs on 4" centers. Then, between several of the large pegs, I centered a smaller Shaker peg. I placed the tool rack high enough so that my longest tool hung about 4" off the benchtop (you don't want your planes crashing into your hammers when planing across the grain of a wide panel).

I hung my large saws above the rack (also on pegs) and now everything is right where I need it. Some tools I can grab without even looking up from my work. It's a right-powerful way to prevent you from walking all over the shop, opening drawers and toolboxes.

To be certain there are disadvantages of tool racks (aside from the dust). You have to be careful when moving assembled pieces around on your bench. It is too easy to knock into tools on the rack, denting the work. Or when planing, it's easy to bump a tool in the rack and bring it crashing onto your work. Finally, if you have the rack in front of the window, the tools will block a surprising amount of light.

So while racks are probably the easiest storage solution, they aren't the end-all, be-all.

Leather-faced Dogs

If you've made it this far in the book, you know that I like to add little bits of leather to my vises to increase their grip. Wooden bench dogs are part of a vise and so they don't escape my leather fetish either. Gluing rectangles of leather to the faces of your wooden dogs just might make you think twice before buying steel dogs.

Holdfast Pad

This is a trick I picked up from retired blacksmith Phil Koontz, who made hand-forged holdfasts. Like the leather-clad canines above, this improvement falls into the category of small tricks that also help protect your work. When using a holdfast you should protect your work with a wooden pad. Holdfasts can leave an impression. This little pad

is always right where you want it and swung out of the way if need be. The pad should be about ⅜" thick, wider than the pad of your holdfast and longer than the reach of the holdfast. The hole for the pad should be about ¼" larger in diameter than the shaft of your holdfast.

Bench Hook

Two huge misconceptions about sawing: Freehand sawing requires great skill. Immobilizing your work for sawing requires a serious vise. Both are false, thanks to a bench hook. These three pieces of wood are so essential to good woodworking that I think you should finish reading this section, put down the book and go down to your workshop and build a bench hook.

With a bench hook, you can saw (and sometimes plane) workpieces anywhere you have a stable top. I have used a bench hook on a kitchen counter, a dining table, a table saw wing, a stair tread and a cinderblock.

Here's why they get my vote for the most ingenious shop device ever: The *hook* of the bench hook braces against the edge of your work

ULTIMATE SAWING ACCESSORY: A bench hook and a sharp backsaw will change your woodworking. Saw cuts that seemed like they might require a maestro are within your grasp. Saw cuts that seemed foolhardy are simple and safe.

HOOKED: The second bench hook slides along the benchtop to support long work. You could put a fence on it, but if you don't position it perfectly, it could interfere with holding your work against the fence of your other bench hook.

surface. The fence of the bench hook immobilizes your work with the assistance of a little bit of hand pressure from your off hand and the cutting force of the saw itself. The fence also assists you in sawing square crosscuts by guiding your eye.

The bench hook lets you quickly position your work, hold it without clamps and saw pieces of any size. No more cutting 1" off a ¼" dowel on your 12" miter saw. Once you have a bench hook and a backsaw, you will stop with the foolish jiggery needed to cut small parts or just the foolish foolishness (which is what usually happens).

My bench hook is the deluxe model. The fence and the hook are trimmed off the ends of a ⅝" x 5" x 12" piece of ash. The fence and the hook are 1½" long. I glued the hook to the underside of the jig as shown. I trimmed a ½" off the width of the fence and glued it to the top of the jig. This avoids cross-grain construction, which is what causes these jigs to self-destruct or go out of true after a while. Then, to further add to the de-luxe-ness of the jig, I marked out a small scale on the fence between 0" and 3" in ⅛" increments. I use a spring clamp as a fence when cutting small parts.

I also use the bench hook as a planing accessory. I brace small parts against the fence, using it as a planing stop. I also use it as a quick shooting board for trimming end grain. Flip the bench hook over. Use the fence as the hook against the benchtop. Place your work against the full-width hook (now used as a fence) and place your

plane against the edge of the bench hook. You can now shoot the end grain of small pieces: dowels, muntins to perfection.

As you are making your bench hook, also make a second one without a fence. The second fence-less bench hook is used with the bench hook to support long stock on your bench.

Shooting Boards

Shooting boards are like bench hooks. They hold the work so you can concentrate on guiding the plane through the cut. There are many kinds of specialty shooting boards. The three most common include one that looks like an oversized bench hook (for shooting end grain), a miter shooting board (for shooting 45° cuts) and a long shooting board designed for shooting long edges of boards.

I don't think you need to build the shooting board for long edges. You only need one of those if your workbench cannot hold pieces on edge to work them. It's far simpler (and smarter) to either clamp a board in your vise and shoot the edge than it is to build a big shooting board that has to be dragged out and set up every time you shoot an edge. Plus, many need to be adjusted for different widths of boards being trued.

As you can guess, I see little use for these long shooting boards for edges. Build a good bench and they are like your appendix or vestigial gill slits.

SHOOTING ENDS: Use a heavy plane that is easy to grasp for shooting. This shooting board has a separate track for the plane. If your benchtop is flat you can just run the plane on the benchtop.

TINY RABBETS: The first time you use a shooting board the iron of your plane will cut into the long edge of the appliance, cutting a small rabbet. After a couple strokes the sole at the side of the mouth will stop the plane from cutting. Note to user: Don't use a rabbeting bench plane for shooting because it will never stop cutting the shooting board.

The other shooting boards are useful, however. The one for shooting end grain is built just like a bench hook, but it's longer and wider. I like to use plywood for these shooting boards for its dimensional stability and (relative) flatness. When attaching the fence, strive to get the fence dead square to the working edge of the shooting board. You can make the fence adjustable if you like. Mine is. The fence is screwed to the bed using pan-head screws I drove through oversized holes (Note: the screw hole near the fence is not oversized. I use it as a pivot point for the fence.)

The underside of the fence has sticky-back sandpaper adhered to it. This works fairly well to keep the parts aligned.

A couple important details about shooting: People ask how you prevent the plane from cutting the side of the shooting board. You don't. The first two or three passes with a plane removes a tiny corner of the shooting board. Then the edge of the mouth (by the sidewall of the plane) prevents the tool from cutting the shooting board any more. Try it, you'll get it as soon as you do.

When I shoot, I work to a knife line. I cut it close with a saw and then use the shooting board to take the end down. The first strokes are rough. Then the shavings will become more regular. When you get to the knife line, stop planing.

Here's what the mechanics feel like: Brace the work against the fence only – I don't like to press it against the sole of the plane. Immobilize the work with your weight. Use your right hand to push the plane forward into the cut. Your right hand should focus your efforts on keeping the tool pressed both down and against the shooting board.

Practice with some narrow scraps. Soon you will be able to shoot those so you are reducing the length of your board in .001" increments (try that with a table saw). Then move to the wider stuff.

Miter shooting boards are great if you can get them in alignment and keep them that way. They shoot a perfect 45° after you saw a less-than-perfect 45°. That's dang handy.

With my miter shooting board, the 45° fence is actually cut from a square piece of stock that is sliced across its diagonal, making two triangular pieces. If the piece started square, then the triangular section will be at 45° – or at least complementary angles to one another.

SHAVE YOUR MITERS: This traditional design for a miter shooting board allows you to trim miters going either direction, which reduces the times when you will get tear-out on a moulded, show surface.

Mortise the fence block into the bed of the shooting board. You should leave a little play in the mortise to adjust the fence at the end. Other than that, the mechanics of the miter shooting board works just like the end-grain shooting board: Brace, slice, repeat.

Sticking Boards

Sticking boards are useful for forming rabbets and mouldings. They were designed for use with moulding planes and rabbet planes, but they also work with routers. A sticking board is a long section of stout wood with a low fence along one long edge. It also has some kind of restraint or stop at one (or both) of its ends.

After you secure your sticking board to the bench (there are many ways to go about this) you nestle your work in the rabbet created by its bed and fence. Then you adjust the stop of the sticking board so that it will restrain your work without interfering with the cutter or fence of your tool.

BEGIN AT THE END: When planing moulding, some begin with short strokes up by the far end of the moulding. Gradually increase the length of your strokes. This process creates a track for your plane to ride in and makes cleaner profiles. Note that my left hand pushes the tool against the fence. My right is pushing forward. Each hand has but one job.

SIMPLE STICKING BOARD: My sticking board is immobilized by other accessories on my bench. At the end, my planing stop holds it, and the dogs brace the sticking board from the side. As a result my sticking board is two pieces of wood and four screws. Note I'm using only one screw to cut this ³⁄₁₆" beading profile in some walnut.

My sticking board uses four screws. I move the screws up and down (or remove them) to accommodate different mouldings. Then you plane or rout the work. Note that with a moulding plane you will plane from right to left. With a router, you will rout from left to right. So you might need stops at both ends if you use both kinds of tools.

Shop-made Planing Stop

There are many ways to restrain your work with a planing stop. Planing stops come in many sizes and materials. I prefer one that crosses the width of the benchtop (so I can plane panels) and is thin (just shy of ¹⁄₄" thick) so I can plane thin stock.

Here are the details: The stop itself is ¹⁄₄" x 8" x 24". Why so wide? To add stiffness to the stop so it can be that thin. Glue and screw one end of the stop to a short section of scrap that you can secure in your face vise. I used pan-head screws – a countersunk screw hole would split the thin stop.

This stop is adjustable, quick to make and dirt simple – all the things I like about good workbench appliances. Woodworking author Nick Engler once told me he never wanted to build a jig that had more than 10 parts. I agree.

THROUGH THICK OR THIN: What I like about this stop is that it is thin enough to restrain small pieces of work (top). And you can tip it up to stop thick boards. The width of the stop (8") and its stout nature (oak) allow this to really work.

MORTISING MADE EASIER: This simple board holds your work on your benchtop and allows you to clamp it right where you should.

HALF FRAME; HALF SHUTTER: The planing board is an odd assembly. The slats float free in a ⅜" x ⅜" groove. The tenons on the rails are glued into the stiles.

Mortising Board in a Vise

This "jig" is taken directly from Robert Wearing's book *Making Woodwork Aids & Devices*, but I have found it so handy for hand-mortising that I feel compelled to show it to you.

I put jig in quotes because it's just a single board that you clamp in your face vise with one long edge proud by 2". Then you clamp your door stiles or legs to this board, stand yourself at the end of the bench and waste out your mortise. You can get a clamp directly across the end of the stile to help prevent splitting, and because of the position of your face vise, you're mortising right where you should be: off the end of the bench and right over a stout leg of your bench.

Planing Boards

A planing board is useful if you have a thin benchtop, a warped benchtop or no benchtop at all. It offers a flat and stout surface with stops that you can plane against. Some planing boards are pieces of plywood with a thin lip all around. This works great (as long as the plywood is flat). The planing board can raise your work off the bench a bit if your bench is low. It also can raise your work too high.

Make your planing board large enough to accommodate your work. If you are going to build cabinetry, make it about 24" wide and 36" long. That will accommodate most case sides. Just as with your sticking board, you can come up with a variety of ways to secure your planing board to your bench. I recommend a hook on the front edge of the tray and then some sort of way to restrain it from sliding off the end: a holdfast or a bar clamp across the benchtop.

I made a planing tray with the theory (unfounded) that benchtop flatness is a red herring. If you work a lot on a bench that isn't flat, you'll see it affect your work. A low spot in the top will prevent you from planing the middle of a board. You'll only be able to plane the ends of the board.

One solution to this problem is that woodworkers who toiled on less-than-ideal benches would use a planing board. I first stumbled on the idea in *Modern Practical Joinery* (1902) by George Ellis.

I made a planing board using Ellis's description and text, and it works quite well. It's an unusual piece of work: It's a frame assembly that contains seven slats that float in grooves and can be slid a bit back and forth. Here's where it gets a bit odd: The frame's rails and stiles are 1⅜" thick; the slats are 1½" thick. The slats are proud on the bottom of

PORTABLE PLANING: I use a planing tray when I'm headed someplace where I know I'm going to need to plane things but I'm not sure about the workbench. My planing tray hooks over any work surface, and I can constrain it with one or two bar clamps across my work surface.

the planing board. The top of the planing board is cleaned up flat and flush all around.

The differing thicknesses, I believe, might keep the whole thing flatter in the end. The center of the planing board will always be planted on the benchtop. You can easily true the underside because it is proud and then flip the thing over and true the whole thing. That's a working theory. I have a few others as well.

There are two planing stops at the end that adjust up and down. You can also restrain work for cross-grain planing by inserting wedges between the slats and pushing the work against the wedges.

And how do you keep the planing board on your bench? The book is quiet on this. I have mine pinched between dogs and against a dog at the back of the bench. I'm going to change this arrangement this weekend. I plan to put a hook on the front edge (just like on a bench hook for sawing). And then I'll push the thing against a planing stop in use. There's no need to have a tail vise here.

After dressing your stock, plow a ⅜" x ⅜" groove down one long edge of each stile. Cut ⅜"-thick x 1¼"-long haunched tenons on the ends of the rails. Cut matching mortises in the stiles. Cut the ⅜" x ⅜" stub tenons on the ends of the slats.

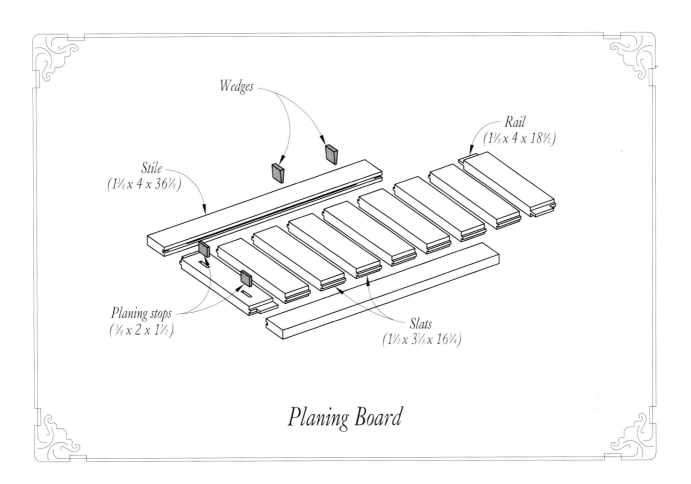

Wedges

Rail
(1⅜ x 4 x 18½)

Stile
(1⅜ x 4 x 36⅛)

Planing stops
(⅜ x 2 x 1½)

Slats
(1½ x 3⅞ x 16¼)

Planing Board

INGENIOUS WEDGES: The slats move so you can press wedges between them. The wedges allow you to hold your work in a wide variety of ways fore and aft. The more wedges you have, the more you can do.

NO CLAMPS; NO BATTENS: Working cross-grain is always tricky. With a planing board, small wedges between the slats prevent the board from skittering across the bench.

Bore the two ³/₈" x 2" through-tenons in one rail for the planing stops. Dry-assemble the frame, clamp it up and make sure the slats will move when the assembly is put together. If everything works, glue up the frame and clamp it. When the glue is dry, dress the underside of the planing tray flat. Then flip it over and dress the entire top surface flat. Fit your planing stops and get a few wedges you can insert between the slats.

Planing Board

	NO.	PART	SIZES (INCHES)			NOTES
			T	W	L	
❑	2	Stiles	1⅜	4	36⅛	⅜ x ⅜ groove
❑	2	Rails	1⅜	4	18½	1¼ tenons
❑	7	Slats	1½	3⅞	16¾	⅜ x ⅜ tenons

ANOTHER SUNDAY IN THE SHOP: These joiners had a lot in common (vests and pocket watches), but they had different benches. The man on the left has no tool tray, whereas his partner had a large one (that's filled with junk, I might add). Sadly, we don't get to see their vises.

Chapter Ten

Epilogue: Invent Nothing

I lost confidence a couple of times while writing this book. Not in the writing itself. Or in the workbenches I've built. Instead, I lost heart in the idea that a good workbench is an essential part of good woodworking.

In 2002 I got to visit Sam Maloof's new workshop and home in Southern California. We were expecting a tour of the place by one of his assistants. But instead, Sam himself took us around the establishment and spent hours showing us all the inside corners of his curvaceous furniture, plus his workshop and his cave-like wood-storage sheds filled with wood that you never see in Southern California.

Sam's whole place is arranged like a walled compound, but there is nothing closed about it. The Maloof homestead is filled with pieces of his work you can touch and sit on, from his early days as a struggling woodworker to some of his modern designs that fetch breathtaking prices. In all of his pieces, even the early ones that Sam would call primitive, the level of craftsmanship is quite high.

So when we took a walk through his shop, I was bewildered by his benches. The main workbench looks like a dining room table. Seriously. Take off the Emmert patternmaker's vise, plop it in a SoHo loft and the goateed hipsters would gladly nibble some Brie around it and use words like *ennui*.

The bench is about 30" high and hugely rectangular. There are four tapered dining-table legs. Four wide aprons under its thin maple top. Stretchers below support a shelf that was stacked so full of chair parts that you would never be able to clamp anything to the top.

The bench disobeyed every single rule in this book. And it bore the marks of heavy use. On the day I visited they were assembling a settee on it. The seat and legs were together; the spindles were yet to come. The work was fresh from the rasp and sandpaper that Sam's shop assistants (*the boys* as they are called) use to fair the work.

In other words, this dining bench wasn't just for assembly (they had low carpet-covered trestles for that) and it wasn't just a cart for

parts (they actually used a continental-style workbench for that – ha!). This was a working workbench.

At first I thought: Sam Maloof builds chairs. So he doesn't need much in the way of traditional workholding. But his house is filled with cabinetwork as well as chairs. A lot of world-class woodworking had passed over this bench while under the hands of Sam Maloof.

So, I considered, perhaps workbenches are vestigial to the modern woodworker. They are remnants of a time when we needed bench dogs and bench planes, tail vises and sash saws. Old bench designs survive in the same way that professional woodworkers who have never used a handplane will put a picture of one on their logo or business card.

After all, the best woodworking I've ever seen in my lifetime was built on the worst workbenches I've ever seen.

But my own experiences with workbenches since I was a boy kept me typing, reading and building for most of a year. And as I got to visit shops all over the world and delve into private tool collections (which always have a bench or two) I saw many patterns in the old forms of benches, echoes of cultural migration and tool evolution.

Modern-day workbenches, however, usually seem to fall into two patterns: the poorly conceived commercial brand of bench and the

"Every contrivance of man, every tool, every instrument, every utensil, every article designed for use, of each and every kind, evolved from very simple beginnings."

— Robert Collier (1885 - 1950)
author, publisher

A BASEMENT SHOP: I suspect this guy was a professional woodworker, based on his bench. Manual training benches from this era tended to be spindly.

individualistic design made by someone who was more interested in getting something knocked together than in poking through old woodworking books. Great modern benches exist, but they're rare.

Most modern benches usually fail to satisfy the three basic workholding tasks that all benches should do with ease: to be able to quickly hold boards so you can work on their broad faces, long edges and recalcitrant ends. Why are our modern workbenches so bad? Perhaps we don't need them.

A planer's serrated feed rollers are the 21st-century equivalent of the wrought iron holdfast. A power jointer's flat bed is the requisite flat worksurface required to try and true your cupped boards. Random-orbit sanders don't need boards that are secured with bench dogs. Dovetail jigs can be screwed to an old kitchen table and churn out tight tail after tight tail.

It's enough to make you stop typing, I can tell you.

But then I visited Brian Boggs shop in June 2006 in Berea, Kentucky (before he moved to North Carolina). Boggs, in my mind, is the Eastern Sam Maloof. His chairs are exquisite, and he also builds tables and casework. The back of his old shop looked like a laboratory more than a shop. He's assembled a robotic army of router jigs built using extruded aluminum 80/20 hardware. He's built a machine that turns hickory bark into a flexible seat material that, when woven, can endure hundreds of years of Thanksgiving dinner abuses.

But at the front of his shop were two huge traditional workbenches – one old, one new. Both of them saw heavy use. The Ulmia workbench was about worn out from all the work Brian and his employees gave it. The replacement, a Lie-Nielsen bench, was only a

year old but looked about 10 years old and Brian was worried he was wearing out the bearings in one of the vise screws.

When he worked on these benches, it was like watching two dance partners. Boggs was at ease. The vises spun in and out. He secured the work without a glance and began to saw, plane or file. This is exactly how I feel when I'm at my workbench. Workholding is easy, leaving me to worry if the surfaces are true or if my joints fit. I almost never have to stop and ask: How will I hold this part to work on it? This freedom makes me less of a jigger and rigger and more of a joiner. And that I like.

So here's the message I leave you with today: No matter what sort of projects you build. No matter what sort of tools you use. No matter what your skill level. No matter what kind of joints you use. A good workbench will make every workholding task easier.

And here's the best part: You don't need to invent anything, patent anything or manufacture anything to create a workbench that's better than what's lurking in the aisles of many stores today. Workbench designs evolved into their highest form more than 300 years ago.

And they are just waiting to be rediscovered by anyone who can understand that though things are always changing, that doesn't mean they are always improving.

Christopher Schwarz
February 2007,
Fort Mitchell, Kentucky

Sources of Bench Supplies

Benchcrafted
Cedar Rapids, IA
benchcrafted.com
Vises

Highland Woodworking
1045 North Highland Ave. NE
Atlanta, GA 30306
800-241-6748
highlandwoodworking.com
Benches, hardware, plans, vises, workbench
tops & accessories

Hovarter Custom Vises
Howell, MI
810-545-6179
hovartercustomvise.com
Vises

Lake Erie Toolworks
1234 Irwin Drive, Unit #22
Erie, PA 16505
814-528-4337
lakeerietoolworks.com
Wooden-screw vises

Lee Valley Tools
P.O. Box 1780
Ogdensburg, NY 13669-6780
800-267-8735 (U.S.)

P.O. Box 6295, Station J
Ottawa, ON K2A 1T4
800-267-8761 (Canada)
leevalley.com
Benches, hardware, plans, vises, kits
& accessories

Lie-Nielsen Toolworks
P.O. Box 9
Warren, ME 04864-0009
800-327-2520 (U.S.)
207-273-2520 (international)
lie-nielsen.com
Benches, hardware, vises, & accessories

Maguire Workbenches
Bramble Barn,
Saleby,
Alford,
Lincolnshire,
LN13 0DU
07920423123
rm-workbenches.co.uk
Workbenches and vises

Rockler Woodworking & Hardware
4365 Willow Drive
Medina, MN 55340
800-279-4441 (U.S.)
763-478-8200 (international)
rockler.com
Benches, hardware, plans, vises,
& accessories

Tools for Working Wood
32 33rd Street 5th floor
Brooklyn, NY 11232
800-426-4613
toolsforworkingwood.com
Holdfasts, plans, vises, & accessories

Woodcraft Supply
1177 Rosemar Road
P.O. Box 1686
Parkersburg, WV 26102
800-225-1153
woodcraft.com
Benches, hardware, plans, vises
& accessories

TIGHTEN UP: Drawboring is a simple and fundamental skill that will radically transform your joinery. The few extra steps it requires will virtually eliminate gaps in a mortise-and-tenon joint – even if the wood still needs to reach equilibrium with its environment. Plus, drawboring reduces clamping and the need for a perfect fit.

Drawboring Resurrected

Drawboring is one of the simple reasons that so much antique furniture survives today, some of it as sound as the day it was made.

What is drawboring? It's a technique that strengthens a mortise-and-tenon joint, transforming it from a joint that relies on glue into a joint that has a permanent and mechanical interlock. In essence, you bore a hole through both walls of your mortise. Then you bore a separate hole through the tenon, but this hole is closer to the shoulder of the tenon. Then you assemble the joint and drive a stout peg through the offset holes. The peg draws the joint tight.

Drawboring offers several advantages compared to a standard glued mortise and tenon:

- The joint will remain tight. A common problem with mortise-and-tenon joints is that the joint can open up and develop an ugly gap at the shoulder. Sometimes this is caused by the wood shrinking as it reaches equilibrium with a new environment (such as your living room with its forced-air heat). Sometimes this gap is caused by simple seasonal expansion and contraction, especially with woods that tend to move a lot, such as flat-sawn oak. The peg in a drawbored joint keeps the tenon in tension against the mortise during almost any shrinkage.
- The joint can be assembled without clamps. Drawboring is excellent for unusual clamping situations. Driving the peg through the joint closes it and clamps are generally not needed. Chairmakers use drawboring to join odd-shaped pieces at odd angles. It's also an excellent technique when your clamps aren't long enough. Or when you don't have enough clamps. Drawboring also allows you to assemble a project one piece at a time if need be.
- The joint can be assembled without glue. There is good evidence that drawboring allowed early joiners to assemble their wares without any glue. This is handy today when you're joining resinous woods (such as teak) that resist modern glues or when you're assembling joints that will be exposed to the weather, which will allow water to get into them and destroy the adhesive.
- The joint doesn't have to be perfect. The mechanical interlock of drawboring means that your tenon's cheeks don't have to have a

piston fit with your mortise's walls. In fact, you might be surprised at how sloppy the joint can be and still be tight after hundreds of years. Drawboring requires you to be careful only when fitting the tenon's shoulder against your mortised piece. The other parts of the joint are not as important. And while I never argue against doing a good job, drawboring ensures that every joint (even the less-than-perfect ones) can be tight for many lifetimes. For this reason, I think drawboring is an excellent basic skill for beginning woodworkers.

So why has drawboring become an almost-lost art? It's a good question, and one that I cannot fully answer. I suspect that modern glues and machine-made joinery made the technique less necessary, particularly for manufactured furniture. Drawboring does require several extra steps, and the benefits of it — particularly the long-term durability of the joint — is not something that is apparent to a customer.

Another reason the technique has fallen out of favor, I suspect, is that manufacturers have stopped making drawbore pins. These tapered steel tools allow you to temporarily assemble the joint to check the fit and to ease the path that the wooden peg will later follow. You can drawbore without drawbore pins by relying on the peg (and luck) alone. But once you use a proper set of drawbore pins, you will wonder why they are not in every tool catalog.

"(Drawbore pinning) is chiefly confined at the present time to rough outside work, or imitation mediaeval joinery, as it is neither so effective or of so good an appearance as a glued and wedged joint."

— George Ellis
Modern Practical Joinery (Linden)

Drawboring Basics

1 Bore a ¼"-diameter hole through both mortise walls. The center of the hole should be ⅜" from the edge of the mortise.

2 Assemble the joint. Mark the hole's center on the tenon using a ¼" brad-point bit.

3 Remove the tenon and shift the mark closer to the tenon shoulder – ¹⁄₁₆" to ³⁄₃₂". Use the same bit to bore a ¼"-diameter hole through the tenon at the offset mark.

4 Reassemble the joint. Twist the drawbore pin into the joint to check the fit. Ensure there are no gaps in the joint.

5 Whittle the end of a ¼" peg to about ⅛" diameter at the tip. Add glue to the joint and peg. Assemble the joint and hammer the peg through the offset holes.

6 Saw (or chisel) the protruding peg material flush with the work.

INSIDE THE JOINT: I sawed apart a drawbored joint to show how the oak peg bends through the offset hole. This was a ³⁄₃₂" offset in ash.

Joint Details

I have drawbored many joints during the last five years or so and have found the methods described to be highly effective. My method is based on historical descriptions of the process from the 17th century as well as my own work.

The first detail to tend to is the size and location of the hole through the mortise. I have found that a ¹⁄₄"-diameter hole is good for cabinet work. For larger-scale work (workbenches, doors and windows for homes) a ³⁄₈"-diameter hole is better because the peg is stouter. In general, place the hole ³⁄₈" from the opening of the mortise in furniture work and ¹⁄₂" in larger work. Make the hole as deep as you can. Usually this requires boring it through the assembly, though the hole can be stopped in thick stock. The goal is to ensure that the untapered part of the peg passes into the other wall of the mortise.

Historically, many of the drawbore pins I've encountered are a diameter that's best suited for a ³⁄₈"-diameter hole and peg. Entryway doors and large windows are appropriate for this larger hole and peg. I have encountered (and own) a set of old pins that work with a ¹⁄₄"-diameter hole, however, so this approach is historically accurate.

The next thing to consider is how much to offset the hole in the tenon. The bigger the offset, the sounder the joint, but the bigger the risk that you'll destroy the tenon or peg during assembly.

The traditional joiner was advised to offset the holes by the width of a shilling, according to Joseph Moxon's *Mechanick Exercises*, a 17th-century how-to book on woodworking. I had difficulty locating a shilling from the middle to late 17th century (I did try), but according to one knowledgeable collector of English coins, a 17th-century shilling would be about ¹⁄₁₆" thick.

An offset of ¹⁄₁₆" will always work and is easy to assemble. But I've found that it's sometimes not enough to get the job done. Some of the joints I assembled with this small offset were just a bit wiggly. For furniture-scale work, I prefer a ³⁄₃₂" offset. For big-scale work, I'll push that offset to almost ¹⁄₈" if the parts of the joint are large and the wood is a tough species, such as ash or elm. Experience will be your guide. Begin with small offsets in a sample joint and gradually increase them. You'll know when you've found the sweet spot.

Marking the offset on the tenon must be done with care because small changes can make a significant difference and cause the tenon to split in fragile woods, such as cherry. If you mark the offset with a slightly dull pencil, it can shift your mark by ¹⁄₃₂" or so. I recommend you use a sharp mechanical pencil or (even better) a knife.

HOMEMADE TOOLS: Making your own drawbore pins is easy using an inexpensive alignment pin and a scrap of sawn (or turned) hardwood.

The shape of the peg is important, too. I whittle mine so the last ¹⁄₂" tapers to an ¹⁄₈" tip. In almost all cases, I use straight-grained white oak for my pegs. It must be completely dry; wet pegs will shrink in time and allow the joint to loosen up. Typically I'll split out my pegs from some dry oak using a pocketknife and mallet. This is called *riving*, and it is a technique used by chairmakers to produce durable chair parts. Wood that is shaped by riving is stronger because it splits along the wood's grain lines. Sawing cuts across the grain lines, which can create a more fragile peg in some cases.

I then whittle the pegs round or roughly octagonal. Another option is to pound them through a steel plate with the correct-size hole bored in it. When pressed for time, I'll use dowel stock, which I have found to be satisfactory as long as I choose dowels with straight grain.

When you knock the peg home, you'll sometimes create a small gap between the hole and the peg as the peg leans into one side of the mortise as it makes its path through your joint. If this gap is unsightly, try a different strategy on your next joint. Whittle your pegs slightly larger in diameter and switch to an octagonal shape. Again, a bit of practice in a couple sample joints will help you get it right.

Despite everything I know about drawboring, I still glue most of my joints and even coat the peg with glue before driving it in. It cannot hurt. But I do take great satisfaction in knowing that when that modern glue has given up, the peg will still keep everything in place and the joint will be just as tight as the day I made it.

Moxon's Double-screw Vise

If you cut dovetails by hand, then I'm sure you're aware of the other part of your anatomy that is involved: your back.

Bending over rows of tails and pins all day is murder when you try to stand up straight. Several people have come up with solutions, including a cute mini-bench that you park on your full-size bench to raise your work. Other woodworkers have built benches with higher benchtops that are designed just for hand-joinery.

Of course, like most things in woodworking, someone had already come up with the solution several centuries ago.

'Mechanick Exercises'

Joseph Moxon wrote the first English-language book on woodworking titled "The Mechanick Exercises" in 1678. In it he showed many of the tools used by the contemporary joiner, from the workbench down to the dividers.

In one part of his book he discusses the "double-screw" vise. It looks like a twin-screw vise with two jaws that has been affixed to the front of a workbench.

But the text discusses how the vise can also be clamped down to the top of the workbench.

When that piece of information sunk in, I got excited and built a prototype. After a few revisions, here is what I came up with.

Back to the Future

This vise might not have originally been intended for cutting dovetails, but boy is it great for it. It raises your work, then stows away when you don't need it.

This vise solves a lot of problems that we joiners have. It allows you to hold stock of almost any size (mine holds up to 24$^{1}/_{8}$"-wide material) with an incredible grip.

More so, it raises your work above your benchtop surface. The vise as shown is 6" high, so the top edge of the vise is 39" from the floor. The board I've clamped in the vise is 44" off the floor and is as stable as something clamped between two boulders.

What does that mean? No more stooping to saw dovetails, tenons or other joinery. And because the vise is portable, that means I can:

1. Put the vise wherever I want on the bench — the end, the back edge, wherever.

2. Remove it when I don't need it and hang it on the wall — most woodworkers don't need a twin-screw vise every day.

3. Leave it unclamped on the benchtop, and use it like a giant handscrew clamp (Peter Follansbee at Plimoth Plantation hipped me to this function).

The vise is quite easy to build — I used some scraps. The only other key piece of shop equipment is a 1$^{1}/_{2}$" wooden thread box and tap, which is available at many suppliers for less than $50.

TAP THEN TAP: Place the front jaw on the rear jaw. Drop your Forstner in the hole. Tap it with a hammer. Then drill the hole in the rear jaw and tap that.

Joseph Moxon's Double-screw Vise

NO.	PART	SIZES (INCHES)			NOTES
		T	W	L	
☐ 2	Bench screws	2	2	12½	7" of screw is 1½" dia.
☐ 1	Front jaw	1¾	6⅛	32⅛	
☐ 1	Rear jaw	1¾	6	36⅛	
☐ 1	Rear brace	1¾	2	30	

PROFILE

ELEVATION

Tap the Jaws

The first step is to cut the 1½"-diameter clearance holes in the front jaw. Position the holes so you'll have 24⅛" between them.

Then center the front jaw on the rear jaw and clamp them together. (Note: The front jaw is wider than the rear jaw so that it is easier to line up the rear jaw with the front edge of your benchtop.)

Drop a 1½" Forstner bit into each hole and tap the end with a hammer – this transfers the centerpoint of the hole to the rear jaw.

Unclamp the jaws and drill 1⅜" holes though the rear jaw. Then use your tap to tap the holes in the rear jaw (a little linseed oil or a non-drying vegetable oil makes a good lubricant).

TWO SCREWS FROM ONE STICK. The two vise screws are made from one octagonal piece. Turn down the middle. Cut the piece in half. Thread the round sections.

Turn and Thread the Screws

The vise's screws are made from 2" x 2" walnut. I planed a 25"-long section to an octagon then chucked that in the lathe. I turned the middle 14" down to just a shade less than 1½". Then I crosscut the piece, ending up with two 12½"-long handles.

Clamp a vise screw with the round section facing up and use your threadbox to thread the round section. Test the results in the rear jaw. If the screw squeaks or doesn't turn freely, adjust the cutter in the threadbox so it cuts slightly deeper.

Add the Rear Brace

The vise will be more stable if you glue a rear brace on the backside of the rear jaw, which will increase the surface area that contacts your bench. Glue and clamp the rear vise in place.

Add some details if you like. I chamfered the front edges of my front jaw and the ends of the vise screws. I applied a couple coats of an oil/varnish blend finish.

I also glued on a layer of suede to the inside face of the front jaw, which improves the vise's grip even more.

I've been testing the vise for more than three months (and I made versions for coworkers and friends). If you cut dovetails, I think this vise is well worth making.

Your back will thank me.

The Milkman's Workbench

One of the best things about working with hand tools is you don't need much shop space – often a corner of a bedroom provides enough space. And a complete tool kit fits in a box the size of blanket chest.

As a result, many apartment-dwellers work with hand tools because they are compact, relatively quiet and fairly easy to clean up after. But there is one huge thing missing from the above – a good workbench.

Woodworking is much easier with a solid workbench that is equipped with vises and bench dogs. Good workbenches are usually massive and enormous, and they might not fit in tight quarters. A big bench can also be intimidating to build for a beginning woodworker. And small commercial benches are generally too spindly for real woodwork.

Enter the "Milkman's Workbench" – a small, full-featured bench-top that clamps to any solid surface – a dining table, dresser or kitchen island. And it's not just for the apartment-dweller. This is a great bench for traveling, demonstrating at woodworking clubs or even for working in the living space of your home if you have a shop without HVAC.

It offers a lot of features for such a small thing. You can dovetail boards more than 19" wide in its twin-screw vise area. You can pinch boards almost 24" long between dogs, and you have a decent worksur-face for chopping. Best of all, you can attach it to something sturdy using only two F-style clamps, do your business then put the bench away in a closet or under a bed.

I first saw a commercial version of this bench on an Australian auction site. Then I had a student, Jonas Jensen, whose father owned one. He had bought it from the town's milkman. I purchased the original from Jonas' father, studied its construction and worked with it for months. I concluded it was nearly perfect.

The version in this article is almost identical to the original with only slight changes to make it easier to clamp to your work surface.

Construction Overview

There's little joinery in this bench. The corners of the frame are joined by bridle joints that are pinned with 3/8" dowels. The frame is screwed to the benchtop it surrounds. The benchtop is just glued together with edge joints.

The only tricky part of the bench is the wagon vise. It's a block of wood that slides in two grooves plowed into the internal surfaces of the bench.

All the vises are powered by $1^{1}/4$"-diameter threaded wood screws, which I made with a lathe and a threading kit from Beall Tool Co. (see "Make Threaded Wooden Screws" on page 183 for details on the system). You don't have to invest in a threading system to make

ESSENTIAL GROOVES. Before you do any assembly, cut the grooves for the wagon vise.

DIGGING FOR DOGS. Cutting the dog holes using a dado stack makes for crisp work.

SNOUTS FOR DOGS. These notches allow the dogs to rest below the benchtop when not in use.

bench. You can purchase three veneer-press screws for less than $20 each and use those instead of the wooden screws. You can also simplify construction by installing round dogs instead of square ones.

The place to begin your bench is at the lumberyard.

Stable, Dry and Straight

The original bench looks to be made of beech. Because beech is hard to come by in the Midwest, I opted for red maple, though almost any wood will do. What is more important than the species is that the grain is straight, the stock is dry and there isn't a lot of internal stress in the wood.

I purchased about 8 board feet of 8/4 maple for the bench.

Using my cutting list, I milled all the stock close to size – 1" overlong and $1/4$" over-wide. As I progressed through the project I brought the pieces I needed to final size.

Assemble the Middle

The benchtop inside the frame has three significant pieces: the rear benchtop, the middle benchtop and a thin strip that covers the dog holes. Before you can glue the rear and middle benchtop together, you need to plow a stopped groove in the rear benchtop for the wagon vise. This groove is $1/2$" wide x $3/8$" deep x 7" long. It's centered in the thickness of the rear benchtop. After you cut this groove, cut a similar groove – but 8" long – in the front frame. That's the other groove for the wagon vise.

Glue the rear and middle benchtop pieces together. When the glue is dry, level the seams then lay out the location of the $1/2$" x $1/2$" dog holes on the front edge of this assembly. You can cut these by hand with a backsaw and router plane. Or you can use a dado stack installed in your table saw.

Whichever way you go, it's best to cut the dog holes so they are angled about 3°. They need to lean toward the wagon vise – this helps the dog pinch your work against the benchtop.

"People love chopping wood. In this activity one immediately sees results."

—Albert Einstein (1879-1955), theoretical physicist

With the dog holes cut, you need to make a notch at the top of each hole for the snout of the dog. The notch is $1/4$" x $1/2$" x $1/4$" deep. Chop out the notch with a chisel and finish the floor with a router plane.

Then glue the $1/4$"-thick strip over the front edge of your benchtop. When the glue is dry, level the seams and square up the ends of the benchtop. You are ready to make the frame.

The Frame: Bridles and Screws

Cut your frame pieces to their final lengths by using the assembled benchtop as a guide. Then cut the bridle joints at the corners. Note that the "slot" half of the bridle joint has to be cut on the front piece of the frame. Otherwise the groove you already milled for the wagon vise shows.

After the bridle joints are cut and the frame wraps around the three sides of the benchtop, you should bore the four holes for the movable vise screws in the front piece of the frame and the end piece where your wagon vise is located. If you are using the Beall $1 1/4$" threading kit, you'll need to bore $1 1/8$"-diameter holes. Use the drawings to lay out their location. Bore all the holes then tap them for the threads.

TAP THE HOLES. A simple pair of locking pliers can help you turn the tap into the holes in the frame.

The Milkman's Workbench

NO.	PART	SIZES (INCHES)			MATERIAL
		T	W	L	
☐ 1	Rear benchtop	$1\frac{5}{8}$	$2\frac{3}{8}$	28	Maple*
☐ 1	Middle benchtop	$1\frac{5}{8}$	$1\frac{7}{8}$	21	Maple
☐ 1	Dog cover strip	$\frac{1}{4}$	$1\frac{5}{8}$	21	Maple
☐ 1	Front frame	$1\frac{5}{8}$	1	30	Maple
☐ 2	Frame ends	$1\frac{5}{8}$	1	$7\frac{3}{8}$	Maple
☐ 1	Spacer block	$1\frac{5}{8}$	$1\frac{1}{2}$	$1\frac{7}{8}$	Maple
☐ 1	Vise block	$1\frac{5}{8}$	$2\frac{5}{8}$	$4\frac{3}{4}$	Maple
☐ 1	Garter	$\frac{1}{4}$	$1\frac{5}{8}$	2	Maple
☐ 3	Vise hubs	$1\frac{3}{4}$-dia.		$2\frac{3}{8}$	Maple
☐ 2	Face vise rods	$1\frac{1}{4}$-dia.		5**	Maple
☐ 1	Wagon vise rod	$1\frac{1}{4}$-dia.		$7\frac{3}{4}$	Maple

*Any seasoned, straight-grained wood will do; **Trim to fit vise block

3D VIEW

VISE BLOCK DETAIL

DOG HOLE DETAIL

Next you need to cut the spacer block that holds the frame away from the benchtop, making room for your face vise and your wagon vise. Cut two identical spacer blocks. One will be bolted in place permanently in your bench. The other will help you keep parts aligned as you assemble.

The best way to assemble the frame is to first attach the front piece and the end piece that does not house the wagon vise. Leave the other end piece unattached for now so you can fit the wagon vise.

The front part of the frame is bolted to the benchtop spacer block with a $\frac{3}{8}$" x 4" lag screw (don't forget the washer). The end piece is glued and screwed to the benchtop with three #10 x $1\frac{3}{4}$" wood screws.

Make Threaded Wooden Screws

Wooden vise screws are quite durable (as long as you don't abuse them). Once you have a rig to make them you'll be eager to make your own handscrews, panel clamps and other useful shop gizmos.

Sadly, the modern manual wood-threading kits are fragile and fussy – I've burned through four sets. So when it comes to making precise, clean threads, the best method is the Beall Tool Co. wood-threading system (bealltool.com, 800-331-4718).

This American-made and patented system uses a router-powered threader to create the threads. The tap is hand-powered. But it uses an ingenious pilot bearing to ensure you tap holes dead straight.

The instructions and enclosed DVD are quite good, but here are some tips that aren't covered.

1. Precise and sturdy stock is imperative. Home-center dowels don't work, but hardwoods with tight, straight grains work best. Turn your own (I did) or buy some tight-tolerance dowels from Beall.
2. Soaking the dowels in alcohol or linseed oil overnight makes for cleaner threads.
3. Despite what the DVD shows, don't back out your threaded rods from the jig while the router is running.
4. Longer lengths of dowel are better than short lengths. Threading 12" lengths (at minimum) is best.
5. The depth of the cut on the router is critical. A few thousandths of an inch makes an enormous difference in the shape of your threads.
6. Test every screw in a tapped sample hole before you commit to using it.

Here's how I made the vise screws for this bench. I sawed some straight stock into 1⅜" octagons. I turned down the octagons into 1¼"-diameter cylinders. I turned them just a few thou shy of 1¼". Then I cut the threads on these dowels with the Beall system.

I then chucked the dowels back in my lathe and turned 1"-diameter tenons on the ends of the dowels. I crosscut the threaded rods to the desired length.

Then I turned the hubs on my lathe from 1¾" stock. When the hubs were complete, I bored 1"-diameter holes to receive the tenons. I glued the threaded rods to the hubs using epoxy.

MAKE CLEAN THREADS. The Beall system makes crisp threads, once you dial in the right settings and have some good stock to work with.

TURN WITH CARE. Turning the dowels slightly undersized pays off when cutting the threads.

TURN WITH MORE CARE. Keep the dowel moving forward into the jig with steady hand motions. Eventually, you will need to turn the dowel with one hand on the infeed side and one hand on the outfeed.

TENONS ON BOTH ENDS. Here's the threaded dowel for the wagon vise. One end goes into the vise block, and the other into a hole in a hub.

GROOVE FOR A GARTER. Now I'm turning a ¼"-wide x ⅛"-deep groove for the garter in the wagon vise.

HUBS & SCREWS. Here you can see how the hubs and threaded screws are assembled. The longer turned portion fits into the hub.

Vise Block Construction

A CLOSE FIT. The vise block needs to move smoothly. The less it wobbles in its grooves, the better.

POKE THE BLOCK. Mark the centerpoint of the hole for the threaded screw using a Forstner bit. Layout is then almost fool-proof.

VISE BLOCK. Here you can see the garter, the underside of the vise block and the completed threaded screw.

Underside of block

HOLD-DOWNS. These 2"-long sections of angle iron are easily screwed to the benchtop and then clamped to any surface with F-style clamps.

around the circumference of the end of the threaded screw. You also need to make a "garter" – it's a block of wood that fits in a mortise in the vise block and intersects the blind hole. The garter locks together the threaded screw and the vise block. The photos do a better job than words can.

But before you make the garter, you need to shape the vise block so it slides smoothly in the grooves in the bench. So cut stub tenons on the ends of the vise block. The block should fit without wobbling like a loose tooth, but it should slide back and forth with fingertip pressure.

With the vise block fit and in place, clamp the still-loose end of the frame to the benchtop. Place a 1^{1}/$_{8}$" Forstner bit in the hole in the end and prick its center point on the vise block. Remove the vise block and drill a 1"-diameter x ^{7}/$_{8}$"-deep hole in the vise block, using the center point to guide you.

There are two more steps to complete the vise block. First add a ^{1}/$_{2}$" x ^{1}/$_{2}$" dog hole. You can make this hole in a variety of ways – chop it out by hand, use a hollow-chisel mortiser or bore a round hole then square it up. Next, add the snout like you did for the other dog holes. Last, you need to chop the mortise for the garter. That mortise is ^{1}/$_{4}$" wide x 1^{5}/$_{8}$" long x 1^{1}/$_{4}$" deep. It is centered on the hole for the vise screw. And it's ^{1}/$_{4}$" from the end of the vise block. Whew.

To complete the work on the vise block, you need to fit the garter into the mortise you just cut and fit it to the groove in the end of the threaded screw. Again, words are not the ideal medium for comprehending this 3-dimensional construction.

When everything in the wagon vise moves smoothly, glue and screw the end to the benchtop. Peg the bridle joints with ^{3}/$_{8}$"-diameter dowels. Now turn your attention to making the threaded screws and hubs (handles).

Clamping Hardware & Finish

The original bench had wooden clamps below the top that would allow you to attach the benchtop to a table or other stout surface. These clamps, however, were easily worn out and pulled out of their mountings.

After many experiments, I settled on attaching 2"-long sections of angle iron to the rear edge of the benchtop and at the end of the bench opposite the wagon vise. These little bits of metal allow you to clamp the benchtop to any surface with F-style clamps.

With the benchtop complete and functioning, take apart everything you can and prepare the surfaces for finishing. I use a finish that is equal parts varnish, boiled linseed oil and low-odor mineral spirits. Wipe the finish on with a rag. Remove the excess with a dry rag. Two coats should be enough for a bench.

Make some wooden dogs to suit your dog holes (there's a free on-line tutorial available on how I made mine). They are pieces of maple that are friction-fit into the holes. And get to work – in the kitchen, in the bedroom or anywhere else you can find a stout surface.

Drill the clearance holes and counterbores for all the hardware. Glue the corner of the frame then clamp together the two frame pieces, spacer blocks and the front of the frame.

When everything is where it should be, drill your pilot holes for your hardware. Drive in the three #10 screws. Use a socket wrench to install the lag screw. Let the glue dry, then level the joints and turn your attention to the wagon vise.

The Wagon Vise

If you have never built a vise like this, some of the parts – a garter? – can be baffling. But the photos and drawings will help the words do their job.

Here's how it works: The vise block is pushed forward by the threaded screw. The end of the threaded screw sits in a blind hole in the vise block. So far, so good. Now, here's where people get confused.

If you want the threaded screw to also retract the vise block, you need to do two things. You need to cut a ^{1}/$_{4}$"-wide x ^{1}/$_{8}$"-deep groove

15 Years of Building Workbenches

It's difficult to believe that I've been researching, writing about and building workbenches for only 15 years. Using the terms of our craft, those 15 years would be called "a good start" – and little more.

But thanks to a near-vacuum of information on historical workbench forms, a lot of helpful readers and a few strokes of luck, the world of workbenches became much more diverse during the beginning strokes of our new century. We rejected the spindly or complex forms of the 20th century and embraced the simple, robust workbenches that were ideal for handwork and (as luck would have it) machine-based woodworking as well.

It is my opinion that this sea change had little to do with any printed matter about workbenches. It would be easy to trace the "modern" French bench back to Rob Tarule's 20th-century Roubo bench that was featured in *The Workbench Book*. (Taunton). Or to chart the popularity of the French form in tandem with the sales numbers of the 2007 version of the book you are now holding.

But I'll be honest: Books (or magazine articles about these books) had little to do with the renaissance of the classic workbench. That credit goes to the Internet.

When *Workbenches: From Design & Theory to Construction & Use* was first published, the response from readers was silence. Believe me, I was listening. It was my first book, and so I was hoping for some sort of response. Curious interest? Outrage? Anything?

Nothing.

For months after the book was released, the only questions I received were from people asking what wood species they should use for their European-style workbench. They really wanted to use steamed beech, which was expensive, but did I think that hard maple would be OK?

Yes. Maple is OK.

About six months after the book was released I had moved on. I was building other workbench forms and investigating a lot of back alleys I had discovered during my research. But then something out there clicked.

Someone decided to build a French workbench from my book and wrote about the process on a woodworking forum. When he finished his bench, he was thrilled with the result and wrote a love letter to the form.

Other woodworkers built the French bench and wrote about their experiences. Soon there were hundreds (probably thousands) of French-style workbenches being built all over the world. And to find them, all you had to do was type in "Roubo workbench" into the search field of your computer's browser.

For many years, I tried to keep up with each and every woodworker who built one of these workbenches or its variants. But it became an impossible task. My back-up plan was to keep every photo of a finished workbench that people sent to me. And I still have all of those images on my hard drive.

And the entire time I collected these "baby photos," I prepared for a backlash. I knew that eventually people would tire of the novelty of the form and woodworkers would start evaluating these ancient benches on their merits, divorced from the novelty.

There was indeed a backlash; there always is. But the backlash was – and I use this word sparingly – pathetic.

These old forms of workbenches are immune to any significant criticism. They represent the most highly evolved form of bench during the high point of our furniture-making history. The benches were simple. They were easy to make. They didn't require a lot of complex mechanical vises to work. They could be built using only one joint: the mortise and tenon.

So there was no doubt in my mind that once these benches infected the minds of woodworkers that they would be never forgotten or rejected again. They are simply too useful – something I have proved to myself every day I have worked at one of these benches. And they are too easy to make – something I have proved more than 30 times in teaching classes on these benches in Europe and North America.

I don't dislike European, Dutch, Scandinavian or other workbench forms. Honest. As long as a workbench can hold boards so you can work on their faces, edges and ends with ease then it's a good bench.

My only complaint about these other European forms is that they are more complex than they need to be. I'm not interested in building mechanical workbench gizmos. I'm interested in building furniture.

If that's your thing as well, then you have found the right book. Examine this book's bench plans. Figure out what workholding is best for you. Build your bench and then put down this book (or give it away to a fellow woodworker) and get started building furniture.

There are few workbenches in our cultural museums; yet there are thousands of gorgeous chairs, tables and chests on display. Though I love my workbench, I know that it's going to end up in a barn or (even worse) a Manhattan kitchen as a wet bar. And I'm going to end up in a pine box.

But the things my bench and I can make together – those are the real prize.

Christopher Schwarz
August 2015,
Fort Mitchell, Kentucky

Index

Popular Woodworking Books
An imprint of Penguin Random House LLC
penguinrandomhouse.com

Copyright © 2015 by Christopher Schwarz

Printed in the United States of America
20 19 18 17 16 15 14 13 12 11

ISBN 978-1-4403-4312-4

Edited by Scott Francis
Designed by Terri Woesner and Angela Wilcox

READ THIS IMPORTANT SAFETY NOTICE

To prevent accidents, keep safety in mind while you work. Use the safety guards installed on power equipment. When working on power equipment, keep fingers away from saw blades, wear safety goggles to prevent injuries from flying wood chips and sawdust, wear hearing protection and consider installing a dust vacuum to reduce the amount of airborne sawdust in your woodshop. Don't wear loose clothing or jewelry when working on power equipment. Tie back long hair to prevent it from getting caught in your equipment. People who are sensitive to certain chemicals should check the chemical content of any product before using it. The authors and editors who compiled this book have tried to make the contents as accurate and correct as possible. Plans, illustrations, photographs and text have been carefully checked. All instructions, plans and projects should be carefully read, studied and understood before beginning construction. Due to the variability of local conditions, construction materials, skill levels, etc., neither the author nor Popular Woodworking Books assumes any responsibility for any accidents, injuries, damages or other losses incurred resulting from the material presented in this book. Prices listed for supplies and equipment were current at the time of publication and are subject to change.

METRIC CONVERSION CHART

Inches. . . . . Centimeters		2.54
Centimeters . . . . Inches		0.4
Feet . . . . Centimeters		30.5
Centimeters . . . . Feet		0.03
Yards . . . . Meters		0.9
Meters . . . . .Yards		1.1